Advance Praise for Lawrence M. Stein's *Value Investing* . . .

"Larry Stein's book, *Value Investing,* is excellent. It's well thought out, easy to read, and instructive, using the best of fundamental and technical analysis to search out good investments. Definitely a book worth reading."

> Leo Fasciocco
> Stock Market Columnist
> *Investor's Daily*

"A fascinating blend of fundamental and technical concepts of value. Stein's insightful, disciplined approach to investing should appeal to novices and pros alike."

> Carlene Murphy
> Mutual Fund Manager
> Stein Roe & Farnham

"*Value Investing* is a refreshing return to no-nonsense basics, with no get-rich-quick gimmicks. Stein makes his case in a clear, straightforward manner, without resorting to buzzwords or cliches."

> Sallie Gaines
> Financial Writer
> Chicago *Tribune*

"Larry Stein demystifies the stock market, making it logical and understandable. His work makes a significant contribution to the current body of investment knowledge and is probably one of the best investments that an investor can make."

> Stephen E. Scherer
> Instructor, UCLA Extension
> Attorney and President
> Private Financial Counseling

"In an easy to follow, well-documented book, Larry Stein shows how both fundamental and technical analysis can be used to form an effective value-based investment strategy. . . . Stein's new book is must reading for the serious investor."

> Dick Davis
> Syndicated columnist
> Miami *Herald*
> Publisher, *Dick Davis Digest*

VALUE INVESTING

VALUE INVESTING

New Strategies for Stock Market Success

Lawrence M. Stein

JOHN WILEY & SONS

New York   Chichester   Brisbane   Toronto   Singapore

Library of Congress Cataloging in Publication Data:

Stein, Lawrence M.
  Value investing.

  Bibliography: p.
  1. Investments—Handbooks, manuals, etc. 2. Stocks—
Handbooks, manuals, etc. I. Title.

HG4527.S816   1987   332.63′22   87-23152
ISBN 0-471-62875-1

Printed in the United States of America

10 9 8 7 6 5 4 3 2 1

To Susan, my love and my friend

Acknowledgments

Although the writing of this book was a solitary venture, it would be foolish to believe that it is the product of one individual. The concepts contained are a conglomeration of influences from other people. I hope that each of you who has played a role in my life can point to a place in this book and see your reflection.

Like most endeavors, its creation was characterized by fulfilling highs and somewhat debilitating lows. For all of the people with whom I shared either end of the half-filled glass—I thank you.

This book may not have come to fruition without the offerings of some wonderful people. Susan, my wife and best friend, hung in there well beyond the bounds of the conventional marriage. Her love and patience served as a powerful source of encouragement, giving me the drive to carry this work through to its full maturity.

My parents have always been a source of inspiration, and indeed, probably laid the seeds for this book. My mom, Bobbe, fostered an interest in expressing my thoughts through writing. And my dad, Floyd, introduced me to the stock market as a child and sparked the desire to delve deeper. Like the two of them, wedding the stock market with writing seemed to be a natural. They, my sister Sheri and brother Marty, and a supporting cast of terrific friends became my unwitting cheerleaders, a position on my team that I was fortunate to have so ably filled.

On the professional end, special thanks to Mike Lewis, an economist, who edited Chapter Three with tremendous care and precision; and to JoAnne Pekin, who assisted as a sounding board thoughout the book; and to Mark Achler, a fellow aspirant who lent me use of his computer equipment for graphics; and to Clare Kerner and Henry David Thoreau, teachers of different times, who together unhinged my mind afloat. And finally, to a series of people and events that led a dreamer to assess his world realistically enough to write the beginning chapter, and hopefully a lot more.

Contents

PART FOUR   THE STRATEGIC VALUE INVESTOR

Why Read This Book?

In recent years, droves of individual investors have become disillusioned with the stock market. They fear its volatility, the often unfair influences of corporate raiders and insider trading, and perhaps most of all, the overwhelming presence of mammoth investment institutions. For many, the stock market has become a source of intimidation, a place where common sense has been supplanted by the deadly calculations of computer-generated trading.

To these investors, I would like to suggest that these confusing changes are largely irrelevant. Frankly, I do not think the stock market has changed very much at all. The market has always been superficially affected by a bombardment of confusing events and those investors who try to understand each market movement will be paralyzed by uncertainty.

But behind this mesmerizing smokescreen, the stock market is still a market of stocks. Quality companies that are undervalued can still be bought and held over the long-term to produce sizable profits. The investor's job is not to decipher the stock market, it is to buy shares in companies that will be worth more in the future than they cost today.

Success in the stock market does not require the insight of a guru; just a bit of common sense and a measure of discipline. Of course, over the years, the stock market has seen its share of gurus pique the curiousity of the investment public. Eventually, the market reaffirms its superiority, another stock market messiah is humbled—and his followers join the swelled ranks of the disillusioned.

By contrast, *value* is something we have been trained all of our lives to understand. Whether in the purchase of a house or a household product, we seek investment in things that will produce returns greater than their cost. Investment in shares of a company should be no different.

When I was in my early teens, trying to learn about the stock market, I found plenty of books on the subject, but some were too general to be of real worth, while others boasted too many promises to be believable. Nearly all of them seemed to be based on methods that could be reduced to an insightful hunch, which didn't seem to be an intelligent way to invest my hard-earned money.

This is the book that I wish was available in my early investing years. I wrote this book to give both novice and experienced stock market investors an honest method of investing that can produce consistent, worthwhile returns at a reasonable risk. Some of the strategies presented are logical extensions of sound investment principles that successful investors have been using for years. Other methods are unique to my work, which has been a quest to make sense out of that riddle called the stock market, a riddle that defies perfect solution.

I cannot promise that *Value Investing* will make you rich, but I can assure you that adherence to its strategies will eliminate many of the errors that most investors make. And this should lead you to become a consistently successful investor over the long term.

Charles D. Ellis, speaking to clients of investment institutions in his brilliant book *Investment Policy*, claimed the stock market is a "loser's game." He likened investing to flying commercial airplanes. "For example, 60 or 70 years ago only very brave, athletic, strong-willed young people with good eyesight had the nerve to try flying an airplane. But times have changed and so has flying.

If the pilot of your 747 came aboard today wearing a 50-mission hat with a long, white silk scarf around his neck, you'd get off. Such people no longer belong in airplanes because flying today is a loser's game with one simple rule: Don't make mistakes." In other words, Ellis believes that today the object in stock market investing is no longer to win but *not to lose*.

Paradoxically, this negative-sounding statement can serve as a very positive beacon for individual investors. While few investment institutions may ever be able to win the "loser's game," individual investors can cross the threshold into successful investing by taking a realistic approach to the stock market.

As Ellis eloquently argues, institutions face such pressure to show superior performance on a quarterly basis that it forces them to take a short-term view of the market. If institutional clients could instead accept the ups and downs of the market and allow their investment managers leeway in short-term performance, then perhaps institutions could take the longer term investment approach necessary to improve their performance.

I agree wholeheartedly with Ellis's argument. All of the tremendous research and brainpower in Wall Street cannot compensate for the short-sighted approach of many institutional investors. And as in most endeavors, you can gain a decisive advantage by capitalizing on the failings of your competitors.

Herein lies the reason to read this book. As an individual investor, you don't have to play the institutional game, because as an independent decision maker, not subject to client pressures, you can stay with an investment strategy over the long term. Because institutions have such power in the market and compete on a short-term basis, stock valuations are pushed to extreme highs and lows which are recognizable by value-oriented techniques. Given a long enough investment perspective, individual investors can profit handsomely by buying undervalued stocks and holding them until they are overvalued. Through long-term value investing, they can win the "loser's game."

The finest insights of the investment world do not produce winners; they minimize the cost of errors. But, in the course of minimizing errors, value investing should produce a very high percentage of winners, some of which will be quite substantial. Most important, the value of your portfolio will grow steadily as the success of the winners is minimally impacted by the number of losers. Over the long term, this consistency should become the hallmark of your stock market success. If you are willing to take a realistic approach to the stock market, I think we will get along pretty well through this book, and maybe I can help you get along a bit better with the stock market.

Note that the masculine pronoun has been used throughout in order to preserve the readability of the book. No offense was intended toward my female readers.

LARRY STEIN

Chicago, Illinois
October, 1987

Part One
A Value
Perspective

1

A Realistic
Approach to the
Stock Market

Investors in the stock market typically run into problems managing their portfolio because of an unrealistic approach. They may be unrealistic in the results they expect and buy dramatic turnaround situations, hoping to make the illusory "big kill." Perhaps they see the stock market as a source of quick profit, leading them to trade aggressively, which results in a large number of minimal gains and not-so-minimal losses that add up to very little.

Both types of investors are making unrealistic assumptions about the nature of the stock market and their investment abilities which limits the possibility of making long-term gains in their portfolio. They stack the deck against themselves by raising the risk of their stock transactions to levels that cannot consistently produce a profit. Unless you approach it in a realistic manner, the stock market can be an exhausting exercise in futility.

To make the stock market work to your advantage, you must be realistic in your expectations, methods, and strategies. This requires a businesslike approach, quite similar to that of a businessman who acquires companies as investments for his financial empire.

Buying a share of stock is almost identical to buying a share of a business. The businessman scours the country, perhaps even

3

the world, looking for businesses that fit his investment criteria. Regardless of what method he employs, a common objective is shared with other acquisition-minded businessmen: to try and buy a company at a discount of its future value. In other words, he is a value investor.

The ordinary individual cannot afford to buy major corporations for his personal portfolio, but he does have the opportunity to buy shares in such corporations through the stock market. What the investor sacrifices in his lack of control in management decisions, he benefits from gaining liquidity. If the investment goes sour, he has an instant market for selling his shares. The businessman, by contrast, is stuck with a poor investment which can take months or longer to unload.

This wonderful aspect of liquidity is the investor's advantage over the businessman. Unfortunately, it breeds overconfidence in the minds of many investors. The stock market becomes a candy store for some investors, leading them to buy and sell shares of stock as if they were buying bubble gum. If they do not like the gum, they can spit it out and find plenty of other candy at a minimal cost to take its place. All they have lost is a few cents, or in the case of an investor, a relatively minor amount in the form of commissions and capital.

In truth, these seemingly minor losses can add up over the long term to depress the performance of most any portfolio. Remember, any loss in capital is also a loss in the opportunity to make a gain. Not only have you lost money, you have also lost the opportunity to make a gain in another investment. This doesn't mean you shouldn't take losses now and then, only to say that once you have committed your capital, you have eliminated the opportunity to make gains in other stocks. Therefore, the acquisition of a stock carries a dual responsibility, both to the choice of the stock and how the investment is managed.

For most investors, the bubble bursts when their stock does not perform up to expectations. Usually these expectations are too short in scope, placing the investor in the unrealistic position of expecting instant gratification from gains in the price of his stocks. As we will see throughout this book, short-sightedness is the primary downfall of the common investor.

Ironically, many of these investors have more invested in their egos than in their stocks, believing that a stock price should rise immediately after they buy it. Before we continue, let's establish one humbling fact:

The stock market is its own master and nothing we do has any effect on its movement. The most an investor can do is intelligently manage the risk of his investments.

Despite the advantage of instant liquidity, the stock market investor should assume a similar degree of care and diligence as the businessman in selecting and managing his investments. The purpose of this book is to give you, the individual investor, the knowledge to implement a realistic strategy for making consistently successful investments in the stock market.

THE TWO SCHOOLS OF ANALYSIS

The stock market has been mistakenly understood as a game, with its players competing to outdo each other. In this quest, two primary schools of stock market analysis have taken shape: fundamental and technical. In this book, rather than claiming to have done a better job of fine tuning either system, we will apply *both* methods as a way of realistically evaluating value in individual stocks and the stock market as a whole.

Fundamental analysts try to buy stocks that are priced below their potential value in the marketplace by assessing the value of a company's assets or its expected earnings power. Of course, there are several other ways that fundamental analysts study the stock market, such as evaluating economic factors and talking to management. However, few individual investors have the training to make economic forecasts or the intimate ties to major corporate managements to study the stock market this way. For most investors, or perhaps all investors, consideration of value characteristics is the most realistic method of investing.

The asset value approach attempts to determine the value of a company's assets by analyzing its balance sheet. Some analysts try to buy a stock below its expected liquidation value or at a low price relative to the company's net assets (equity or book value). Others may look for "hidden assets," such as appreciated real estate or vast natural resources that have not been properly valued by the marketplace. The aims of both are similar—to buy a stock that is undervalued by the stock market.

Those who focus on the expected value of a company's earnings power take a different approach to the same objective. Some seek to buy stocks that have shown tremendous increases in sales or earnings. Others might look for solid companies whose stock price is at a low multiple of its sales or earnings. Again, the fundamental analyst, regardless of the approach, is trying to buy stock in a company whose value is not adequately reflected in its stock price.

Technical analysts take an entirely different tack. Technicians view stock as a commodity, a product that is the object of competitive bidding by a free-flowing marketplace. They study the market behavior of individual stocks and the entire market as a whole, looking for indications in market activity that portend a rise or fall in prices. The technical analyst may look at price, volume, or any number of factors to assess market behavior on the premise that the market itself is the best indicator of what stock prices are likely to do in the future.

This places the two schools in obvious conflict with each other. Fundamental analysts consider it positively blasphemous to recommend a stock solely on the basis of a chart pattern, without understanding the workings of a company or its intrinsic value. Conversely, technical analysts doubt not only the ability of fundamental analysts to forecast earnings or asset values accurately, but they also question the relevance of such factors to the price of a stock. Thus we have two schools of thought, mutually exclusive, each with no allowance for the other.

The conflict of the two competing schools is like the two-party system of politics in the United States. Both are trying to do what is right, but each has its own ideas on how to accomplish the same objective. Stock market literature is littered with categorical battles between the two schools, each casting the other as a charlatan. Indeed, most stock market books are either fundamentally oriented or technically oriented, without consideration of a peaceful co-existence. In truth, the fundamental and technical schools have nothing to lose, but rather have a great deal to gain by bridging the two thought processes under a universal concept of value.

A UNIVERSAL CONCEPT OF VALUE

The universal concept is based on the assumption that all intellectual disciplines have similar veins of knowledge that can be transplanted and used effectively in other disciplines. Specifically, in the stock market, although the fundamental and technical schools are in obvious conflict, they are not as far apart as it might seem. The technician's objectives are identical to those of the fundamental analyst: to buy stocks that will be worth more tomorrow than they are today. In other words, both are really value investors seeking to recognize value that is not reflected in current stock prices.

The universal concept suggests that the dichotomy traditionally thought to exist between the fundamental and technical schools of stock market analysis is more of an intellectual shading than an impassable chasm. The universal concept, applied to the stock market, recognizes that: *value is value, whether it is expressed in fundamental or technical terms*.

The universal concept of value can be expressed in an equation:

$$Value = \frac{Perception}{Reality}$$

Regardless of whether the value question is approached from the technical or fundamental viewpoint, if market perception—that is, the perceived value of a stock—is greater than reality, then the marketplace is overvaluing the stock. If perception is less than reality, then it is being undervalued.

In fundamental terms, if a company has a liquidation value of $100 per share, but because of some near-term problem that is clouding its future, it is selling for only $50, the market is undervaluing the stock. Because the market has such a pessimistic perception, it is ignoring the reality that the company can be instantly liquidated for twice the current market value. Because perception is less than reality, the stock is undervalued.

Notice that it took a pessimistic perception to drive the price lower. "Pessimism" is ordinarily a term of technical analysis, yet it is used here to describe an instance of fundamental valuation. This should reinforce the notion that fundamental and technical value cannot be divorced from each other—they should ideally be considered together within a universal concept of value.

Suppose there is rampant speculation occurring in a small group of stocks that is pushing the market averages to record levels, but large amounts of stock are being sold by corporations (secondary distributions) and corporate insiders. The technician sees the internal structure of the stock market becoming fragile, with corporate insiders selling out to the less-knowledgeable public at inflated prices. Because a technical evaluation indicates that market perceptions are greater than reality, the technician's judgment suggests the market is overbought (overvalued) and likely to fall from current levels.

The objective of both schools is obviously the same: to run profitable stock market operations. To do so, each school has identified conditions that lead to higher or lower stock prices. Ideally, these conditions depict extreme valuations which will lead to extremely large profits.

In fundamental analysis, extreme valuations are called overvalued and undervalued conditions. In technical analysis, extreme valuations are termed overbought and oversold conditions. Both schools seek the most effective method of valuation, hence a universal concept of value (see Figure 1-1).

	Fundamental	Technical
Bearish	"Overvalued"	"Overbought"
Bullish	"Undervalued"	"Oversold"

Figure 1-1. Fundamental and technical views of market valuation conditions.

Generally, the most important market tops and bottoms are formed when fundamental and technical values reach extremes at the same time. These extremes in universal value also define the best times to buy and sell individual stocks, since the overwhelming majority of stocks follow the conditions of the general market. Even though fundamental analysts focus more on individual stocks and technicians usually center on the market as a whole, proper application of the two schools should lead to the same conclusions at the same time.

LIFE-CYCLE THEORY AND THE UNIVERSAL CONCEPT

Stock market value moves in a complex network of cycles which mirror the cycles of everyday life. This, of course, is another universal concept which states that the progression of stock market value is the same as the progression of value in other things. For example, let us examine one of the more universal principles, the life process. Life can be divided into basic cycles: birth, development, and death. This may sound irrelevant to the stock market. But keep in mind, the stock market was created by man, is operated by man, and functions by the participation of man (see Figure 1-2).

In the stock market, the birth–development–death cycle is expressed in rising and falling stock prices. The stock market does not continually rise, it moves up and down in a cyclical motion. A cycle spans one rising motion and one falling motion.

For example, the beginning of a bull market is the birth of a cycle. The bull market develops, carrying stock prices higher, eventually leading to a peak. The topping process leads to a decline in stock prices, which is still part of the development cycle. Finally, the bear market concludes, marking the death of this cycle. However, this is only the conclusion of a smaller cycle within a larger cyclical structure. The cyclical process continues, with smaller cycles passing through a framework of larger, more important cycles.

The only obvious difference between the cycles of man and the stock market is that the life of a man does not continue after death,

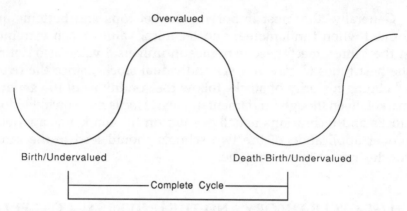

Figure 1-2. An idealized cycle shows the pendulumlike motion of the stock market, swinging from one extreme valuation to another. The cycle is born at undervaluation, develops to an overvalued peak, and dies at undervalued levels, which gives birth to a new cycle.

at least in the conventional sense. But this obvious difference is really no difference at all. Each man, by his influence, whether significant or minimally so, leaves a legacy that shapes the development cycle of the next generation. A man dies, but his influence passes through the system like a smaller cycle within a larger cycle. Indeed, in the overall progression development of man, we are but a passing fancy. Like man, each stock market cycle leaves an influence on the overall cyclical structure.

The cycles of the stock market follow an orderly progression that parallels the human experience. Each stock market cycle builds on the last cycle in a logical progression. The 1929–1932 depression years marked the death of a long-term cycle, but this was just a smaller cycle within the cyclical development of the United States that dates back to the late 1700s. Out of the ashes of the 1929 depression was born another long-term cycle that is still in the process of development (as of 1987). And within this most recent long-term cycle, we have witnessed several smaller cycles that have better defined the character of the 1932–present cycle.

LIMITATIONS OF FUNDAMENTAL ANALYSIS

Academic studies have argued vehemently—and sometimes persuasively—that the stock market moves in a random fashion and that no amount of analysis can improve investment results. Obviously, if I accepted this as entirely true there would be little reason to write this book, much less for you to read it.

Stock prices *are* largely unpredictable, but there are still ways to make intelligent—and not-so-intelligent—decisions about stocks. Intelligent decisions are based on judgments regarding value, technically or fundamentally oriented, but do not claim any precision in price movement or timeliness. They are merely value judgments, attempting to minimize and manage risk, which in the stock market also works to maximize consistency.

The great investor dream of the perfect predicting indicator is simply a dream without substance. Many great minds have spun many of the greatest computers of our time, searching for the perfect indicator or methodology. To date, they have not found it.

It is unfortunate that many of us who are not geniuses or armed with powerful computers have spent countless hours looking for the perfect stock market formula. I have tried it myself. Such a formula does not exist. While this book does contain a few suggested formulas, they are only meant as tools to aid judgment within an overall strategy of investment.

Fundamental analysts of large investment houses often spend a career following a handful or two of stocks in a single industry group. They analyze a company up and down, learning more than the average investor could ever hope to, spewing thick reports that contain their findings and highly educated conclusions. And yet they are unable to predict consistently, with any accuracy, the earnings per share for many of the best-known corporations in the world. And certainly, their forecasts are further off the mark for lesser-known companies.

For example, with all of the analysts following IBM, perhaps the most scrutinized company in the world, should there ever be any surprises in their earnings? Absolutely not, unless it was simply impossible to predict accurately earnings on a consistent basis. Yet, at the beginning of 1986, the consensus of Wall Street analysts estimated that IBM would earn over $12.50 per share for 1986. After several "surprises" during the year, actual earnings for 1986 came in at only $7.81 per share.

Does this invalidate the work by the legion of Wall Street analysts? No. Are these unintelligent people? I doubt it. In fact, it would be safe to say that they represent some of the brighter minds in the country. It is just that the task is impossible to perform with any precision on a consistent basis. The work is good and the forecasts are fine, it is just that the expectations of using the predictions are overambitious. It is simply unrealistic to base investment decisions on estimates of future earnings.

However, due to the competitive nature of stock market decision making, many investment houses base their recommendations on these estimates. To compete successfully, they try to foresee future earnings on the assumption that they have an information advantage over the rest of the marketplace. While it can be helpful to use this information as a guide, if it proves to be incorrect, it can be worse than not having any insight into the future at all.

Investors should realize, then, that predictions of earnings are just as difficult as predictions of market movement. A good analyst should be able to predict with reasonable consistency over the near term whether a company is likely to continue intact or whether it is headed for trouble. Beyond that, the forecast takes on a risk of its own.

The more ambitious the forecast, the less realistic, and the more likely it is to be wrong. The more an incorrect prediction is relied on, the more likely it is to hinder investment performance. Therefore, the more ambitious the forecast, the more likely it is that investment performance will suffer.

LIMITATIONS OF TECHNICAL ANALYSIS

Technicians are just as imperfect in their attempts to predict the future. Bookstores and computer software stores are filled with information purporting to predict swings in the general market or in individual stocks. But no mechanical system is likely to be able to predict shorter-term (less than a year) movements in the stock market.

Even if one could develop such a system, it would not be effective for very long, as masses of investors would begin using it. Once it became used on a widespread basis, it would be of little benefit to its users because everyone would have the same information and ability to predict the future. Stock prices would quickly rise or fall to reflect the change in investors' expectations, thus preventing all but a very few "early birds" from profiting. Hence, the suppliers and users would have incompatible desires, a relationship that would almost guarantee that such a product is useless.

Value Investing is based on value concepts that have been used successfully in the stock market for generations. Because the methods are derived from universal concepts, it is very unlikely that widespread use of these methods would render them useless, since they have been used already for years.

Another popular notion among technicians is the idea of trend-following, using moving averages to jump on trends at their inception and hang on until they terminate. Trend-following systems work fine as long as the market is in a definite trending pattern. But over the long haul, the stock market spends a large amount of time in trendless basing or topping patterns to prepare for a trend. As a result, trend-following systems may be successful for perhaps half the time, but eventually give back their profits during the other half.

My first draft of this book began with over a hundred pages describing my technical work, hoping to give the average investor an extra edge in analyzing the market. But the truth is, while I do spend a lot of time with this type of analysis, it ends up having a very minor impact on my investment decisions. In addition, the consistency of my work or that of any other "expert" (if there is an expert market timer) is not good enough to become the basis of any investment program. If so many so-called experts working day and night to predict short-term moves are not able to be consistently accurate, how can anyone expect to pick up a book and be successful at this pursuit on a part-time basis?

Stock market folklore is littered with stories of legendary speculators who used their technical savvy to build phenomenal fortunes by short-term speculation. Unfortunately, these speculators are equally famous for their penchant for making it big and then going broke several times over. I am making the assumption that you can fulfill your passion for living on the edge with some other pursuit and desire somewhat less thrilling—and more consistent—results from your investments.

The truly great investors, those who have amassed fortunes without giving them back, have been investors, not speculators. They did not jump in and out of the market, but rather stood back from the crowd and recognized the longer-term trends. Regardless of their technique, most of the great investors recognized opportunity and the opportunity to protect their profits. In other words, they developed methods to manage risk, generally based on some judgment of value. When the value was there, they seized it. When it was not, they were content to walk away and wait until an attractive value presented itself.

Remember, the object of the market timing techniques presented in this book is to help manage risk by identifying characteristics of overvalued or undervalued markets. We are not trying to call each market move, but rather to recognize periods that have more risk than others and adjust our exposure to the market accordingly. Admittedly, this is a form of market timing, hence the free use of the term in the book. Nevertheless, I am not advocating that investors place money in and out of the stock market on the basis of shorter-term timing considerations.

As this book was being written, articles appeared in the same week by two of the most expert individuals in market timing, each with a track record of impressive successes and highly respected by their peers and critics alike. One expert foresaw disaster, while the other was looking for the Dow to double.

Is one smarter than the other? Probably not; both are extremely intelligent. At least one of the two will be proven terribly wrong and could possibly suffer tremendous losses (in invested money or missing the opportunity of investing money) if they placed all of their money on one side or the other. I have a feeling that both men, intelligent as they are, have not placed their bets in a way that would seriously endanger their portfolio. In other words, while they have offered bold predictions, which is fine, chances are they have taken measures to minimize the risk of their predictions.

Their decided differences do not invalidate the work of market timers. Their work is important in trying to assess market risk. But just as in fundamental analysis, it would not be wise to base your entire investment portfolio on the basis of a forecast. Many investors have placed their investment fortunes in the hands of a moving average or a chart pattern, blindly putting money into the market on a favorable technical pattern and pulling it out when it becomes negative. This is highly unfortunate, because a moving average is simply an addition and division of numbers, which has nothing to do with the potential of an investment. A chart pattern is a historical record which gives a clue to the future, but again, it is not going to provide a degree of consistency that would make it worth trusting. Remember, you're still buying a share of stock—a share of a real-life company.

It is better to trust facts that we know rather than forecasts about what we do not know. When we become so confident as to trust our hard earned money to predictions instead of common sense, we have stepped out of the bounds of realism and into a dangerous overconfidence.

According to the universal concept of value, when the market is over-confident, it is likely to stumble; so too will investors.

This type of risk is unnecessary. Risk can be managed by an intelligent application of some basic investment principles, many of which are based on the way businesses have been successfully acquired for generations. Granted, we are giving up hope of precisely calling the market or buying the biggest winners on the exchange, but such hopes are never realized on a consistent basis anyway. It is better to accept a realistic methodology that has a desirable probability of success than to struggle with lofty expectations that cannot be achieved.

BACK TO THE BUSINESSMAN'S APPROACH

Warren Buffett has been widely recognized by the investment community as perhaps the greatest investor of this generation. He is the chairman of Berkshire Hathaway, a company he controls, which acts as a convenient vehicle for his investments. Rarely available for interview, many lovers of the stock market own a share of his company's stock (traded over the counter) merely to get a copy of its annual report, which contains Buffett's personal message to shareholders, noted for its sagacity.

On November 17, 1986, investors were treated to a lesson in investing by the legend himself. Buffett placed an ad in the *Wall Street Journal* with the headline, "We want to buy businesses worth $100 million or more before December 31, 1986." The ad stated some requirements for the businesses, none of which included moving averages, chart patterns, or an earnings prediction.

Here are four of the six prerequisites he listed:

1. "Demonstrated consistent earning power (future projections are of little interest to us, nor are 'turn-around' situations)."
2. "Businesses earning good returns on equity while employing little or no debt."
3. "Management in place (we can't supply it)."
4. "Simple businesses (if there's lots of technology, we won't understand it)."

Does this say enough? Here one of the greatest stock market investors of all time has clearly listed his criteria for considering an investment. Acknowledged by many as an extraordinary genius, all that Buffett is looking for is an established business of reasonable size that has proven itself as an efficient generator of earnings from its base of equity, but with little debt. He had "little interest" in projected earnings or turnaround situations. As they said on "Dragnet," "Just the facts."

As you will see in Chapter 7, I believe that being an efficient generator of earnings is the single most important quality of a good company. Rather than finding companies with a strong return on equity and little or no debt, I prefer to place equity and debt together to equal total capital, resulting in a return on capital equation. Interviewed in John Train's superb book, *The Money Masters*, Buffett listed "a good return on capital" as his first characteristic of a "wonderful business."

In his offer to buy businesses, Buffett is assuming a role similar to a stock market investor. Since he cannot supply the management, he will have to place a certain amount of trust in the people already doing the job. And it does not matter what type of business it is; in other words, Buffett is not forecasting or targeting any particular segment of the economy. His only industry-specific qualification is that it must be a business he can understand, nothing of the exotica that seems to catch the fancy of many more ordinary investors. An examination of his company's investment portfolio in its annual report shows a strong penchant for just the same type of stocks: solid companies with proven track records that he has waited patiently for the opportunity to acquire at attractively low valuations.

THE LONG-TERM PERSPECTIVE

There was one more comment in the ad that should be of interest to investors, but was probably overlooked by most; the simple line, "We buy to keep."

The investor's time perspective is discussed fully in Chapters 10 and 11, but let us take a brief look now at why time is perhaps the most important element to your investment success. Buffett buys companies (or shares in companies) to keep them. If an investor can buy a good company at a good value, as long as it remains a good company, its value will grow over time. The more time a good company is given to mature, the more growth can be expected.

Sometimes a company reaches a point of limited growth potential—when it has become so mature in its businesses that its ability to grow further is severely impaired. But this rarely occurs in a good company, since competent management will ordinarily take the necessary steps to use capital from the matured business to fund a diversification effort into other growing businesses. As long as strong management is in place and actively seeking to maximize the earnings potential from its base of invested capital, corporate maturation should rarely be a problem.

The basic reason for a long-term perspective is to allow for the stock market's unpredictability. The more we constrict the duration of our investment viewpoint, the more vulnerable we are to this unpredictability. Although we can make educated judgments about whether the market and its individual stocks are under- or over-valued, even the most intelligent observations are likely to be inaccurate at times. However, given enough time and a quality company, the company will prosper and its stock price will accurately reflect the growth of the company. In this way, we can show superior performance without requiring stock picking or timing precision because we are using time as an ally to increase the worth of our investments.

By allowing a stock price to mature with the growth of the company, we are significantly reducing the risk of our investment by giving the stock a chance to grow through the progression of market cycles. Of course, with successful judgments about the value of a stock price, we can tremendously increase the consistency and magnitude of the gains in our portfolio. *Nonetheless, time, more than timing, is the key to superior long-term portfolio performance.*

THE ADVANTAGE OF CONSISTENT RETURNS

I am obviously a proponent of consistently successful investing. A few isolated big winners among a sea of losers does not advance the ordinary investor's purpose of building and maintaining wealth to any meaningful extent. Suppose your portfolio begins with $100,000 in year one. Suppose that by the end of year one, you lose 50%. In the next year, you would have to gain 100% just to make it back to your original $100,000.

By contrast, a conservatively managed portfolio earning 12¼% per year will double in just six years. Taken over a 20-year period (a common length of time for a retirement portfolio), that $100,000 would build to $1 million. Taken over a 40-year period (a common length of time for a person's total involvement in the investment marketplace), that $100,000 would become $10 million. Neither of these examples includes the likely addition of more funds to the original kitty.

This simple math shows the power of compounding money at a consistently moderate rate of increase. That should be enough to silence the aggressive instincts of the get-rich-quick crowd who takes unnecessary risks in search of the big kill. By consistently compounding moderate gains, it is very possible to become a millionaire over the long term strictly from stock market invest-ments. Even just a $5000 investment in mutual funds at age 25 would build to well over a million dollars by age 65 at a 15% rate.

The next question should be: "How can we accomplish these results consistently?" The answer does not lie in the dazzle of formulas or the contemplations of great minds, but instead, a realistic focus on what makes a good investment, and what makes that investment a good value, and finally, the ability to realize you have a good thing and have the patience to let the investment mature to a ripe value.

STRATEGIC APPLICATIONS

The stock market investor should take the approach of a busi-nessman, waiting patiently to buy quality businesses at distressed values. Once acquired, investments often require long periods of time to mature and reach well-appreciated values. Such a long-term approach allows for the inherent unpredictability in the stock market by reducing the necessity for precision timing.

Long-term value investing is a realistic approach to the stock market. Overambitious investors who fail to recognize the limi-tations of stock market analysis or their own investing ability are destined to embark on an exhausting exercise in futility. Rather than assume unnecessary risk, a diversified portfolio of quality companies held over the long term should provide consistent investment returns that compound impressively over time.

2

Cycles of Stock Market Value

Stock prices are based on intrinsic economic value, but this alone does not fully explain market movements. For example, the U.S. economy has gradually grown over the years, and the stock market's average value generally reflects this growth. But the economy does not rise 50% over a three-year span and then fall 40% over the next two as the stock market sometimes does.

Moreover, it is doubtful whether a quality company like IBM would be powerful one year, incur difficulties that would seriously injure the prospects of the firm the next year, and then bounce back to be the powerhouse of the American economy the year after that. Yet, the price of IBM (and other stocks) can double in a bull market and halve in a bear market. Is the company twice as strong one year and then half as strong the next? Probably not. Market psychology is at work, exaggerating both the highs and the lows in the company's fortunes.

The price of any stock can be explained as the composite of:

1. The company's fundamental value
2. Market participants' perception of the company
3. Market participants' perception of the stock market

4. The competitive position of the stock market versus other investments

In Chapter 1, we defined stock market value as the relationship between perception and reality. A company's fundamental (intrinsic) value, coupled with the relationship of the stock market to competing investment opportunities, creates a fair value (reality). *Then psychology takes over.* Because the stock market is a marketplace of competing buyers and sellers, the stock market does not trade at fair values, but rather at *market values* that are influenced by market psychology. In a sense, because of the impact of market perceptions, the market becomes its own reality.

Market psychology inflates (and deflates) stock prices according to the perceptions of the participants. Psychology doesn't create value, but it does translate fair stock value into market value. Therefore, a universal concept of stock market valuation must include the study of cyclical market psychology.

Why "cyclical market psychology?" Because market psychology moves in cycles, creating waves of popularity that sometimes inflate prices and sometimes deflate them. Because the consensus of investors actually creates market psychology, it is very difficult for investors to stand apart from the crowd and recognize the often unrealistic perceptions around them. In this chapter, a cyclical perspective to stock market valuations that can help you better understand and follow the logical progression of value in market cycles will be introduced.

CYCLES OF INVESTOR PSYCHOLOGY

The stock market is like any other market. The goods (stocks) of the market are attractively packaged to entice buyers to pay a marked-up price. Each stock has a fair value, which is either inflated or deflated by the perceptions of market participants. Buyers and sellers haggle back and forth, finally exchanging goods for what each considers an advantageous price. In time, depending on the future movement of the stock's price, only one of the two parties will be happy with the transaction; the other will prove to be the poorer for his decision.

Consistent money can be made in the stock market only as it is made in any other business: by buying goods at a bargain value and selling them at a marked-up price. Bargains are created by market pessimism or disinterest. Once a bargain advantage is recognized by the marketplace, prices are propped back to normalized levels by the market's valuing mechanism and may become inflated by optimistic public expectations.

For example, bib overalls used to be worn exclusively by farmers and were not sold in general retail clothing stores. The demand was not sufficient, so the profit margin and volume didn't warrant a retailer's carrying them in his store. In the mid-1970s, overalls became the rage. Urban and suburban retail clothing stores began stocking them next to their shirts and sweaters as popular clothing. Overalls were no longer considered farm clothing; they were fashionable.

Prices for overalls soared based on increased public demand for an item that was previously regarded merely as work clothing. Overalls did not improve in quality, but the new public *perception* of overalls served to increase prices and sales volume.

The investment market is no different from the retail market. In this market, however, what changes is the fashion for different types of investment. Sometimes financial assets like stocks and bonds are in style; sometimes real assets like gold and real estate capture the fancy of the public. The more "in" the stock market is, the higher stocks are likely to be valued above their fair values. When the stock market is out of favor, stocks are likely to trade below their fair values.

Market psychology is not created out of the whim of investors, but is usually a logical response to a change in the economic environment. Very often, that change is a publicized event such as interest rates. Other times it is something as inconspicuous as a change in the regulatory climate. Regardless of what triggers a new cyclical trend, it is important to realize that the underlying intrinsic values have not necessarily changed, but something in the environment dictates that stock prices will be revalued.

Interest rates are a crucial environmental factor influencing stock prices. If they move lower, stock prices will usually rise, because their earnings and dividends attributes are worth more. And sometimes, just an increase in stock prices encourages investors to rush in and bid prices higher still. Whatever the catalyst, stock prices are pushed by investors' perceptions of these environmental changes to overvaluation, undervaluation, and back to overvaluation in the form of cyclical waves.

In time, all stocks reflect their intrinsic value. But because of the competitive bid nature of the stock market, prices will bound above and below intrinsic value based on the perceptions of market participants. This forms the link between cyclical value and the behavioral cycle of market psychology.

THE PSYCHOLOGICAL DILEMMA

The stock market poses a psychological paradox that works relentlessly to confound investors. *When the market appears hopeless, it's the best time to buy. And when the market appears to be a sure-fire road to riches, it's time to sell.* This is true because the stock market is a very accurate barometer of investor perceptions. For example, when the stock market reaches a bottom, investors perceive the worst possible conditions. Because the worst is perceived, the only direction for prices to go is up.

Falling into the traps of the psychological dilemma persuaded me to refine my thinking about technical analysis, subordinating it from my primary investment method to a way of better understanding market valuations.

Traditional technical analysis takes the form of glorified trend-following, often leading investors into the cruelest traps of the psychological dilemma. By buying after "break-outs" on charts or moving averages, these trend-followers usually purchase stocks well into their uptrend, often very close to the top. Conversely, selling rules for trend-followers make it advisable to sell once the price falls below its support level. The trend-follower ends up executing a strategy that dictates "buy high and sell low,"—exactly the opposite of a value-oriented strategy.

Disillusioned trend-followers often quit the stock market and find success investing in areas like real estate or other businesses. These are investments in which they can use their business acumen to buy properties at a reasonable value, develop them, and later sell them at inflated prices. This certainly makes a lot more sense than trying to buy runaway uptrends in stock prices. They might say, "those chart patterns and moving average tricks work now and then, but who can rely on them for consistent profits?" And they are absolutely right.

It is unfortunate that some people fail to apply the same logic they use in the real estate or business markets to the stock market. All markets are fundamentally the same. In real estate, they bought property at cheap valuations, fixed it up, and then sold it at inflated prices. They could have done the same thing with their stocks. Rather than fix up the company themselves, investors entrust that job to corporate management. Eventually, the market realizes the value added by management, and in a period of optimistic perceptions the stock can be sold at an inflated price.

This illustrates the advantage of buying quality stocks at bargain valuations and holding them through market cycles until they become overvalued. Equally important, it should expose the folly of buying stocks on the basis of breaking a moving average or a resistance level. Technical analysis can help to explain market behavior, but in reality, an investor buys a share of a business. The price of a stock is not going to rise because it share price broke a moving average line. The price is going to rise because other investors recognize that the market is undervaluing a stock relative to its potential value.

Fundamental analysts are not immune to the psychological dilemma either. When the economy is heating up, earnings begin to rise, sending fundamental analysts into heat with their forecasts. It is easy for analysts to get caught up in the psychology of the times, making forecasts of spectacular earnings on the assumption that the economy will maintain its powerful pace. Unfortunately, many underestimate the possibility that the economy will slow

up or sour, a common occurrence when expectations are at their
peak. As stocks rise, their recommendations tend to become still
bolder, eventually assuming too much risk.

But even those fundamental analysts who moderate their forecasts can run into traps of the psychological dilemma by neglecting
interest rates. Remember, stock market valuations are not just
based on intrinsic values, but are also the product of environmental
factors, especially interest rates. When the economy is hot, interest
rates usually begin to rise, which works to lower the relative value
of earnings and dividends. Therefore, even if the analyst forecasts
a company's earnings correctly, he can be entirely wrong about
the stock market because of the dampening effect of rising interest
rates on stock prices. The converse is true also. In fact, most bull
markets begin with the economy in terrible shape, because interest
rates are generally brought down to help pull the economy out
of a recession.

*Contrary to what most investors think, recessions often produce bull
markets, while booming economies usually create bear markets. This is
primarily because of the influence of interest rates on stock market value
and the extreme perceptions of market participants regarding economic
conditions.*

THE CONTRARIAN APPROACH

The psychological dilemma has led some in the financial press to
lionize the contrarian investor. A contrarian claims to only buy
stocks when no one else will buy—when fear is in the streets and
once-wealthy widows are selling their blue chips for pocket money.
Conversely, a contrarian will not sell until there is so much optimism
that their shoeshine boy is discussing the trading of stocks rather
than the latest baseball trades. While I agree with the contrarian
strategy in principle, there are better ways to measure extremes
in market psychology than a sampling of local shoeshine boys.
Some of the more reliable indicators of market psychology will be
discussed in Chapter 5.

The true objective of a contrarian is not simply to be a contrarian, just as the objective of a corporate raider is not to wreak havoc in management boardrooms. Contrarianism is a by-product of intelligent value investing, since the basic value strategy of buying stocks at distressed values and selling stocks at overinflated values (both of which have been created by the extreme emotional reaction of other investors) is essentially a contrarian one.

The contrarian recognizes that when crowd psychology has reached such a feverish pitch, it must be incorrect. This is because when such high expectations are built up, any minor disappointment will ruin investor confidence in their perceptions. Once the bubble of confidence is popped, the market is extremely vulnerable to a return to levels more approximating fair values.

Anticipating the possibility of this occurring at extreme valuations, a smart investor will often go directly against the general market consensus. This is not done for the sake of being a contrarian; it is just a matter of following the parameters of value that good sense dictates.

A contrarian investor recognizes the opportunity to seize value when others can only recognize fear or greed.

THE BEHAVIORAL MARKET CYCLE

Extremes in market psychology do not occur by accident; instead, they are a regular occurrence that is best understood by briefly returning to our earlier example of the life cycle.

The life and death of a bull market parallels that of a man. Each human life is different, each with its own unique course of events. But there are certain life processes that transcend human choice. Babies are not born by their own choice, nor do adults grow old and frail of their own accord.

The stock market is no different. While the stock market continues to amaze its legions of watchers by finding new patterns to its lifetime, the cyclical characteristics that begin and end bull and bear markets are very definable and very consistent. Indeed, one truly amazing quality of the stock market is the orderly way in which the stock market processes extraordinary events into very ordinary results. Though the event may be unprecedented, the processed result will fit into a familiar pattern. This is because the stock market is shaped by the forces of human behavior, and the range of human behavior has remained relatively constant over recent generations. After all, people are people (see Figure 2-1).

As a human creation, then, the stock market complies with the life-cycle process of advance and decline for all living things, be they human, or human-created phenomena like the stock market. The behavior of market participants conforms with the behavioral cycle found in nature, rising from overpessimism (birth of a cycle) to overoptimism (development) and declining back to overpessimism (death and then rebirth).

The idealized behavioral cycle shown in Figure 2-2 graphically shows the link between stock price cycles and market psychology. We can also add fundamental and interest rate attributes to the cyclical structure. This forms my system of cyclical benchmarks, which holds that certain fundamental, technical, and interest rate attributes tend to characterize each point in the market cycle. If you learn to recognize these attributes, you will be better able to understand and perhaps anticipate movements in the market.

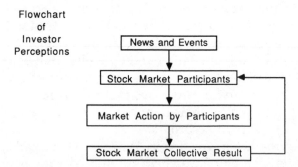

Figure 2-1. A flowchart representation depicts how investors receive new events and process their perceptions into a collective market result, which essentially, is the change in stock prices. The actual content of the news is not what moves stock prices, but rather the processed reaction to the news by the marketplace.

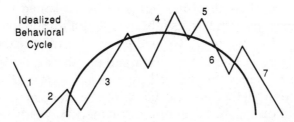

Figure 2-2. The idealized behavioral cycle gives detail to the thick-lined idealized cycle. The psychological elements of each phase within the cycle are numbered: (1) overpessimism, (2) reconstruction, (3) growth, (4) optimism, (5) overoptimism, (6) decline, and (7) overpessimism; and the cycle repeats indefinitely.

BASIC TERMS TO UNDERSTAND

We will now take a look at the basics of fundamental, technical, and interest rate value and see how they usually progress and develop along the cyclical structure. However, before we get started, let us quickly introduce a few helpful terms that may be unfamiliar to some of you.

Fundamental Terms

Fundamentalists price stocks according to the value of the company's assets or equity, earnings, or dividends. Stocks spend most of their time near fair valuations of these attributes. But in overpessimistic periods, stocks can fall so sharply that they become undervalued relative to these attributes. Conversely, in overoptimistic periods, stocks can rise so far that they become overvalued. The cycles swing from periods of undervaluation to overvaluation.

A stock's *price-earnings (p/e) ratio* is simply the stock price divided by the company's last 12 months of earnings per share. If the market is optimistic, rising stock prices will raise p/e ratios. And if the market is pessimistic, falling stock prices will lower them. Historically, a low p/e ratio for the average stock is 8, and a high p/e ratio is 16. In other words, suppose the average stock earns $10 per share. If the market was very pessimistic, it might sell for $80 or less. But if it was optimistic, it might sell for $160 or more.

(Keep in mind, like all of the terms to be explained in the next several paragraphs, this is a slight oversimplification to introduce the concept. In Chapter 7, we will go much further in depth.)

A stock's *dividend yield* is the dividend per share paid for a stock over the last 12 months divided by its stock price. Like the p/e ratio, dividend yields rise and fall with the stock market, but in the opposite direction. In an optimistic market, yields tend to be low; in a pessimistic market, they are usually high. Historically, a low dividend yield for the average stock is 3% and a high yield is 6%. Suppose the average stock is paying a $1 dividend. If the market was very pessimistic, it might sell for $17 or less. But if it was optimistic, it might sell for $33 or more.

Interest Rate Terms

The Federal Reserve (Fed) is an independent body empowered by Congress to manage U.S. monetary policy and therefore to a large extent, economic policy. They encourage economic growth by lowering interest rates and inhibit economic growth (and inflation) by raising rates. The Fed is constantly caught up in this tug of war between economic growth and inflation—a war that strongly influences stock prices.

Stock prices compete with bonds and other investments for the investment dollar. The more money going into the stock market, the more likely stock prices will rise. If interest rates are low, the rates of return from bonds are usually less than stocks, making stocks more attractive to investors. When the economic cycle overheats and the Fed becomes concerned about the problems of inflation, it might raise interest rates, which can cut off the demand for stocks and consequently lower their price. In this way, interest rates have a preponderant effect on how the market values its stocks.

Technical Terms

There are three basic sets of terms in technical analysis to consider: *overbought* and *oversold* conditions, *confirmation* and *divergence*, and *support* and *resistance*.

Overbought and *oversold* conditions, as we have already explained, are extreme moves in price or other market attributes that are equivalent to the fundamental terms of overvaluation and under-valuation. During overoptimistic periods, the market will explode to the upside and become overbought, while in overpessimistic times, stocks will fall sharply to become oversold.

Confirmations are signs of a healthy market, with new highs (or new lows) in the market averages being "confirmed" by a variety of technical indicators. *Divergences* are caused by the failure of the market to show confirmations. In a classic divergence, the popular market averages move in one direction while the internal dynamics of the market, as evidenced by trading statistics, move in the other direction.

For example, if the Dow advances to record levels, but the number of stocks reaching new lows is roughly equal to those setting new highs, this is a negative divergence (bearish). This often occurs at market tops, and it suggests that the market is not as strong as the popular market averages portray. If the Dow is falling to new lows, but other market averages like the Dow Jones Utility Average and Transportation Average are showing good strength, this is a positive divergence (bullish) which often occurs at market bottoms. This indicates that the market may not be as weak as the Dow is showing.

Support and *resistance* are two terms of art in charting. Support is the point where the marketplace recognizes value and buying demand props (supports) prices that were previously falling. Resistance is just the opposite of support. It is the point where sellers overpower buyers and form a ceiling (resistance) against further price gains. Bottoms form at support, tops form at resistance.

AN INTRODUCTION TO CYCLICAL BENCHMARKS

Now that we have a basic handle on the terms, let us see how fundamental, technical, and interest rate forces interact to make bull and bear markets. As we go along, the important thing is not to memorize the events, but to see how the events evolve in a logically developing cyclical structure.

Long-term stock market cycles begin with stock prices at their lows after suffering sharp declines. The economy was most likely getting a little too strong, forcing the Fed to raise interest rates to combat rising inflation. Eventually, this will cut off economic development, leading to a recession and pessimistic investor attitudes. At this point, p/e ratios may be quite low and dividend yields may be historically high, but stock prices may still be fairly valued because of relatively high interest rates.

Once the Fed begins lowering interest rates, the balance of value soon swings toward an undervalued stock market. Stock prices may not rise immediately, but as the Fed becomes more accommodative, the historically cheap p/e ratios and high dividend yields become more attractive to investors, who are unable to receive such good returns on other investments. Market psychology was already so pessimistic that it would take very little in the way of positive developments to send rays of hope into the environment.

A bull market is born, and it grows with favorably lower interest rates. Technically, the market is somewhat pessimistic about future advances, but the internal dynamics are healthy, with each new high in the market being confirmed by strength in a variety of technical indicators.

As the market cycle matures, cracks in the technical picture appear and negative divergences seep in to weaken the market structure. Eventually, often spurred on by higher interest rates which effect a swing toward fundamental overvaluation, the weakened market structure collapses, and stocks begin a broad decline. The bottom occurs the same way as described earlier, with interest rates swinging the balance of value toward undervaluation and overpessimism.

To summarize: At market bottoms, overpessimism creates tremendous selling pressure, causing oversold conditions at a point where stock prices are unrealistically undervalued because of falling interest rates. Buying surfaces, creating support for a future rise in stock prices. At market tops, overoptimism creates tremendous buying pressure, causing overbought conditions at a point where stock prices are unrealistically overvalued because of rising interest rates. Selling surfaces, creating resistance against a future rise in stock prices.

The following is a basic description of the qualities that identify each part of the market cycle like a personal signature. If we can identify the qualities, then we can identify which part of the cycle the market is in, thereby giving us an overall understanding of which direction stock prices are headed. Obviously, these benchmarks are generalized and should not be construed as absolute qualities that *must* appear. However, understanding the general progression of cyclical benchmarks can give an investor important insights into future movements of the market.

Market Cycles and Their Benchmarks

1. Overpessimism
   a. Stocks are grossly undervalued
   b. Investors have unrealistic fears of severe price declines
   c. Downtrend is deeply oversold with positive divergences building
   d. Interest rates are very high, but reaching a peak

2. Reconstruction
   a. Stocks are still grossly undervalued
   b. Hope is beginning to surface
   c. Oversold conditions are relieved with positive bias to market direction
   d. Interest rates are falling quickly

3. Growth
   a. Stocks are moderately undervalued
   b. Investors recognize an improvement in economic conditions
   c. Uptrend is strong with constant confirmation
   d. Interest rates are still falling

4. Optimism
   a. Stocks are nearing full valuations
   b. Investors are optimistic toward economic conditions
   c. Uptrend is nearing overbought levels, but still being confirmed
   d. Interest rates are nearing their bottom

5. Overoptimism
   a. Stocks are grossly overvalued
   b. Investors are overoptimistic toward economic conditions
   c. Uptrend is deeply overbought with negative divergences building
   d. Economic expansion causes interest rates to rise slightly

6. Decline
   a. Stocks are still overvalued due to earnings declines or sharp increases in interest rates
   b. Investors are still optimistic toward a rebound in stock prices
   c. Downtrend is strong with constant confirmation
   d. Interest rates continue to rise

7. Overpessimism
   a. Stocks are grossly undervalued
   b. Investors have unrealistic fears of severe price declines
   c. Downtrend is deeply oversold with positive divergences building
   d. Interest rates are very high, but reaching a peak

THE HURST STUDY IN CYCLES

Stock market cycles move within the constraints of time, just like most other cycles. Our everyday world is filled with time cycles, many of which we take for granted: the rising and setting of the sun, the four seasons, and so on. Like most natural cycles, the stock market regenerates, repeating the same progression of cycles with regular frequency.

J. M. Hurst wrote a fascinating account on the time element of cycles in his book *The Profit Magic of Stock Transaction Timing*, which is a complex study of cyclical principles. The book contains many ambitious attempts to predict cycles with moving averages and other techniques that do not fit into my work. However, I have adapted some of my cyclical concepts from Hurst's book and it is recommended reading for those interested in cycle analysis.

Hurst designed a table of expected cyclical periods for the stock market, which he called *nominal durations*. These time periods could be expected to vary slightly from cycle to cycle, but over the long haul, they approximate the average lengths of the appropriate cycles (see Table 2-1).

Hurst spoke of five principles that govern cyclical movement in the stock market. His verbiage is a little difficult to understand without the complete text, so I have quoted his words and have added my interpretations directly below.

1. *Summation Principle.* "Cyclicality in price motion consists of the sum of a number of (non-ideal) periodic-cyclic components" (p. 32).

A cycle is the sum of many cyclic components. In other words, all of the cycles are in progress at all times, but certain cycles dominate others. If five different cycles are in an uptrend position and only one cycle is pointing downward, the five cycles will

TABLE 2-1   Durations of Cyclical Periods as Described by J. M. Hurst

Years	Months	Weeks
18		
9		
4.5		
3		
1.5	18	
1	12	
.75	9	
.5	6	26^a
.25	3	13^a
	1.5	6.5
	.75	3.25
	.375	1.625

[a] The 26- and 13-week components often appear in data as a combined effect of 18-week nominal duration.

ordinarily dominate and the uptrend will continue. The cycle would be formed by the sum of the six cyclic components.

2. *Commonality Principle.* "Summed cyclicality is a common factor among all stocks" (p. 32).

The summation principle from rule 1 applies to all common stocks, and all stocks have similar cyclic durations. I do not apply cycle analysis to individual stocks because the variances among different stocks can be too misleading. However, since most stocks have similar durations, they generally move together. Therefore, if the stock market as a whole reaches a cyclical bottom (or top), it can be assumed that a great many stocks have reached a bottom (or top) as well.

3. *Variation Principle.* "Each cyclic component varies from the ideal in that magnitude varies slowly as time passes. As magnitude increases, duration also increases. As magnitude decreases, duration also decreases" (p. 33).

Magnitude is the amount of price movement from the top to the bottom of a cycle. A cycle that began from 1000 and rose to 1200 at its peak would show a magnitude of 200. The length of each cycle of each stock varies somewhat. The variation is due to the magnitude of the cycles. The greater the magnitude, the longer the cycle is expected to last. This causes each cycle to vary from the nominal lengths listed in Table 2-1, but the variances should equal out over time to approximate the nominal lengths.

4. *Nominality Principle.* "The effect of the variation principle is to force the use of a nominal cyclic duration in the quantification of the cyclic model" (p. 33).

Despite the variations in cycle lengths, because of the commonality of cyclic behavior, we can derive nominal cycle lengths. These are the expected lengths of the cycle about which the cycles are expected to vary. Those cycle lengths are shown in Table 2-1.

5. *Proportionality Principle.* "The greater the duration of a cyclic component, the larger its magnitude" (p. 33).

The longer the cyclical length, the deeper the cycle. For example, from top to bottom, a four-year cycle is expected to show a much greater point spread (gain or loss) than a six-week cycle.

The Hurst study has had a profound influence on my approach to cycles. Cycles form a progression, not only of psychological development, but also of time. In the progression of human life, the infant cycle supports the development of childhood, which leads to adolescence, and so on. Each cycle requires a certain amount of time to develop to be able to move on to the next cycle. Maturation time can be expected to vary from person to person, but measured over a great many people, the variances of each cycle even out to an average that will hold true for most people.

The summation principle suggests that the market spends a great deal of time moving in a trendless sideways motion, preparing for relatively short advances and declines. This is easy to understand, if you relate the pattern of cycles to market psychology. Changing market trends is like changing jobs. It takes time to make the decision to job hunt, send out résumés, then interview for the new post. Transition periods take time in human life, and since the market is composed of human decision makers, stocks spend a great deal of time wading through smaller cycles of sideways movement.

Ambitious market timers often lose a lot of money because of this problem. Because sideways motion is just as (or even more) prevalent than advancing or declining movement, it demands more precision than is consistently possible to catch the occasional "intermediate term" moves that market timers so cherish. These moves of 10% or more usually happen so fast that by the time a technician has reversed positions, most of the move has already occurred and the market is usually ready to head back the other way (see Figure 2-3).

Moreover, because smaller cycles make up larger cycles, trying to catch the shorter-term moves often results in missing the larger and more profitable ones. Without a *long-term* cyclical perspective, the sideways moves can be excruciating. Intermediate-term timers bite their nails looking for the perfect time to jump in the market. They know that such precision is necessary because the move will terminate relatively quickly.

Because the sideways motion often looks like the beginnings of a move, ambitious market timers are often whipsawed into buying near tops and selling near bottoms. And since a large part

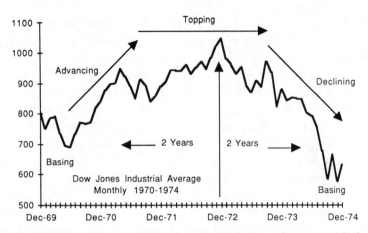

Figure 2-3. The 1970–1974 cycle is typical of most cycles, spending a great deal of time in sideways motion, either in topping or basing movement. The propensity of the market to move sideways makes it unrealistic to practice shorter-term market timing.

of market movement is either downward or sideways, aggressive timers have a lower probability of making consistent profits because they are likely to have as many losing transactions as winning ones.

The commonality principle suggests that, because most stocks generally move together, timing for the entire market can be a valid way to improve investment performance. Since most stocks have the same cycles, and all cycles have cyclic attributes, we can use our system of cyclical benchmarks to improve our market timing. It also points out the importance of market timing as a method of risk management. For example, in a bear market, most stocks are likely to undergo a severe decline with the rest of the market.

The variation and proportionality principles suggest that shorter-term timers will end up with smaller price increases, because the larger the move, the longer it takes to develop. A shorter-term investor does not give his investments enough time to build up the bigger moves. Smaller holding periods result in smaller profits, because shorter cyclical durations result in smaller magnitudes. By going in and out of stocks on a shorter-term basis, investors have a very low probability of making large profits.

Moreover, because the timing and magnitude of moves varies, an investor is never really sure whether a move is finished or not. This makes the shorter-term investor inconsistent to the point where timing will ordinarily hinder investment performance. By trying to catch short-term moves, the investor limits his profits by trying to call several smaller moves that have smaller rewards. In addition, because the moves are smaller and happen so quickly, this type of investing demands a precision that is unsustainable over time.

The long-term investor knows that several of these perfectly called smaller moves add up to one large move that he can catch by simply remaining invested. This is another way in which long-term value investors strategically stack the deck in their favor. Equally important to note is the converse—the way that aggressive timers stack the deck against themselves by assuming unnecessary risks.

THE FOUR-YEAR ECONOMIC CYCLE

Larry Tisch, chairman of Loew's Corporation and one of the great investors of our time, explained his simple investment philosophy in John Train's book *The Money Masters*:

> I'm a pragmatist, I just wait until the fourth year, when the business cycle bottoms, and buy whatever is offered, whatever I think will have the biggest bounce. Coming off the bottom, lots of things will double or triple before the next peak in the cycle, two or three years later. You never know what they'll be.

Since the "four-year cycle" doesn't last exactly four years, but rather varies between about three and five years, let us call it the economic cycle (see Figure 2-4).

The economy rises and falls in approximately four-year cycles. The stock market, as an excellent leading indicator of economic activity, tends to lead the economy in its movements. (The stock market has been recognized by economists for its forecasting ability to such an extent that it is an official component of the Index

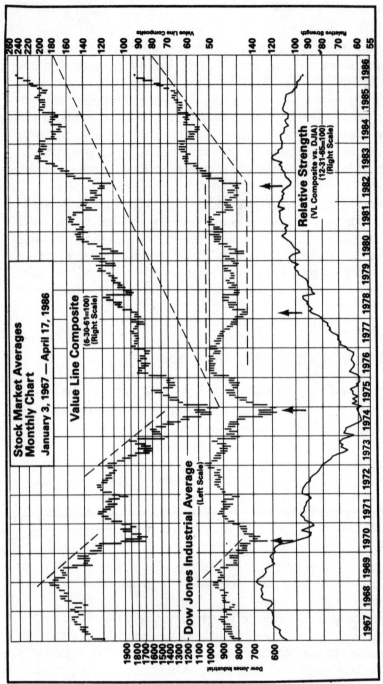

Figure 2-4. Arrows show market bottoms on the Dow Jones Industrial Average. The bottoms are approximately four years apart, suggesting the influence of the four-year economic cycle. Between 1976 and 1982, the dashed line at 1000 on the Dow chart shows resistance, while the dashed line at 740 illustrates support, and the rising dashed lines illustrates an uptrend. *Courtesy:* Value Line, 711 Third Avenue, New York, NY 10017.

of Leading Economic Indicators.) The lead time is impossible to judge, but the most commonly quoted figure is six to nine months. Thus, if the economy is rising out of a recession, the stock market has probably already been rising for several months.

Of course, because the stock market is a leading indicator, economic forecasts are of less utility for the stock investor, because they are always late to a significant degree. As mentioned earlier, by the time the economy is judged to be in a booming condition, the stock market is often building a top formation because interest rates are rising to meet increased credit demands and combat inflation. This makes the stock market a far better predictor of economic activity than the reverse.

It is perhaps no coincidence that a U.S. president is elected every four years. And accordingly, since the depression, the stock market has *never fallen* in the year before a presidential election year. The politics of the nation, as we will see in Chapter 3, have a great deal to do with the stock market. Before a presidential election, the incumbent party does its best to paint a pretty picture of the country, which includes lowering interest rates and pumping up public perceptions of the economy—two of the most telling factors of stock market value.

As it has for Tisch, this creates an investment opportunity for investors as well. This is not to suggest that long-term investors try to turn into precision market timers to catch the four-year cycle. Although we can only guess when the cycle will begin and when it will end, we can gain some security knowing that a long-term move requires a matter of years to build rather than just a matter of weeks. Furthermore, we can use our system of cyclical benchmarks to fit the qualities into the cyclical structure to achieve some advance warning.

For example, suppose the stock market is exhibiting the classic cyclical benchmarks of an important bottom: grossly undervalued, deeply oversold, and overpessimistic, with interest rates at a peak and beginning to fall. In this case, knowledge that the market has reached an important low approximately four years before and approximately four years before that for decades on end, can lend confidence to your assessment that the market is near a cyclical low. Since downside risk is minimal, the market represents a

terrific buying value on a long-term basis on the expectation that
the forthcoming upswing will last for several months (or years)
and result in sizable price gains.

OTHER CYCLES

In assessing the four-year economic cycle, it is important to maintain
a cyclical perspective and be tolerant of the minor ups and downs
that occur along the way. Once the cycle begins, it will usually
be quite powerful, but this does not preclude occasional corrections
that can be somewhat scary. Remember, market movement is the
net result of several conflicting cycles of varying duration and
power, both dominant and recessive—like genes. Usually the
dominant cycles control the trend, but occasionally the recessive
cycles exert a corrective influence within the dominant trend.

Much of the time, the net result is a blending of the dominant
and recessive cycles, resulting in sideways market movement. In
general, the longer-term cycles create the general environment,
but the shorter-term cycles define the current activity.

For example, a long-term uptrend will go through a number of
corrections during its cycle. Within the context of this long-term
uptrend, if the shorter-term cycles are positive, the market will
advance strongly. But if the conglomeration of shorter-term cycles
is negative, the market is likely to have a correction within the
uptrend. For the long-term investor, following the shorter-term
nuances is not important and so this exceedingly complex and
often ineffective body of knowledge is not fully addressed in this
book.

Nevertheless, there are more cycles to be aware of than just
the four-year economic cycle. Four-year cycles join together to
form even longer cycles. For example, two 4-year cycles formed
together to create the 1966–1974 decline. And the 1974–1982 market
action can be characterized as a largely sideways movement. Now
in progress, the 1982–19xx period is an upward move. It has been
disputed whether the 1974–1982 period was the beginning of a
bull market cycle that continues today (1987) or was just a continuation of the 1966–1974 decline. As fully discussed in Chapter
9, I tend to believe the latter.

The basic lesson here is that smaller cycles fit together in different configurations to form larger cycles. In Table 2-1, the Hurst nominal lengths are multiples of each other, suggesting perhaps that three 1.5-year cycles come together to create one 4.5-year cycle. The behavioral cycle contemplates three advancing waves (reconstruction, growth, and optimism) that fit into each complete market cycle.

In view of our inability to time short-term moves in the market consistently, the shorter nominal cycles suggested by Hurst are of limited use to the long-term investor. At best, they can be put together like building blocks to get a better understanding of how the four-year and longer cycles are put together. This is a humbling concession to our limitations, but given the difficulties posed by timing shorter moves, most experienced investors would probably agree that this bit of wimpishness is good advice.

For those interested in tracking shorter-term cycles, the Elliott Wave Principle attempts to predict market movement from a well-developed network of cyclical analysis that contemplates cycles lasting from a matter of minutes to a number of centuries. My behavioral cycle uses the Elliott Wave Structure and Elliott's work probably inspired my system of cyclical benchmarks and the universal concept. For a better understanding, read Robert R. Prechter and A. J. Frost's fascinating account of R. N. Elliott's cyclical wave work in their book *Elliott Wave Principle*.

Although I do not ardently study the Elliott Waves by delving into the smaller cycles, I do maintain an awareness of how the larger waves are unfolding. Just having an awareness is helpful to value decisions, since it can be a guide to where the market might be in its long-term cycle. As for the shorter cycles, I do not believe in my ability to follow consistently the progression of smaller cycles. Therefore, I reserve its use for long-term awareness.

STRATEGIC APPLICATIONS

As we have seen, stock market value is a combination of fundamental (intrinsic), technical (investor perceptions), and interest rate value. Fundamental value is inflated or deflated by investor perceptions and interest rates in a cyclical fashion. Each stage in the cycle has its own personality, indicated by cyclical benchmarks, which serves as a signature of its unique market attributes. Investors should follow the progression of cyclical benchmarks to better understand current market action and the movements that are likely to follow.

Several cycles move in different directions at any one time, creating a net market result that spends a great deal of time moving in a sideways motion and relatively little time producing trends that yield good profits (uptrends or downtrends). Because it is too difficult to catch the trending moves with any consistent precision, shorter-term investors, who are often underinvested, are likely to do worse than long-term investors. By buying when market valuations are on the low side and holding on to investments, the long-term investor has an inherent edge over the short-term investor because time is working to progress the development of the cyclical price structure.

Part Two
A Value Approach
to Market Timing

3

Understanding
Interest Rates

Chapters 2 and 3 stressed the importance of viewing the stock market with a universal approach, taking full consideration of all three aspects of stock market value (fundamental, interest rate, and technical). As discussed, fundamentals create intrinsic value, interest rates turn intrinsic value into fair value, and technical factors translate fair value into market value.

If money is tight (rates are relatively high or rising), then stocks are worth less. And if money is easy (rates are relatively low or falling), then stocks are worth more. If an investor could perfectly predict interest rate movements he could probably be extremely successful in the stock market without knowing very much about individual stocks. All that he would have to do is invest in the 30 companies of the Dow Jones Industrial Average according to his expectations of changes in interest rates. That is how much interest rates influence stock prices.

This chapter is not intended to turn you into an expert on interest rates, but it should provide an adequate background regarding interest rates for most investors and their investment activities. Chapter 4 will delve into the tremendous impact that interest rates have on stock market value. We will now see what moves interest rates and investigate how we can better understand why they fluctuate.

THE FEDERAL RESERVE

Interest rates are more than just another market indicator, they are perhaps the most important tool that the government has in its arsenal to influence the national economy. Moreover, as the economics of the United States becomes increasingly intertwined with other nations, the interest rate policies of major European and Asian industrial powers, such as West Germany and Japan, play a crucial role in setting U.S. policies, a topic to be discussed later in this chapter.

The Fed is the decision-making team for interest rates in the United States. Interest rate policy is managed by the Fed's Federal Open Market Committee (FOMC) a 12-person panel comprised of 7 governors (Board of Governors) and 5 regional Fed bank presidents. The Board of Governors are appointed by the president of the United States (with Senate approval) to 14-year terms. The five presidents are chosen by the chairman of the Fed (with Senate approval) and rotated annually from among the 12 regional Fed banks which influence more than 6000 member banks.

The FOMC directs the monetary policy of the United States by controlling the level of the Federal funds rate, a pivotal, short-term interest rate that tends to lead changes in other interest rates. Through management of the Federal funds market and other facets of the banking system, the Fed controls the flow of money, and therefore, strongly influences which investment markets receive inflows of investor capital.

Specifically, the FOMC indirectly controls the Federal funds rate, other short-term rates like U.S. Treasury bills, bank free reserves, and the money supply. The Board of Governors directly controls the discount rate, stock margin requirements, and bank reserve requirements. Even though each commercial bank sets its own prime rate, the Fed has a very strong influence on the prime rate, since its discount rate and Federal funds rates have such a preponderant effect on the borrowing costs of banks.

Although seven governors and five regional bank presidents comprise the FOMC, it is the chairman (one of the seven governors) who is generally in the spotlight, setting the tone for interest rate policy. While the other members can act independently in their decision making, most members tend to follow the policy leads of the chairman. As head of the Federal Reserve System, he directs policy and is the most public voice of that policy to the stock market and the rest of the world.

The chairman of the Fed is often referred to as the "second most important man in the country," although such distinction is often more a function of the individual than the office. In the case of a powerful leader like Paul Volcker, who was chairman until mid-1987, when Alan Greenspan took over, this is probably a true statement, leading Wall Streeters to measure his every action and nonaction.

POLITICAL INFLUENCE AND THE FED

Interest rates are a way in which the federal government gets involved in the nation's economy and still can call it a free economy. To increase economic expansion, it lowers interest rates; to slow expansion and control inflation, it raises interest rates. The stock market would be easy to predict if investors knew exactly what the Fed was doing and was planning to do. However, the Fed, for the most part, keeps its operations and objectives secret to the public. This has led to the art of "Fed-watching," analysts who attempt to piece together clues laid by the Fed in their market behavior and public statements to better understand Fed policy.

The Fed is meant to be entirely independent from the White House. It is supposed to be free of political influence and act as an independent body in the nation's economic welfare. As a matter of practical operating procedure, the White House is able to exert a certain amount of pressure on the Fed, much of it depending on the political power of the Fed chairman.

The president has the ability to influence directly the course of the Fed by appointing new members when a 14-year term is completed or a board member resigns. This influence is even more pronounced if that appointment is for the chairmanship of the Fed, which is chosen every four years. Even if the appointment is for one of the six nonchairman seats, the president and his political party can build important unspoken alliances by choosing individuals who have an economic orientation similar to their own.

From a longer-term perspective, this can also give a measure of cooperation to the ideals of one political party over another. But, from the past experiences of appointed board members, most individuals take a middle-of-the-road approach once they join the Fed, leaving behind the political ambitions of the president who appointed them. Their ideals and economic orientation may not have changed, but most Fed board members tend to act with an objective clarity of purpose that is fairly devoid of political influence.

But there are examples of political influence. In 1985, President Reagan publicly argued with Fed chairman Paul Volcker to lower interest rates and encourage more economic growth. Volcker held firm to his goal of keeping a close rein on inflation. Vice-chairman Preston Martin and Martha Seger were both Reagan appointees. Both were pushing for lower rates, actively criticizing Volcker's policies as being too restrictive. In 1986, two board posts opened up and Reagan added two more of his appointments to the board.

The vote for a discount rate change by the Fed is by majority. Having four appointees gave the Reagan camp a majority in Fed decisions, leading the press and the financial markets to question the power of Volcker to rule over Fed policy. This became a major political story, particularly as the Fed made a decision to cut the discount rate against the vote of the Chairman. To save face for the Chairman, the Fed agreed internally to forestall the rate decrease until a condition desired by Volcker was met.

The condition (important to the global discussion later in this chapter) was not to cut the discount rate until Japan and West Germany lowered their central bank interest rates in a concerted global interest rate cut. Soon after the cut, vice-chairman Martin, the most vocal Volcker critic, resigned from the board, restoring the political power of Chairman Volcker. Of course, it should be noted that since Volcker has control over the choosing of the five regional presidents of the FOMC, he still maintained control of the FOMC and the Federal funds rate.

This example should make it clear that although the Fed is meant to be immune from influence by the other branches of the government, in truth, there is considerable political pressure on the Fed. This is becoming more a reality, as Fed policy decisions have an increasing impact on the global economy and vice versa. The Fed can no longer consider the effects of its actions within the vacuum of domestic policy, but must assess the impact that its decisions will have in the international political and economic arena.

GROWTH VERSUS INFLATION

The Fed is constantly caught in a delicate balancing act between promoting economic growth and fighting inflationary pressures. Every action that the Fed takes has an influence on the push-pull of this equation. If the Fed takes an accommodative stance to promote economic growth, then it risks heating up the fires of inflation. Should the Fed assume a more restrictive posture to control inflation, then it risks pushing the economy into a recession. There is rarely a perfectly obvious path for the Fed to take, so every decision is scrutinized by the financial markets for its effects on the growth-versus-inflation equation.

As an example of the economic tug-of-war between growth and inflation, let us take a brief look at the monetary policies in the first half of the 1980s. From 1979 to mid-1981, the Fed and Chairman Volcker decided to fight a raging inflation by raising the discount rate to 14%. Federal funds were pushed up to 20%. Banks responded by raising the prime rate as high as 21½%. Consumer debt had risen to dangerously overextended levels, but the high interest rates eventually choked off spending and inflation. The high rates also inhibited corporate expansion, which slowed oil consumption and later contributed to a worldwide oil glut.

By 1982, the economy was in the throes of its worst recession in several years. The Fed had no choice but to adopt an accommodative stance, forcing rates down as it maintained a watchful eye toward inflation. By late 1985, the inflationary spiral seemed well contained, perhaps even dead, leading the Fed to ease sub-

stantially, although certainly not as much as some proponents of
economic growth would have liked. But Wall Street liked the
results well enough, as the Dow rose about 25% in 1985.

In November 1985, the dampening effects of high interest rates
on worldwide industrial expansion were to make their impact felt
in the crude oil markets. Crude oil prices fell from over $30 a
barrel in late November to under $10 a barrel by March 1986. In
the 1970s, it was commonly believed that the key to snapping the
inflationary spiral of high oil prices was to place political pressure
on the Arab oil-producing nations. In retrospect, Volcker and his
monetary policies probably had more to do with the lowering of
oil prices than any single force in world politics.

This is just one example of the awesome power of the Fed, a
power that must be used with the utmost of care. The Fed has
the capacity to turn on or off the fuel to economic growth—money. The stock market, as we will see, is not so concerned with
economic growth as it is with the flow of money. This accounts
for bear markets starting during heated economic growth and bull
markets beginning in the latter stages of an economic recession.
Wherever interest rates go, stock prices are likely to run in the
opposite direction.

INTEREST RATES AND THE BUSINESS CYCLE

Earlier, we discussed the impact of the four-year economic cycle
on stock prices. Since 1960 alone, long-term bottoms in the stock
market have occurred in 1962, 1966, 1970, 1974, 1978, 1982, and
late 1985. Of course, the four-year cycle might be influenced by
the presidential elections, but a more concrete argument can be
found in the relationship between interest rates and the business
cycle.

Figure 3-1 shows that when economic growth becomes so strong
that it threatens to raise inflationary fears, the Fed steps in to raise
rates. When the economy is stuck in the doldrums, the Fed tries
to stimulate growth by lowering interest rates. This is the basic
battle between inflation and economic growth and its impact on
interest rate policy.

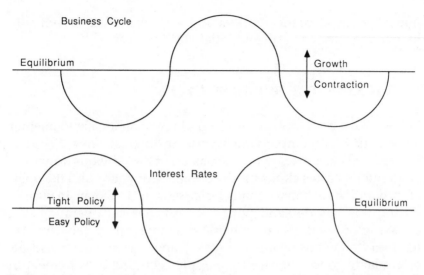

Figure 3-1. The path of interest rates is shown against the movement of the business (economic) cycle of growth and contraction. Note how easy money leads to economic growth, which eventually leads to the need for tighter monetary policy, which results in a contraction of business activity.

The politics of this issue are fairly obvious, but they can become extremely entangled during election time. A posture favoring economic growth (lower interest rates) is politically favorable in that it should improve employment and income, the way to most voter's hearts. A firm stance against inflation (higher interest rates) may anger voters, as the short-term damage to their pocketbooks usually overcomes their concern for the long-term health of the economy.

Furthermore, rising interest rates usually mean a weak stock market (a political issue in itself), since the market is perhaps the most publicly watched barometer of economic conditions. In truth, a strong stock market is often indicative of sluggish business conditions (because interest rates are lowered), but most voters are not aware of this. To them, a strong stock market usually means a strong presidency.

In this way, stock market performance can be linked to the presidential elections and the elections linked to interest rates. As noted earlier, since the depression, the stock market has not fallen in any year prior to a presidential election year.

TRACKING THE BUSINESS CYCLE

Let us take a brief look at the chronology of an idealized business cycle with its accompanying swings in interest rates. Seeds for the upward cycle are sown by the ashes of the previous downturn. High interest rates choke off the demand for goods and the ability of corporations to borrow funds for expansion. To remain in business during this low-demand period, companies cut operating costs by laying off workers and lowering manufacturing capacity. This has the effect of raising unemployment and lowering the inventories of available goods. In essence, supply is cutting back to meet the slumping demand.

Due to the lack of demand, inflation is under better control but the economy is faltering badly. To stimulate economic growth, the Fed turns to a policy of lower interest rates. At some point, falling interest rates ignite more active business conditions. Demand for goods rises, working off the inventories from the previous business cycle. Eventually, heightened demand encourages companies to increase their production of goods to the marketplace. To do so, they hire new workers and build plants to increase their manufacturing capacity.

However, the optimism soon leads to new inflationary pressures. Low interest rates have provided a favorable environment for corporations to make sizable investments to cash in on the economic boom. Consumers enjoy the low rates and enrich their lives by extending themselves with cheap loans for purchasing new homes and other discretionary purchases, such as automobiles. By this time, inflationary pressures are rising, reaching a level that causes concern among the monetary authorities. The Fed constricts the supply of free reserves in the money markets, putting a brake on the supply of available money. The borrowing pressures on the banking system heat up, causing interest rates to rise.

The rise in rates is not able to overwhelm the pace of economic growth immediately, but the restrictive forces gradually take their toll on business decisions. Rates continue to rise, as corporations who made business decisions predicated on low interest rates are forced to either cancel or scale back expansion plans or accept the higher rates. Eventually, the expansion cools as corporations and consumers are slowed by tighter monetary conditions.

The Fed is consciously slowing the growth of the economy, trying to keep it out of a severe recession. At this point, an assessment of inflationary forces is crucial. Should inflation be in a runaway situation, the Fed may be forced to continue raising interest rates as it did in 1981 to choke off inflationary expectations. This fear of inflation must be balanced against the potential damage to the domestic economy, the global economy, and the basic welfare of the American people. Eventually, as inflationary pressures ease, the Fed decides that economic growth is becoming more of an imperative than inflation, rates are lowered, and the business cycle begins again.

The preceding paragraphs described a simplified and idealized business cycle, but they illustrate the balancing act that the Fed plays between economic growth and inflation. The Fed often adopts a stance, whether to err on the side of inflation or the side of economic growth. Investors should always be aware of which way the Fed wants to lean. As a rule, the Fed feels a certain responsibility to act as the independent crusader for the economy against the ravages of inflation. But as long as inflationary expectations are constrained within an acceptable limit, the Fed will encourage economic growth by offering favorably low interest rates.

GLOBAL CONSIDERATIONS

The Fed is concerned with more than just the American economy. Increasingly, the worldwide economy is very much subject to the swings of U.S. interest rates. By virtue of the dominant status of the United States as a world economic power, the state of the global economy is highly dependent on the level of U.S. interest rates because of its influence on U.S. spending and currency. If interest rates in the United States are high enough to slow spending, then the global economy suffers because of the lack of U.S. dollars buying foreign goods.

The investment world is an increasingly global community, with competition to receive investment dollars among the major world markets. The United States is generally viewed as a safe and liquid haven for investment, largely devoid of the political upheavals that endanger investments in many other parts of the world. There have been times when world opinion has turned skeptical toward the United States, but in general, the U.S. is recognized as the most stable country in the world. This safety and liquidity feature gives U.S. securities an inherent edge in buying demand over the securities of many other nations.

If interest rates are higher in the United States than in other foreign countries, then investment capital will flow into the U.S. financial markets, buoying them higher on the strength of new infusions of capital. Initially, most of this capital will flow into the bond markets. By the end of 1985, reliable estimates were that the Japanese were buying about 15% of all Treasury bond and bill offerings. This is due to the fact that U.S. interest rates were about three points higher than those available in Japan.

The tremendous inflows of capital sopped up the excess supplies of securities, allowing the Treasury to place large offerings onto the bond markets and still have the capacity to lower interest rates. Without such participation by the Japanese and other nations, the United States might not have been able to finance its bulging budget deficit without incurring much higher interest rates.

The relative exchange rates of the two currencies were crucial to maintaining this arrangement. If the U.S. dollar were to fall to very low levels against the Japanese yen, it would lessen the advantage of investing in U.S. securities because the risk of currency transaction losses to Japanese investors could outweigh the benefits of higher U.S. interest rates. Also, as the dollar falls, interest rates might fall also, further reducing the advantage. Should the inflow of capital slow, demand for Treasury offerings would be severely affected, leading to a rise in interest rates. This rise would be expected to continue, perhaps until interest rates became attractive enough again to lure foreign capital back to the U.S. markets.

The increasing global scope of the U.S. economy is ushering in a new era of cooperation among industrial nations. In 1985, inflation and interest rates were low, but the U.S. dollar was setting record highs, causing a serious trade deficit in the United States. In September 1985 the United States and the four largest industrial (non-Communist bloc) nations, dubbed the "Group of Five," signed an agreement to lower the value of the dollar and reduce the U.S. trade deficit, thereby hoping to rejuvenate the ailing industrial sector of the United States.

The political aspects of this type of an agreement, regardless of its ultimate success, cannot be divorced from the role of the Fed. Again, the Fed is not supposed to be subject to political forces, but in this case, it would have been political suicide for the Fed and the United States (as a participating nation in the Group of Five agreement) to raise interest rates. Obviously, if rates were raised, it would probably raise the value of the dollar, working against the goals of the international agreement. Though not actually written, but almost implicit in the arrangement, was an understanding that the Fed would not raise interest rates to undermine the objective. Situations like these have a tremendous impact on the financial markets and underscore the importance of understanding the role of the United States in the global economy.

ECONOMIC INDICATORS

As an investor, you should be able to digest basic economic facts and understand how economic events might affect interest rates. The single most important relationship to recognize is that the interest rate markets are encouraged by weakness in the economy and hurt by strength in the economy. In other words, good news to the economy is bad news to the credit markets. This also means that good news to the economy is often bad news to the stock market, unless inflation is under good control. That bad news to the economy is usually good news to the stock market, unless the economy is perilously weak.

This is the main reason that the stock market is able to act as such a wonderful leading indicator of the economy. Once the economy strengthens too much, rising interest rates will push the stock market lower, soon to be followed by an economy weakened by tight credit conditions. Conversely, stock prices rise on lower

interest rates, which eventually lead to economic expansion by
virtue of easy credit conditions. In this way, the stock market is
a better predictor of the economy than the economy is a predictor
of the stock market.

The following is a simple list, certainly not all-inclusive, of nine
conditions that might encourage the Fed to tighten money. They
all deal with the relationship between economic fact and policy
objectives. Should economic reality project more growth than is
suitable, the Fed might need to tighten its hold on monetary
policy. The converse would be true for loosening monetary policy.

Economic Conditions That Might Encourage a Money-Tightening Policy

1. Inflation rises, particularly if it exceeds policy limits
2. Money supply (M2 and M3 only) rises above policy objectives
3. Employment figures are stronger than forecasted
4. The U.S. dollar is too weak to achieve policy objectives
5. Consumer or corporate debt rises above policy objectives
6. Retail sales rise quicker than policy objectives
7. Industrial capacity utilization is at high levels
8. The gross national product rises quicker than policy objectives
9. Personal income rises quicker than policy objectives

INDICATORS OF FEDERAL RESERVE POLICY

It is sometimes possible to get an indication of Fed reactions to
economic reports by watching the trend of the Federal funds rate
(the interest rate charged to member banks on loans by the Fed).
The Federal funds rate and other Fed actions have a strong influence
on several other short-term interest rates, all of which can be used
as indicators for determining the general direction of interest rates.

Interest rate indicators fall into two categories: Fed indicators
and market indicators of interest rates. Some of the indicators of
Fed activity that we will examine are:

1. Federal funds
2. Discount rate
3. Prime rate
4. Reserve requirements
5. Margin requirements
6. Free reserves
7. Money supply

Studying the interest rate markets is very similar to studying the stock market; after all, all markets are basically the same. Interest rates are simply the cost of money, like stock prices to the stock market. Movements in the interest rate markets are influenced by political and psychological factors and by the attractiveness of competing forms of investment, all of which assume cyclical patterns.

One advantage of studying interest rates is the vast and varied number of markets that can be used as indicators of the primary trend. To simplify our discussion, we will concentrate on Treasury bonds and bills. There are also common stocks dependent enough on the level and direction of interest rates that they make excellent interest rate indicators. The market-oriented indicators of interest rates that we will discuss are:

1. Treasury bonds and bills
2. Yield curve
3. Certain common stocks
4. Inflation and commodity prices

FEDERAL FUNDS

The Federal funds rate is the primary tool of the Fed and is its daily message to the world regarding its monetary policy. As a daily indicator of Fed policy, its importance is unsurpassed. Although the Federal funds rate is competitively set by the Federal funds market, comprising several thousand commercial banks and nonbank financial institutions, the Fed is able to influence heavily its rate of interest.

Member banks of the Federal Reserve System are required to hold a certain percentage of reserves with the Fed relative to their deposits. Federal funds are the excess reserves beyond what is necessary by law that is credited to member banks. At any one moment, some banks will have excess reserves and some banks will be short of reserves. The Federal funds market system acts as a network to allow member banks who have excess reserves to lend reserves to member banks who need reserves to fulfill reserve requirements.

Therefore, when banks are experiencing heavy demands for money, reserves are pressured, which raises the demand for available Federal funds to replenish reserves. This demand increases the Federal funds rate. The opposite is true for periods of lighter demands for money, which serve to lower the Federal funds rate. In this respect, the Federal funds rate is set by a competitive market system.

Despite this competitive market, the Fed can influence the Federal funds rate when it is not accomplishing policy objectives by controlling the amount of nonborrowed reserves that it injects into the system. The Fed uses the Federal funds market as a money spigot, turning the amount of reserves that are flowing on or off through the banking system. To encourage more economic activity, the Fed injects reserves into the system to lower the Federal funds rate. To restrict economic growth, the Fed constricts the amount of reserves, forcing banks to borrow at higher rates in the Federal funds market.

Sometimes the Fed will maintain a steady Federal funds rate by targeting a rate to achieve policy objectives through the delicate balancing of reserves. While the Federal funds market is a competitive marketplace, free to set its own market rates, the Fed is controlling the supply of goods going to market. If you can control supply, you can control the price; in this case, the price of money—interest rates. This is how the Fed influences the federal funds rate and thereby influences the rates of interest on all other interest rate instruments to accomplish its monetary policy. The costs are passed down through the money system, creating tight or easy money.

THE DISCOUNT RATE

Changes in the discount rate confirm interest rate policy changes suggested by the Federal funds rate. Through changes in the discount rate, the Fed makes a clearly defined statement about the direction of interest rates and sets the basic course for all other rates. The discount rate is the rate of interest that commercial banks pay when they borrow from the Fed. It is rarely changed, perhaps only a few times a year, sometimes even less. The decision to change the discount rate is solely in the hands of the Fed, voted by a majority of its seven governors. Changes in the discount rate are usually made in half-point increments, although on occasion, the Fed has made quarter- and full-point moves.

The financial media have become a bit obsessed with the machinations of the Fed and have brought the melodrama into the living rooms of the investing public. This adds a psychological element to interest rate announcements by the Fed, since very often market participants have already speculated on the event for several weeks before, pushing stocks higher on anticipation of a rate cut or driving prices lower before a rate hike.

A change in the discount rate does not mean that stock prices will react immediately with a change in the long-term trend. Because of the anticipation by investors, the change in rates may have already been built into the price of stocks. This is another way in which the stock market acts as a predictor of the economy. If further rate reductions are expected, the market may continue to rise after a rate cut. If the instant cut is viewed as the last of a series, stock prices might fall since there are no more positives to look forward to.

The Fed realizes their actions are taken seriously by the financial community, so the discount rate is not manipulated in a yo-yo fashion. A change in the direction of the discount rate is a carefully deliberated statement regarding a shift in monetary policy. Any change in the direction of the discount rate can be expected to have a trending effect on interest rates ranging from a few months to a few years.

For example, on January 15, 1973, the discount rate was raised from 4.5 to 5%. This was the first change in the discount rate in over one year and the first rise in rates since 1969. Besides setting off the brutal 1973–1974 bear market in stocks, this change set off nearly two years of uninterrupted increases in the discount rate that eventually brought the rate up to the 8% mark. The economy plunged into a deep recession, creating the need for lower interest rates to get the economy going again.

On December 9, 1974, the discount rate made its first dip in three years, leading a series of declines all the way back to the 5.25% bottom of November 22, 1976. This two-year decline in rates coincided with the powerful two-year recovery in the stock market. The next rise in the discount rate was on August 31, 1977 to 5.75%, which led to three years of higher interest rates and generally lower stock prices. A monthly history of the discount rate and the Dow Jones Industrial Average thus far in the 1980s is shown in Figure 3-2, which graphically illustrates the preponderant effect of interest rates on stock prices.

It is important to realize that primary changes in the direction of monetary policy occur only once every few years, usually in response to some extreme feared in the development of the business cycle. Because interest rates govern the flow of investment money among the various instruments, broad changes in monetary policy create changes in the long-term trend of the stock market. This is yet another advantage to long-term investing, since money flows generally persist in the same direction for one to four years at a time. A short-term investor would miss out on the full benefits of shifts in monetary policy.

The Federal funds rate may set the course for all other interest rates, but changes in the discount rate (which confirm movements by the Federal funds rate) are more recognized by the public and have become something of a media event. Once the discount rate is changed, particularly if its direction is changed, the other short-term interest rates generally follow suit in a domino-like fashion.

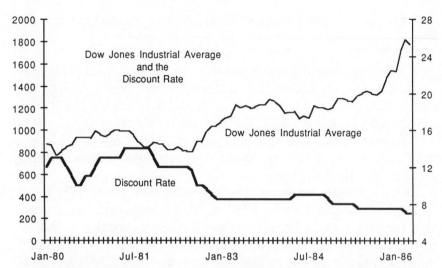

Figure 3-2. Changes in the discount rate are direct statements by the Federal Reserve regarding monetary policy. Since the flow of money moves the stock market, cuts in the discount rate often result in higher stock prices; and vice versa.

Often, the Fed will use the discount rate to confirm their policy rather than as a leader. It will use its influence in the Federal funds market to affect interest rates, thereby letting market conditions lead interest rates to new levels. In this instance, the Fed will make a change in the discount rate to meet market conditions rather than to lead them. This makes it important to watch the Federal funds rate and to consider other interest rates and indicators in your assessment of Fed policy.

AN INDICATOR OF FED POLICY: THE FED FUNDS RATE MINUS THE DISCOUNT RATE

Since the discount rate is controlled by the Fed and the Federal funds rate is strongly influenced by it, the two rates make an interesting comparison that can be used as an indicator of Fed monetary policy. Both represent costs to the banks of borrowing. The Federal funds rate is the cost of borrowing from other banks and the discount rate represents the cost of borrowing from the Fed.

Usually, the Federal funds rate slightly exceeds the discount rate. But in periods of easier money, the Federal funds rate may approach or even fall below the discount rate, signaling that the Fed is being very generous in its credit policy with the banks. This would be signified by the Federal funds rate falling within a half-point of the discount rate. When Federal funds fall below the discount rate, it is sometimes a sign that the Fed is considering a cut in the discount rate.

As an example, suppose the discount rate is 8%. When the Federal funds rate falls to 8.5% or lower, investors can assume that the Fed is pursuing an accommodative policy that is bullish for stocks. If the Federal funds rate is below 8%, the Fed might be contemplating a cut in the discount rate. If the Federal funds rate is over 9%, then money conditions are somewhat tight and potentially negative for the stock market. If it is over 10%, then the Federal funds rate is indicating a tight monetary policy that is bearish for stocks (See Figure 3-3).

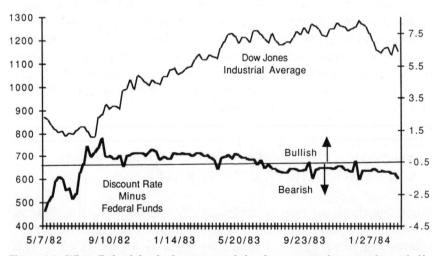

Figure 3-3. When Federal funds do not exceed the discount rate by more than a half-point, it is favorable for higher stock prices. The sharp changes in the thick line at year-end are due to the usual distortions in the Federal funds rate that occur during that time of the year.

From Figure 3-3, it is easy to see that changes in the difference between the two rates often shows a strong correlation with movement in the stock market. This is of great value to the long-term investor, who is merely interested in longer-term money conditions. Since the tendency to tighten or to ease often lasts for a period of several months, or even years, comparison of these two rates can lend insight to the overall trend of monetary policy.

For example, from August 1977 to April 1980, Federal Funds often exceeded the discount rate by more than a half-point, marking nearly three years of uninterrupted increases in the discount rate. As usual, the tight money conditions resulted in poor stock market performance. During this period, Federal funds rose from 5.8 to 19.3% and the Dow fell from 890 to 770. By now, it should be obvious that the Fed does exert a tremendous influence in the stock market. Since these two rates are its most public pronouncement of policy, it pays to watch each of them on a regular basis.

THE PRIME RATE

The Fed does not have direct control over the prime rate, but its influence is so strong that the topic fits in with a discussion of Fed activity. The prime rate grabs more headlines than the discount rate because of its greater applicability to business and the consumer. This media attraction makes the prime rate important to the stock market. The public may not always know the discount rate, but changes in the prime rate always seems to make it into their daily digest of the news.

The prime rate is the rate of interest that commercial banks charge their most favored (prime) customers for short-term loans. To the average borrower, the amount of interest paid over prime represents the additional risk that the borrower poses to the bank. Loans for the purchase of a house or car are often tied to the prime rate, hence the awareness of the consumer. Today, the prime rate is no longer so important to the most credit-worthy corporations because of the wide variety of financing alternatives available.

The prime rate generally follows the Federal funds rate and the discount rate. When the discount rate changes, the cost of funds to Fed member banks is changed and this change in cost structure is passed on to their customer banks in the form of higher or lower borrowing rates. Individual banks set their own prime rates, but at any one time there is one generally recognized prime rate in the country. To remain competitive, once a bank of stature makes a change in its prime rate, most other banks soon follow suit. The prime rate is usually changed in ½-point increments and is changed far more often than the discount rate.

The prime rate offers an excellent example of the domino effect of changing the discount rate. If the discount rate is cut, speculation mounts in the media and trading markets as to whether the prime rate will be cut. Very often, the prime rate is changed within the week. Whether it is intended or not, the Fed has perhaps the most effective public relations methods imaginable. After a discount rate change, banks in every sector of the country change their borrowing rates, garnering significant press in nearly every media source in the nation. By public relations alone, the Fed's actions quickly influence consumer and business spending and the thinking of stock market participants.

RESERVE REQUIREMENTS

The reserve requirement is the percentage of deposits that commercial banks must leave in cash either at their regional Federal Reserve Bank or in their own vaults. By changing reserve requirements, the Fed can influence the amount of money that banks have available for loans or investments. To ease monetary conditions and encourage economic growth, the Fed can lower reserve requirements. Conversely, to tighten money conditions and thereby slow economic growth, the Federal Reserve can raise reserve requirements. Although changes in the reserve requirement are rare and often more related to regulatory issues than to monetary policy, they were mentioned here because they represent a structural change in the flow of money that can influence the course of the financial markets.

MARGIN REQUIREMENTS

Another seldom-used power of the Fed is the ability to change margin requirements, which is the percentage of the total purchase price of stock that must be put up in cash. This power was given to the Fed in 1934 as a direct response to the excessive use of margin debt that contributed to the collapse of the stock market in 1929. The Fed has not changed the margin requirement in over a decade, but it can do so to control levels of margin debt.

Having the power to change margin requirements on stock purchases not only exercises an effect on monetary conditions, it also directly affects the buying power of participants in the stock market. Raising the margin requirements can choke off a rally, while lowering margin requirements can turn a depressed stock market into a new baby bull. The effect of this is often very swift, as a change in margin requirements is one of the boldest statements that the Fed can make toward the stock market.

FREE RESERVES

Free reserves are the difference between excess reserves and money borrowed from the Fed. Free reserves are reported as a daily average of a two-week period and can be found every Friday in the *Wall Street Journal* and other newspapers. The more free reserves in the banking system, the easier monetary conditions are because banks have an easier time replenishing their reserves to meet reserve requirements.

Free reserves = Excess reserves − borrowings from Fed

Since the level of free reserves varies a great deal from week to week, to smooth the fluctuations it is better to take a four-week moving average, like the one shown in Figure 3-4. (A four-week moving average is simply an average of the last four weeks of data.) Easier monetary conditions are indicated when the moving average of free reserves moves above −500 million, especially when it is positive. A drop below the −500 million mark suggests

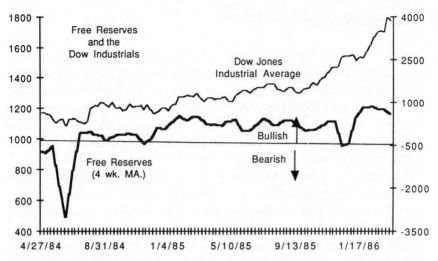

Figure 3-4. When free reserves are averaging more than −500 million per week on a four-week moving average, it suggests that the Fed is supplying easier monetary conditions that are bullish for stock prices.

tighter money. Free reserves can be an indicator of the future direction of Federal funds, the leading indicator for all other interest rates.

THE MONEY SUPPLY

Although the money supply is not a direct market indicator, investors should be aware of its readings because it is an important statement of Fed monetary policy. The Fed uses the money supply to gauge the amount of money available in the economy. It is reported in the *Wall Street Journal* each Friday in the Federal Reserve Data section and can be found in most newspapers across the country.

There are now three different sets of basic money supply figures available, cleverly denoted as M1, M2, and M3. The definitions of each type are a bit cumbersome; just keep in mind that M2 is a broader measure of money available than M1, and M3 is broader still.

M1. The sum of currency held by the nonbank public, demand deposits, other checkable deposits, and travelers checks.

M2. M1 plus money market mutual fund shares, savings and small time deposits at commercial banks and thrift institutions, overnight-repurchase agreements, and Eurodollars.

M3. M2 plus large time deposits and term-repurchase agreements at commercial banks and thrift institutions.

In the early 1980s, the M1 figure was such a hallowed barometer of interest rate activity that its public release used to have a sharp impact on bond and stock prices. At that time, M1 received headline press coverage in the financial media and was the subject of public curiousity. By 1987, the Fed decided that the once-popular M1 figure, which is still considered a good measure of transaction demand, had become irrelevant to the assessment of money supply.

The basic problem with M1 was that its definition included interest-bearing accounts like the popular NOW accounts, which, due to low interest rates, became competitive with other types of investments. Therefore, savings money surged into the M1 category, distorting its usual growth patterns and rendering it less useful to the determination of monetary policy. Although new parameters for M1 will probably be set in the future, I suggest that you follow the lead of the Fed in gauging monetary policy and concentrate primarily on the movement of the M2 and M3 figures.

The money supply measures liquidity in the banking system— how much money is available to flow through the economy. The Fed targets levels of money supply growth for the year and makes it available to the public. One indication of Fed policy is to determine how conscientious it is in keeping the money supply within its targeted growth. A money supply that continues to grow beyond targets without action by the Fed is a sign that it is willing to be very accommodative in its monetary policy.

Although strong money supply growth is positive for stock prices, it can short-circuit a bull market by raging beyond policy objectives. Historically, money supply growth has a long-term correlation to the rate of inflation. Once inflation is perceived to be higher than policy objectives dictate, the Fed is likely to take action to restrict the growth of the money supply until both the money supply and inflation rates are well within policy limits. Such action often leads to higher interest rates and eventually bearish conditions for the stock market.

In short, healthy money supply growth is an accommodative monetary condition that is bullish for the stock market. This encourages business expansion as long as the Fed perceives that inflation is not a serious threat. Once inflation is recognized as a problem, the Fed will restrict the growth of the money supply by raising interest rates. Higher rates eventually lead to a change in the flow of investment capital, driving funds out of the stock market and into other investment markets. This leads to lower stock prices.

The Fed indicators outlined above are not the only ways to gain an understanding of the interest rate situation. Both the credit and stock markets are affected by the Fed and serve as an excellent proxy for interest rate movement.

A BRIEF LOOK AT THE CREDIT MARKETS

The credit markets are broken into different lengths of debt maturity. Basically, there are three lengths to be concerned with: short, intermediate, and long term. Bonds are generally issued in denominations of $1000, which is the amount that is to be repaid when the bond is due. Bonds are quoted in percentage terms. In the newspaper, the par amount of $1000 is quoted as 100. If the amount is greater than 100, then the bond is selling at a premium. If the bond is less than 100, then it is trading at a discount.

The longer the maturity of a bond, the more the price is going to fluctuate. The more time until maturity, the greater uncertainty (therefore risk) involved, and the greater the volatility. Bonds fluctuate inversely in price to the direction of interest rates. So, if rates rise, bonds prices fall; and, if rates fall, bond prices rise.

Suppose a bond was issued a year ago to yield 8% at 100 (par) and new bonds come on the market at 9%. The value of the old 8% bond will fall below 100 because buyers would only be willing to receive a lower yield if they were able to purchase it at a discount.

Conversely, if new bonds came to market yielding only 7%, the old 8% bonds would trade at a premium (over 100) because of the extra attractiveness of the higher yield. Adjustments in price by the competitive marketplace adjust the yields according to maturity, regardless of the rates at their original issuance.

Short-term maturities are instruments like Federal funds, three month to one-year Treasury bills, and four-to six-month commercial paper. Short-term debt is the most sensitive to Fed policy because of the Fed's influence on Federal funds and on the discount rate. Short-term debt is also most sensitive to changes in business conditions, as these funds are most commonly used to finance short-term business needs, like inventories.

The long-term part of the credit market is represented by instruments like Treasury bonds, tax-exempt bonds, or corporate bonds which have maturities of 15 years or more. Treasury bonds are backed by the U.S. government and therefore have the greatest amount of safety in the long-term market. To receive the extra peace of mind of this safety feature, buyers are willing to purchase Treasury bonds with a lower interest rate yield than corporate bonds. Despite the lower yield, the safety feature makes Treasury bonds a far more popular investment than corporate bonds.

Buyers can receive more peace of mind with tax-exempt bonds and corporate bonds by purchasing higher rated securities. Independent rating services like Standard & Poor's and Moody's rate bonds according to their financial quality. The highest Standard & Poor's rating is AAA, followed by AA, A, BAA, and so on. Like Treasury bonds, the highest quality bonds have a lower interest rate because buyers are willing to give up a minor difference in yield to receive the added assurance of safety. Intermediate-length bonds are simply those with a maturity between the short- and long-term bonds, ranging from 1 to 15 years.

THE YIELD CURVE

The short-, intermediate-, and long-term structure of the bond market creates an instant indicator for gauging the credit markets. This scale of maturity versus yield is called the yield curve.

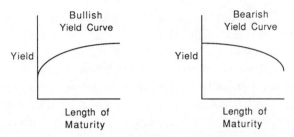

Figure 3-5. The regular yield curve on the left is indicative of easy-money conditions, which are favorable for the stock market. The inverted yield curve on the right signifies tight monetary conditions, which are bearish for stock prices.

We have already discussed how the shorter the maturity, the less uncertain the future, the safer the security, and therefore the less volatile the price of the security. Since U.S. government securities vary in length from 3-month Treasury bills to 30-year Treasury bonds, Treasury securities are ideal for constructing a yield curve. The yield curve usually looks like the chart on the left of Figure 3-5, with short-term rates below long-term rates. This would indicate easy money conditions that are conducive to higher stock prices.

When money becomes tight, short-term securities are in short supply due to heavy demand from borrowers and restricted supply influenced by the Fed. Because credit is scarce, creditors demand higher rates of interest, resulting in a sharp rise in short-term rates. Additionally, because long-term bond prices are more sensitive to changes in rates, tight money creates a "flight to quality," as investors avoid risk-laden bonds and move money into Treasury bills.

In very tight money situations, short-term rates rise above long-term rates and the yield curve becomes inverted like the chart on the right of Figure 3-5, creating an unfavorable condition for stocks. The intermediate-length Treasury yields serve to balance the picture by providing points in between the short- and long-term yield points.

An easier way to approach the yield curve without drawing a lot of points is to simply compare the interest rate of three-month

Treasury bills to the rate on long-term U.S. Treasury bonds. This produces the following yield curve ratio (shown in Figure 3-6):

$$\text{Yield curve ratio} = \frac{\text{Long-term Treasury bond rates}}{\text{Three-month Treasury bill rates}}$$

Historically, very favorable conditions correspond to a yield curve ratio of 1.2 or above. Any reading above one is favorable, and a reading below one is unfavorable. This type of presentation also allows you to keep a chart running over a long time period rather than being restricted to the traditional one-day yield curve chart.

Treasury bills come in several different maturities. The rate we want to monitor for the yield curve and all other analytic work in this book is the rate three months from the current date. Figure 3.7 shows the quote section from the *Wall Street Journal* from May 1, 1987. Looking ahead three months for the most appropriate maturity, we would use the discounted bid rate from 7-30 (circled), which is shown as 5.60.

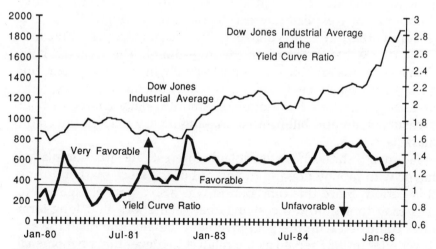

Figure 3-6. When Treasury bond yields exceed that of Treasury bills, the yield curve ratio suggests easier monetary conditions and higher stock prices. Above 1.2 on the ratio is very favorable.

U.S. Treas. Bills Mat. date	Bid	Asked	Yield Discount	Mat. date	Bid	Asked	Yield Discount
-1987-				8-27	5.57	5.53	5.70
5- 7	4.91	4.83	4.90	9- 3	5.57	5.53	5.71
5-14	5.10	5.04	5.12	9-10	5.65	5.61	5.80
5-21	4.89	4.83	4.91	9-17	5.63	5.59	5.79
5-28	3.80	3.58	3.64	9-24	5.63	5.59	5.79
6- 4	5.00	4.94	5.03	10- 1	5.76	5.72	5.94
6-11	5.34	5.28	5.38	10- 8	5.75	5.71	5.94
6-18	5.27	5.17	5.28	10-15	5.76	5.72	5.95
6-25	5.12	5.06	5.17	10-22	5.76	5.72	5.96
7- 2	5.27	5.21	5.33	10-29	5.98	5.96	6.23
7- 9	5.45	5.37	5.50	11-27	6.17	6.15	6.46
7-16	5.43	5.37	5.50	12-24	6.23	6.21	6.51
7-23	5.51	5.47	5.61	-1988-			
7-30	(5.60)	5.58	5.73	1-21	6.17	6.15	6.46
8- 6	5.67	5.63	5.79	2-18	6.31	6.27	6.61
8-13	5.52	5.50	5.66	3-17	6.34	6.32	6.69
8-20	5.55	5.53	5.70	4-14	6.33	6.31	6.70

Figure 3-7. Quote section from the Wall Street Journal, May 1, 1987. Reprinted by permission of the *Wall Street Journal* © Dow Jones & Co., Inc. 1987. All rights reserved.

TRACKING TREASURY BONDS AND BILLS

Treasury bills are redeemed at a face value of 100 and therefore do not pay any explicit interest. Instead, they are purchased at a discount; the difference between the discounted price and face value represents the yield on the investment. The yields of both Treasury bonds and bills are reported daily in the newspaper, but a chart kept on a weekly basis is certainly adequate for long-term investors. *Investor's Daily* offers six-month, daily charts on both Treasury bond and bill futures, making it easy to track the credit markets.

Figure 3-8 shows how the volatile interest rate situation played havoc with money flowing in and out of the stock market during this period. Since this time period was also a part of Figure 3-6, it is easy to see how the swings between short- and long-term rates coincided with market movement. Finally, the push toward lower rates in 1982 served as the catalyst to trigger that phenomenal bull market.

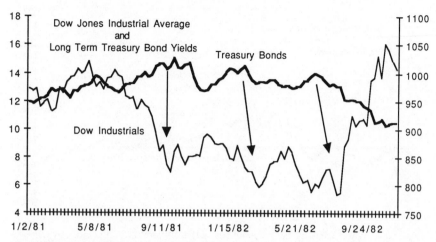

Figure 3-8. Long-term Treasury bonds compete directly with stocks for investor capital. When bond yields decline, the competitive advantage of the stock market is improved, generally resulting in higher stock prices.

TREASURY BILLS AND THE DISCOUNT RATE

Treasury bill yields are set by a competitive marketplace, but are heavily influenced by the short-term machinations of the Fed. The discount rate, of course, is directly controlled by the Fed. When credit conditions are easy, Treasury bill yields fall below the discount rate.

Not only can this be used as an indication of favorable conditions for the stock market, it can also serve as a gauge for when the Fed might be more likely to drop the discount rate. No change in the discount rate over the past decade has occurred without the Treasury bill rate falling below the discount rate. When Treasury bills are above the discount rate, conditions are generally tight and unfavorable for stock prices.

Figure 3-9 shows that when the discount rate is above the rate on Treasury bills (thick line above zero) money conditions are easy and stock prices rise from the inflows of available money. This condition coincided perfectly with the beginning of the 1982 bull market. When Treasury bills moved back above the discount

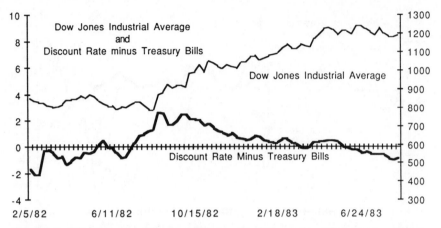

Figure 3-9. When Treasury bill rates fall below the discount rate, it is indicative of easier monetary conditions that ordinarily result in higher stock prices. Of course, when bill rates are above the discount rate, money is tighter and stock prices are likely to decline.

rate in June 1983, the tightened monetary conditions forced a top to the first upleg of the bull market. The condition eased again in November 1984, to kick off a multiyear decline in rates and a boom in stock prices.

STOCK GROUPS

Certain industry groups in the stock market are so dependent on interest rates for their profitability that their price movement can be used as an interest rate indicator. The best known indicator among the industry groups is the utilities, but financial groups like banks, brokerages, and savings and loans are just as applicable. These are all industries which do a great deal of borrowing or that depend on interest rates to boost their sales revenues. Because interest rates often act as the catalyst for major moves in the stock market, these groups often move weeks or even months ahead of the market averages.

The Dow Jones Utility Average of 15 major utilities is available in most daily newspapers and is such a good indicator of interest rates that it tends to mirror long-term bond prices. Somewhat less available, but containing more utility stocks, are the New York Utility Index and Standard & Poor's Utility Index. Ideally, the three indexes should move together, rising to new highs or falling to new lows in unison. If they do not move together, there might be distortion in the Dow Utility Average due to an unusual move in one or more stocks. Furthermore, when the utility averages are not moving in unison with the rest of the stock market, it is often an early warning signal that a change in the direction of interest rates could occur which will impact stock prices (see Figure 3-10).

The New York Financial Index is available in most newspapers and is an excellent indicator of interest rate trends. Like the utilities, the financial stocks, comprised of banks, insurance, finance, and other similar industries, have earnings which are highly sensitive to changes in interest rates and generally lead the stock market to new trends. Other stock groups that can be helpful are the homebuilding and mobile home stock groups. Housing is very sensitive to changes in interest rates and these groups often move in wide swinging trends ahead of the stock market. The prices of financial and housing stocks can become very depressed during

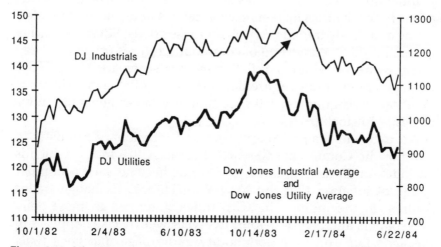

Figure 3-10. Like other interest rate indicators, the Dow Jones Utility Average tends to lead stock market movement. In this case, the Utilities began falling three months before the Dow Industrials to signal the beginning of the 1983–1984 mini-bear market.

periods of unfavorable monetary conditions and can provide terrific price gains to investors when rates are on a downward track.

One single stock to watch is Federal National Mortgage Association. The symbol is FNM, and is commonly called Fannie Mae. Fannie Mae provides supplemental assistance to the secondary market in guaranteed and insured home mortgages. As such, its earnings are directly tied to the movement of interest rates. The stock market may be influenced more heavily by the daily activity of IBM, but the long-term trend of Fannie Mae is one of the best leading indicators of long-term stock market activity because of its intimate link to interest rates.

INFLATION AND COMMODITY PRICES

As seen in Chapter 2, inflation is the enemy of interest rates. When inflationary forces heat up beyond Fed policy objectives, interest rates are pushed higher by a more restrictive Fed to slow the flow of money in the economy. This has the effect of slowing the economy and the demand for goods, thereby slowing the rate of inflation.

Inflation, of course, is a measure of the price growth of goods and services. Futures markets exist in several different commodities, acting as actively traded markets for these goods. For stock market investors, the overall trend of commodity futures prices can keep them aware of whether inflationary pressures are heating up. Rising commodity prices are dependent on inflation and because inflation affects interest rates, commodity prices generally move opposite to stock prices.

An excellent way to keep abreast of inflationary trends is to monitor the Commodity Research Bureau (CRB) Index, which is an index of 26 raw commodities. It has become such a popular gauge of inflation that the New York Futures Exchange trades futures on the index. The CRB index is quoted in most daily newspapers and a very helpful two-year weekly chart appears in *Investor's Daily* on their commodity quote page. *Investor's Daily* also provides 6-month daily charts on 18 different futures markets, which give an overall view of how some of the individual components of the CRB are doing, as well as the progress of the financial and currency markets.

Inflationary trends generally last for a matter of several years, setting the general environment for interest rates, and consequently the stock market. High inflation makes real assets more valuable, moving capital out of the stock market and into real estate and gold. Low inflation slows the price gains of real assets, making financial assets like the stock market more attractive. These topics are discussed in greater detail in Chapter 4.

STRATEGIC APPLICATIONS

Money moves the stock market. The interest rate markets are the mechanism which largely controls the flow of money into the various investment vehicles, including the stock market. The Federal Reserve is empowered by Congress to control monetary policy, making it the source of most interest rate movement, which is the catalyst to a great deal of movement in the stock market. Fortunately, investors can keep track of a few indicators to whether the Fed has made conditions conducive or not to gains in the stock market.

In Chapter 4, we will see how interest rates directly affect stock market value. The stock market is in competition with other financial assets, like bonds and money market instruments, for inflows of investment capital. When interest rates change, they effectively change the balance of value between stocks and other financial assets, which directly affects the direction of the long-term trend. Interest rates are the most common reason for changes in this balance of value, which, as we will see, is the primary reason for making portfolio adjustments to market risk.

4

Interest Rates and Stock Market Value

Interest rates represent the cost of money. As such, interest rates are also the opportunity cost of earning rates of return. Capital available for investment will flow to those markets offering the highest rates of return relative to risk. Investment markets attracting large amounts of capital are likely to rise in price as buying demand outpaces available supply.

The stock market is pitted against the various competing markets on the basis of value, making interest rates a primary element in stock market valuations. In view of this, let us look at the flow of money, how stocks are valued, and how interest rates affect the balance of value among the competing investment markets.

THE FLOW OF MONEY

It takes money to move the stock market. There is a limited amount of capital available in the world to be invested among the various investment instruments. Just like water seeking its own level, money flows to the investments that appear to provide the best return relative to the risk. These competing investment areas can be organized into three convenient classifications.

1. *Financial Assets*. Stocks, bonds, and money market instruments
2. *Real Assets*. Real estate and hard assets (gold, silver, gems, etc.)
3. *Tax Sheltered Assets*. Municipal bonds and other tax shelters

Each area has its merits. Financial assets are generally liquid, safe, and earn rates of return from dividends or interest. Real assets protect against inflation and sometimes provide a return on investment that can be sheltered from income tax. Investors in tax shelters receive a lower return but are compensated by tax-saving advantages.

The purpose of this oversimplification is to clearly delineate the main reasons why investment money goes into areas outside the stock market. Those three reasons are: interest rates, inflation, and tax laws.

The Influence of Tax Laws

In 1986, President Reagan signed into law perhaps the most sweeping tax legislation since the federal income tax was enacted in 1913. A quick examination into the particulars of this law shows the effects of tax policy on the flow of investment money.

Government policy dictates tax laws. Previous policy offered tax incentives to encourage investment in areas that were only marginally profitable, primarily in the energy and heavy industry sectors. This had the effect of subsidizing companies that would have been weeded out by weak performance while taxing the growth of profitable companies. It also had the effect of creating tax shelters for businesses that could not operate without tax advantages, drawing pools of public investor capital from more productive areas of the economy.

Perhaps the successful Japanese invasion of the steel and auto industries made the U.S. government recognize the misappropriation of economic power produced by the old tax code. Encouraging weak companies to remain in business through tax incentives while discouraging the more profitable companies was no longer thought to be conducive to a growing economy. They concluded that free market competition should run the economy, not selective tax breaks.

The long-term effect of the 1986 tax law should be very favorable to the stock market. The demise of most shelters coupled with lower tax rates on individuals will encourage capital to flow away from unproductive tax-induced investments into productive enterprises. Companies which show strong earnings will be subject to lower taxes, encouraging them to build on their successes.

Tax-motivated transactions, mostly in the form of real estate and oil and gas deals, siphoned off large amounts of investment capital in the inflation-driven investment era of the 1970s. Deals offering deep write-offs have been effectively eliminated, which was the primary source of their appeal. Now, with lower tax rates, tax shelters will probably be restructured into income-oriented deals that feature a largely sheltered return on investment and the potential for capital gain.

Municipal bonds may need to offer a higher interest rate to attract investment capital, but should retain their popularity because of the dearth of tax shelter investments. Restrictions on the amount of municipal bond offerings might limit the supply of this market, but not its popularity. In short, the tax-motivated transaction sec-will still be viable, but is not likely to be as strong a force in the competition for investment assets, a long-term bullish development for the stock market.

Real estate was hard hit by the 1986 tax law, but is not likely to slow in its development. Developers should still be able to produce the goods, and brokerages will find creative ways to package and sell it. But the shelter aspects of real estate will be less attractive to investors and should put the stock market on more of a parity. Regardless of the tax law, real estate and hard assets should still be the primary recipient of investment capital during periods of high inflation.

The 1986 tax legislation reduces the attractiveness of assuming debt. After the provisions of the new tax law are fully phased-in, other than home mortgages, consumer debt is no longer deductible, which should lessen the demand for loans. If lower tax rates and reduced opportunities for shelter lead to greater demand for stocks, corporations will be better able to raise substantial amounts of capital by issuing stock, thereby lessening corporate demand for debt. With fewer demands on the credit market, interest rates should be structurally lower, which is a strong long-term positive for the stock market.

The repeal of the long-term capital gains exclusion eliminates investors' incentives to hold stocks for more than six months, since short-term gains will be taxed the same as long-term gains. In a classic contrarian situation, experts in the financial media have encouraged investors to speculate on short-term moves in the market more freely, since the tax consequences are no longer less favorable. Like most highly publicized strategies, this one is likely to be far off the mark. If short-term speculation does become popular, the market is likely to become more volatile, making it yet more difficult for short-term investors to make money in stocks.

Greater short-term speculation would only increase the advantage of being a long-term value investor, allowing you to take advantage of potentially wider swings in stock valuations. In conclusion, the 1986 tax act may cause some problems in the short run, but over the long haul, it should be very positive for the stock market and long-term value investing.

INFLATION—THE DIVINING ROD OF MONEY

Since interest rates are the cost of money and inflation is the increase in the cost of goods and services, inflation is clearly the enemy of financial assets. When inflation heats up beyond the government's liking, the Fed steps in to raise interest rates. But as long as inflation is restrained within policy objectives, interest rates can remain at relatively favorable levels for the stock market.

This makes inflation one of the most important elements in the flow of money. In fact, in general it can be said that low inflation produces bull markets and high inflation produces bear markets.

The effects of inflation on the investment world have been well documented after the experience of runaway inflation in the 1970s and early 1980s. High inflation caused the Fed to raise interest rates until the inflationary cycle was choked off. Once inflation was constrained, the Fed was able to lower interest rates, which set off the incredible 1982 bull market.

Inflation increases the attractiveness of real assets while reducing the allure of financial assets. As inflation heats up, property appreciates in value while money earned from dividends and interest do not. Worse yet, a dollar does not buy as much as it once did, so during high inflation, financial assets suffer a real loss because money is losing value relative to the goods and services it can buy.

This causes a flight to real assets, as investors seek property that is rapidly increasing in value. Since real assets are often leveraged with debt when purchased, during inflationary periods, they offer the additional advantage of buying appreciating property with depreciated dollars.

Inflation travels through cycles that are tied to long-term business cycles. When business is strong and inventories are thin, the demand for goods and materials outstrips supply. Once demand overpowers supply enough to set off the chain reaction of inflation, it takes a long time to work the imbalances out of the economic system. Inflation is not simply a supply/demand problem; it can become a self-fulfilling expectation, creating a spiral that can last for several business cycles.

Since inflation has the power to move money for extended periods of time, these money flows create favorable eras for real assets in high inflation and favorable eras for financial assets during low inflation. The link between interest rates and inflation forms the divining rod that determines which way money will flow.

Recognizing the severity of inflation is one of the most important determinations an investor can make, leaning to real assets during high inflation and financial assets during low inflation.

Of course, bull markets *can* occur during periods of high inflation, but the growth rate of the economy would generally have to exceed inflation by a large margin to sustain the advance. This is unlikely to continue for long, as inflation will eventually eat up gains in economic growth as the business cycle slows. In conclusion, while the stock market can rise during high inflation, the limited life and power of such advances still make inflationary periods undesirable for stock market investors.

COMPETITION AMONG FINANCIAL ASSETS

When inflation is low and interest rates are favorable, how does money flow between the stock and bond markets? We have already seen that money flows to the investment offering the highest return relative to risk. Therefore, the most logical starting point is with a no-risk investment. Later, we will move on to the riskier areas of bonds and stocks.

TREASURY BILLS—THE RISKLESS RETURN

Three-month Treasury bills are widely acknowledged as establishing the riskless rate of return. As we have seen, Treasury bills are issued at a discount and mature at par, leaving the discount portion as "interest" earned by the investor. Treasury bills are also backed by the full faith and credit of the federal government, effectively guaranteeing the principal and interest. With the bought and sold prices known before purchase, as well as the guarantee of the federal government, Treasury bills (T-bills) are truly a riskless asset.

T-bills' status as riskless assets makes them the best benchmark available for measuring the risk element in returns. Since T-bills have the lowest risk, it would be logical that they also offer the lowest return. However, this doesn't necessarily mean that T-bills will always actually yield the lowest interest rate. Sometimes, the yield on T-bills exceeds that of Treasury bonds (T-bonds), causing the yield curve to become inverted. In Chapter 3, we discussed the mechanics of the yield curve; now, let us take a closer look at how the yield curve influences the flow of capital into and out of the stock market.

THE YIELD CURVE IN ACTION

T-bonds are also guaranteed by the federal government, but unlike T-bills, they have substantial risk in market price valuations and a potential loss in purchasing power due to inflation. The longer the maturity, the greater the risk. To compensate for this, a higher rate of interest is usually paid for the long-term bond. However, if the Fed is tightening money to a significant degree, pressures on short-term rates will intensify, sending T-bill yields above those of bonds. This creates an inverted yield curve which is bearish for both bonds and stocks because the riskless return is so attractive.

For example, in May 1981, three-month T-bills completed a two-month rise of 400 basis points (4%) to 16.75%. The stock market was in the final weeks of the 1980–1981 rally that moved the Dow from 750 to 1024—the highest closing peak since 1973. Long-term bond market yields, which are usually slower to respond to higher interest rates, rose only 150 basis points to 13.75% within that two-month period.

Because the yield on three-month T-bills exceeded the yield on T-bonds, the yield curve was inverted, a bearish condition for the stock market. It was no coincidence that the two-month rise in rates and inverted yield curve sent the stock market into a tailspin, with the Dow falling 20% in about four months. It made little sense to remain in the stock market when T-bills offered government guaranteed returns of 16%. The average stock yielded only 5% and was burdened with much greater risk. During this period, money was siphoned off from the stock market and sent into high-yielding, fixed-income securities.

Between May and September 1981, T-bills declined from 16.75 to 14.3%. Long-term T-bonds, however, rose in yield from 13.75 to 15%, exceeding the short-term bill rate and bringing the yield curve back into a bullish condition for the stock and bond markets. The stock market bottomed immediately, but only after sustaining a (previously mentioned) 20% decline. Money moved quickly into long-term bonds to lock-in the attractively high long-term yields. In retrospect, investors who locked up those yields would enjoy several years of yield advantage over other financial assets.

INTEREST RATES—STOCK MARKET CATALYST

On July 9, 1982, one month before the great bull market of 1982 began, T-bills were still above 12% and T-bonds were above 13%. Beginning on July 20, within a single month, the discount rate was cut four times, ½% each time, from 12 to 10%. The stock market exploded after the third cut on August 16, reacting to the tremendous change in stock valuations afforded by lower interest rates (see Figure 4-1).

The building of the incredible 1982 bull market was no accident; it was a direct response to lower interest rates. Rates fell sharply, affecting the relative value of stocks against other competing investment instruments. Because rates fell so quickly, stocks needed to rise just as swiftly to account for the change in relative value.

PRICE-EARNINGS RATIOS AND STOCK MARKET VALUATIONS

The 1982 rush to buy stocks has greater implications than just showing the benefits of a bullish yield curve. It helps show how stock market valuations are directly affected by the level of interest rates. Stocks generally have a higher risk than bonds, so they are expected to have a higher return. When the return on T-bills is higher than the expected return on stocks, money is drawn out of the stock market and prices fall. Given high interest rates, stocks are unable to compensate for their added risk versus the riskless T-bills.

The p/e ratio is the stock market's valuation of earnings. Therefore, the p/e ratio is a measure of investor perceptions. The more favorably an investor views a company, the more he is willing to pay for each dollar of corporate earnings. The same can be said for the entire stock market. Each week in *Barron's*, the p/e ratio for the entire S&P 500 stock index is shown. The higher the p/e ratio, the more confident investors are of future gains in the stock market.

Suppose the earnings for the last 12 months of the 500 stocks in the S&P are $15, slightly higher than they were in the early

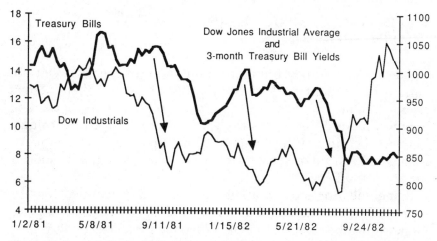

Figure 4-1. 3-month Treasury bill yields generally lead long-term bond yields and represent the riskless rate of return. As such, they directly affect the value of stocks and very often lead changes in stock market trends.

1980s. If the p/e ratio for the S&P is 8, then the market is historically pessimistic and the S&P would be trading at only 120 (15 × 8), its level before the 1982 bull market. If the market is historically optimistic, the S&P might be trading at a p/e ratio of 16, giving the S&P a price of 240 (15 × 16), a mark at which it commonly traded in 1986.

It is important to realize that although earnings hardly changed during the first half of the 1980s, the stock market slid along a scale of investors' perceptions to higher values. Specifically, as shown in Appendix B, the p/e ratio for the S&P 500 rose from 6.96 in April 1980 to 17.16 in November 1986. By March 1987, the p/e ratio rose above 20, an extremely optimistic level. Let us now consider the flip side of value perception—market risk. The higher the market values earnings, the greater is the statement of investor optimism. As seen in our behavioral model, overoptimism is a benchmark for a market top, the maximum point of downside risk. Therefore, in general, the higher the p/e ratio, the greater the market risk. Conversely, the smaller the p/e ratio, the lower the market risk.

RELATING THE PRICE EARNINGS RATIO
TO INTEREST RATES

Interest rates strongly influence the flow of money between the various investment markets and the stock market. When interest rates fall, money pours out of the other markets into stocks, creating buying pressure that raises the value of each dollar of earnings. In effect, because of the competitive nature of the various investment markets, interest rates strongly influence the p/e ratio for the stock market.

Sometimes the stock market's p/e ratio is overvalued relative to interest rates, making it advantageous to sell stocks and place money into other financial assets. When the p/e ratio is undervalued relative to interest rates, the stock market is a bargain purchase compared to other financial assets. Of course, how to measure the valuation of the p/e ratio against competing interest rates is never an exacting procedure, but we can gain a pretty good sense of relative values.

Many analysts try to place benchmark levels for p/e ratios or interest rates, saying that at such a level stocks should always be bought or sold. Historically, p/e ratios below 8 have represented relatively cheap stock markets, while ratios above 17 have been expensive periods. But these are overgeneralizations that can be very costly. For example, the p/e ratio was above 17 for nearly 2½ years between 1971 and 1973. And it was below 8 for most of the time from 1979 to 1982.

While from a very long-term perspective, these were indeed over- and undervalued periods, such a blanket statement about the stock market would not have been good investment advice. For example, between 1972 and 1973, the average stock rose about 30%, an advance that most investors would have wanted to participate in. Moreover, stock market p/e ratios are rarely at such historical extremes, leaving you with no reference point to gauge the values of less-unusual ratios.

The absolute level of the p/e ratio is not a key determinant of value, but rather, the level of the p/e ratio relative to interest rates.

The interest rate markets and the stock markets are in a constant competition for investor funds. As such, the absolute value of one market is not really meaningful. The true significance of a certain earnings valuation or interest rate is in the comparison of one measure against the other.

One famous book said that whenever rates are below 12%, the stock market is a bargain. Written after the high rates of 1981 shocked the nation into a whole different level of expectations for interest rate levels, the author based his 12% benchmark level on the assumption that rates would be high forever. This premise is in itself one of ignorance; the author completely disregarded over 50 years of rates below 12%, not all of which were banner years for stocks.

THE EARNINGS YIELD—EQUATING STOCKS TO BONDS

The p/e ratio is a measure of investment perceptions and risk, but it is also a measure of investment returns. With bonds, the interest rate divided by the price of the bond equals the yield, which represents a return on investment. With stocks, earnings divided by the price of the stock equals the yield, which represents a return on investment. This is popularly known as the *earnings yield*. In this way, we can equate stock market valuations in p/e ratios to the return on interest rate vehicles such as bonds.

$$\text{Bond yield} = \frac{\text{Interest rate}}{\text{Price of bond}} \qquad \text{Earnings yield} = \frac{\text{Earnings}}{\text{Price of stock}}$$

Note that the earnings yield on stocks is just the inverse of the p/e ratio. For instance, if the p/e ratio is 5, then the earnings yield is 1/5, or 20%. This would signify that stocks are priced to offer a return of 20%, since investors would be receiving the potential benefits of one dollar of earnings for every five dollars they paid (1/5 = 20%).

$$\text{Earnings yield} = \frac{1}{\text{p/e ratio}} = \frac{1}{5} = 20\%$$

Obviously, not every stock with a p/e ratio of 5 would return 20%; this is just the potential return equated to an interest rate yield. In fact, it can be said that stocks with a very steady rate of earnings growth are bond equivalents, since the risk of their earnings fluctuations is minimized to levels similar to a bond.

Benjamin Graham, widely recognized as the father of value investing, was perhaps the first to discuss the earnings yield. He suggested that stocks should be bought only if their earnings yield is greater than the current yield on long-term T-bonds. That way, stocks are priced to deliver a higher return than bonds to compensate for their inherently higher risk.

Like most of Graham's maxims, this is often good advice for picking individual stocks, particularly as many stocks are really bond equivalents because of their stability in earnings and dividends. Since both stocks and bonds are financial assets and directly compete against each other for investment dollars, it makes a great deal of sense to buy stocks that offer returns greater than bonds.

While it does make good sense, this strategy automatically eliminates from investment consideration some stocks that have the ability to earn superior rates of return to bonds. In many cases, stocks of such caliber deserve a higher p/e ratio because they are able to generate greater returns from a shareholder's investment. Again, the p/e ratio should not be viewed in an absolute sense, but in a relative comparison against competing rates of return. This subject will be covered extensively in Chapters 7 and 8.

MEASURING STOCK MARKET VALUE AND RISK

The earnings yield concept can be carried one step further to be used as a tool of market analysis to compare stock market value against competing interest rates. In truth, value is really another term for risk. If the market is undervalued, then it carries a lower risk. Conversely, when it is overvalued, it has a higher risk. To best measure value and risk, we need to compare it against a riskless standard. As we have seen, the most recognized measure of a riskless return is the discounted rate (bid) on three-month T-bills.

Since the stock market always has a greater risk than T-bills, it should always offer a higher return. Therefore, its earnings yield should be higher than the T-bills rate, unless stocks are unusually overvalued. For example, if the earnings yield on the S&P 500 is 5% (p/e ratio of 20) rate is 6%, then stocks would seem to be overvalued and pose a great deal of risk.

If the earnings yield was 7% instead, then stocks would offer a greater return than the riskless standard and probably are undervalued relative to competing financial assets. Obviously, stocks have more risk, but as long as their earnings yield exceeds the rate on the riskless T-bills, the potential rewards to be gained over the long term would compensate for the added risk.

We can put this comparison of stock market risk and value into a simple equation that I call the Earnings Value Index (EVI).

Earnings Value Index (EVI) =

$$\frac{\text{Earnings yield on Standard \& Poor's 500}}{\text{Interest rate on three-month T-bills}}$$

Above 1.05 is very bullish

Between 0.95 and 1.05 is moderately bullish

Below 0.95 is bearish

This equation suggests that stocks are fully priced when the rate on T-bills is equal to 0.95 times the earnings yield on the S&P 500—in other words, when the earnings yield is slightly less than the rate on riskless assets. As T-bill rates rise from this point, stocks become overvalued, because their return potential cannot compensate for the added risk. It does not make sense to buy stocks at this point, unless certain ones are unusually undervalued, because the return on the riskless T-bills is too attractive. An EVI greater than 0.95 would be bullish, since again, the potential rewards from stocks can compensate for the added risk.

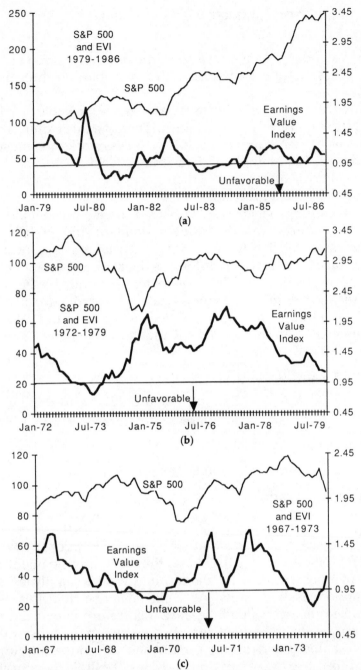

Figure 4-2. The Earnings Value Index measures the relative value of stock earnings against the riskless return from Treasury bills. Below 0.95 is bearish, between 0.95 and 1.05 is moderately bullish, and above 1.05 is very bullish.

Strict theorists might argue that a fully priced EVI should be well above 1.00, because of the added risk in stocks. But this formula is not an attempt to draw a precise correlation, just a helpful guideline. The inconsistencies inherent in the earnings calculation of the S&P 500 make it unrealistic to become too precise, so the dip down to 0.95 is a concession that allows for these imperfections. Also, because we want to remain constructive toward the stock market as long as possible to fulfill our long-term investing goals, only extremes in market overvaluation need to be feared (see Figure 4-2).

The use of the Standard & Poor's 500 p/e ratio is another compromise for convenience. Earnings for the S&P do not perfectly reflect the earnings of the entire stock market. Obviously, the S&P only covers 500 stocks and is weighted according to the market value of its respective stocks. Fortunately, because these 500 stocks comprise a great percentage of total stock market worth, the S&P 500 is a good proxy for the entire market and shows consistently good results in value comparisons. For computation of the EVI, both three-month T-bills and the p/e ratio of the S&P 500 are available each week in *Barron's* and other newspapers.

One difficulty in computing this index is the availability of earnings figures for the S&P 500. Because earnings figures come out a few weeks after each company's year-end, the quarterly earnings for the total S&P 500 are often late by as much as a month or more. However, this will not usually throw the EVI calculation off by an amount that would result in incorrect conclusions. Nevertheless, investors should be wary of this problem. A 20-year history of the Earnings Value Index is given in Appendix B.

THE PRICE-DIVIDEND RATIO—WHY BOTHER?

Many analysts have also placed benchmark levels on dividends, claiming that certain levels of dividend return for common stocks represent overvaluation and undervaluation. To make this simplistic assumption more attractive, they do something very clever. They invert the dividend yield into something that resembles a p/e ratio, calling it a price-dividend ratio. In other words:

Dividend yield of 5%

$$= \frac{1}{20} \text{ , which equals a price-dividend ratio of 20}$$

Unlike the earnings yield, the price-dividend ratio does not facilitate comparisons between dividends and interest rates or any other measure of market value. The dividend yield in its original form *is* perfectly suited to this purpose, and no sleight of hand is necessary.

Putting aside the price-dividend ratio, historical measures on the dividend yield have shown that markets with yields below 3% have correlated to extreme overvaluation, while yields above 6% have been extremely overvalued. Again, markets can survive for several months with these extremes, underscoring the thesis that, like p/e ratios, the dividend yield should not be valued in a vacuum.

A dividend yield is only high or low relative to the level of interest rates, because the two are in constant competition. Dividend yields rise or fall with interest rates, pushing stock prices in the opposite direction. When there is an imbalance in the relationship between dividends and interest rates, an investment opportunity is created to buy undervalued or sell overvalued stocks.

RELATING DIVIDENDS TO INTEREST RATES

Unfortunately, like earnings, comparisons between dividends and earnings are not subject to precision, but we can draw a similar equation. Since dividends are effectively taxed twice, once as earnings to the corporation and once as dividends to the shareholder, they cannot be directly compared to T-bill rates. Furthermore, T-bills are not taxed to individuals on their state returns, so they gain another tax advantage.

To put dividends on an equal footing with T-bills, taxes to the corporation need to be eliminated and taxes to individuals on state returns need to be added back. This led me to my Dividend Value Index (DVI), which compares the pretax dividend yield of the S&P 500 against the rate on three-month Treasury bills. Both are available in *Barron's* and other newspapers on a weekly basis.

Given that the maximum corporate tax rate has been 46% and the average state individual tax rate is about 3%, the total tax advantage to T-bills is approximately 49%.

Dividend Value Index

$$= \frac{\text{S\&P 500 dividend yield}}{(1 - \text{total tax advantage})} \div \text{three-month T-bill rates}$$

Keeping track of the changes in corporate taxes and the variance in individual state tax rates is not really necessary, since the Dividend Value Index is just a rough guideline to value. Since precision is not really an issue, for simplicity, I make the comparison by multiplying the S&P dividend yield by 2.

$$\text{Dividend Value Index} = \frac{\text{S\&P 500 dividend yield} \times 2}{\text{Three-month T-bill rates}}$$

A reading below 1.0 on the Dividend Value Index suggests that stocks would have a difficult time achieving and sustaining higher prices. The stock market might not be poised for an immediate downfall, but if interest rates did go higher from these levels, then stocks would be overvalued relative to interest rates. A DVI above 1.0 suggests that dividends are favorably valued relative to interest rates and can provide a superior overall return over the long term.

Appendix B contains a 20-year history of the DVI and can be used to provide examples for the relevance of the indicator. For example, in January 1973, the S&P 500 had completed a two-year advance of more than 50%. DVI had slipped below 1.0 for the first time since the advance began, suggesting that stocks were no longer providing competitive returns compared to interest rates. Stocks soon turned lower and fell nearly in half before the next major bull market began in 1974.

It is worth noting that in 1974, DVI turned bullish even though the market was still falling. That year represented one of the most undervalued periods in history, and therefore one of the greatest

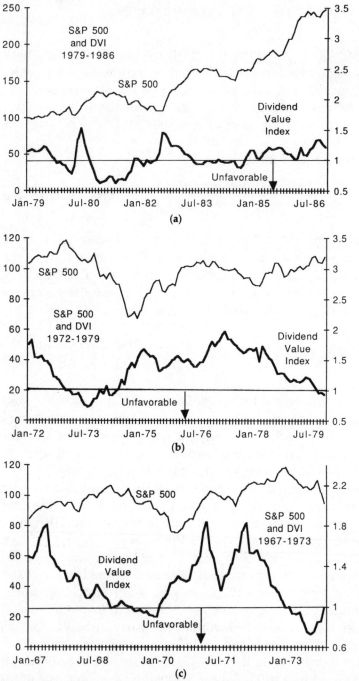

Figure 4-3. The Dividend Value Index measures the relative value of stock dividends (adjusted for taxes) against the riskless return from Treasury bills. Below 1.00 is bearish, signifying that stocks are not competitively valued relative to interest rates.

long-term buying opportunities. At first blush, this would seem
to invalidate the DVI and EVI indexes as good indicators, since
they turned bullish too early. But for the long-term value investor,
this is okay, since we are not so interested in catching exact tops
and bottoms as investing when favorable valuations are available.

Stocks bought in the midst of the 1974 decline would have
shown losses for a year or more, but would have shown astounding
gains of a few hundred percent or more on average within the
decade. The unusually high readings of DVI spanning from mid-
1974 to late 1979 show how severely undervalued the market was
during the late 1970s, an aberration that was corrected in the mid-
1980s. For those of you who wish to see a little more precision in
your indicators, as seen in Appendix B: DVI turned bullish in June
1982, just before the bull market began; turned bearish in June
1983 at the peak; turned bullish again in November 1984, and
remained bullish throughout the incredible 1984–1986 bull market
(see Figure 4-3).

In 1987, the maximum corporate tax rate fell from 46 to 34%,
yet more taxes will be collected from corporations than in previous
years because of other provisions like the minimum tax and others.
In light of this, until the effects of the tax law become clearer,
despite the apparently lower tax, I continue to compute DVI by
multiplying the dividend yield by two. In time, the market should
recognize the lower tax rate, but it is unlikely to make this adjustment
immediately because the collective tax on corporations is actually
higher.

THE BALANCE OF VALUE

The competitive valuation of stocks against interest rates helps to
explain why interest rates tend to lead major moves in the stock
market. Because stock market participants are generally quick to
recognize value, stocks are usually fairly priced relative to the
value of interest rates. The impressive efficiency of the market's
pricing mechanism accounts for long periods of sideways movement
in stock prices and the relatively short periods of wide-swinging
movement.

Occasionally, the pendulum becomes unbalanced. When it does, it is usually due to a sharp move in interest rates, like in 1982, which upset the balance and provided stocks with an advantageous return. For a few years after 1982, the rise in stocks was almost entirely due to a near-continuous decline in interest rates, which made stocks more attractive than competing investment vehicles. In general, interest rates move and the competitive valuation effect sets into the financial markets to realign the balance of value.

This creates a relative value equation, setting movements in interest rates against changes in stock prices. The EVI and DVI are two methods of exposing imbalances in this relative value equation. Once the balance of power is significantly upset, the stock market will usually move swiftly to correct the imbalance by changing stock prices. This accounts for the quick bursts of upside action during bull markets, which often find the short-term investor scrambling to get back into the market while rewarding the long-term investor for his patience in sticking with advantageously valued investments.

EXPECTATIONS IN THE BALANCE OF VALUE

Another reason the balance of value is kept so largely intact, leading to stability in stock prices, is the fact that the Fed uses interest rates to counter perceived undesirable swings in the economy. If earnings are falling, the Fed might lower interest rates to try to keep the economy out of a severe recession. If earnings are rising so fast that inflationary fears are threatening the economy, then the Fed might raise rates to choke off the expansion.

Since interest rates are usually moving counter to earnings, very often the net effect is minimal. This causes the sideways swings in the stock market averages that tend to dominate trading activity.

Since stock market value is a measure of perceptions, market participants try to guess which way each side of the value equation is going, focusing on which way the Fed might move interest rates and where earnings and dividends are headed. Because of the great difficulty of predicting either half of the equation, I strongly suggest that you do not try to predict the direction of rates or earnings. Especially for a long-term investor, there is no reason to throw more uncertainty into the pot by adding predictions. If the experts have difficulty calling interest rates or earnings with any consistency, nonexperts should not expect to profit from their predictions either. *Let the market decide its own direction. When the imbalance occurs, act on it.*

STRATEGIC APPLICATIONS

It is essential for investors to recognize the preponderant influence of interest rates on the stock market. Buying and selling pressure may be a concept of technical analysis, but the primary source of such pressures is from money flows created by interest rates.

Changes in interest rates cause an imbalance of value in stock prices. To better recognize the imbalances, I have offered two measures of stock market value relative to interest rates. The EVI relates earnings to interest rates, while the DVI does the same for dividends. These indicators should serve as helpful guideposts to stock market value, not as substitutes for a careful consideration of the entire investment picture.

Imbalances in the relative value between interest rates and stock prices are often quickly corrected by changes in stock prices. This accounts for the quick bursts of activity in bull and bear markets and the long periods of time when the stock market is relatively stable. The swiftness of the big moves makes it almost impossible to catch the most profitable price action consistently with shorter-term trading strategies. Spurts of sudden market opportunities underscore the importance of maintaining a long-term invested position unless stocks are not advantageously valued relative to competing investments, and undervalued stocks are simply not available.

5

A Framework for Market Timing

A value investor *can* be successful by being strictly a stock-picker, purchasing stocks on the basis of value without regard to the condition of the stock market. Many investors who do this remain 100% invested all of the time simply by staying in the most undervalued stocks. This is usually a good strategy, but it can be a death wish during severe bear markets. In light of the potential dangers, many value investors also use their valuation work to reduce portfolio exposure to dangerous markets.

For instance, the 1973–1974 bear market cut over 40% from the value of the Dow Jones Industrial Average. Investors who remained fully invested, regardless of the valuation of their stocks, would have had several years of previous gains wiped out in less than two years. Between 1968 and 1974 the Value Line Composite, a market average that better portrays the broader market, fell an incredible 75%—a terrifying specter that may have contributed to the boom in real estate in the five years that followed as individuals fled the stock market for greener pastures. Our primary goal in market timing will be to avoid these types of devastating losses.

Market timing can be approached from a value standpoint and become a viable component of an overall value strategy. As the universal concept of value implies, stock market value, determined by fundamental and interest rate value, is also influenced by technical factors like market psychology. Furthermore, extreme valuations are signaled by both technical and fundamental aspects of value in unison. Since the stock market as a whole is composed of individual stocks, a universal approach to market timing can be used to recogize periods of extreme valuation and to adjust the holding of stocks accordingly. In undervalued conditions, market timing can be used to recognize that further bear market risk is minimal, creating the environment for a fully employed portfolio before the next bull market begins. Therefore, market timing is a vital aspect of risk management, not only to reduce risk in bear markets, but also to take full advantage of bull market opportunities.

The best suggestion I can make about successfully implementing a strategy of market timing is this: *be realistic about your abilities, and respect the market's ability to defy consistent prediction.* Stock market movement is a game of value, a tug-of-war between stock market value and competing interest rates. This reality pushes fundamental and interest rate considerations to the forefront, leaving technical work to function as an advance warning system.

Always remember, technical work is based on conditions that have no *direct* bearing on the balance of value. Since I advocate the advantageous use of long-term trends, it would be a giant mistake for you to cut short your gains by overaggressive market timing. A famous economist once said, "I have called 10 out of the last 4 recessions." This is an easy trap to fall into with stock market analysis too, so before you get tempted to pull your money out of the market, go through the upcoming framework and make the conditions prove to you that your portfolio is at extreme risk.

Remember: with regard to the technical side of market timing, *less is better.*

QUESTIONS OF MARKET CONDITION

Now, let us see how you can combine knowledge from our previous discussion of interest rates and stock market value with some of the more reliable methods of technical analysis to produce a universal framework for market timing. This chapter is not intended to be a complete listing of every indicator found in the technical domain; there are plenty of books which fulfill that purpose. The only indicators presented here are those with a long history of success that fit the objectives of long-term value investing. Rather than go through a laundry list of indicators, let us build a market timing framework to answer five basic questions about the condition of the stock market. They are:

1. Where is the market now?
2. Is the market overvalued or undervalued?
3. What is the direction of the long-term trend?
4. Is the trend healthy (confirmation) or deteriorating (divergence)?
5. If healthy, is the trend overbought or oversold?

These questions can be approached in the manner suggested by the flowchart in Figure 5-1. The basic objective of market timing

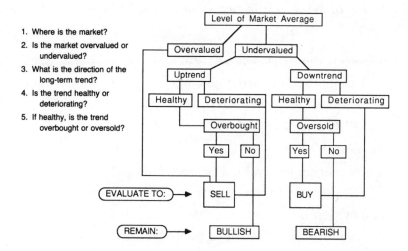

Figure 5-1. This logical framework for market timing addresses the basic questions about the market's condition, giving insight into the direction of its trend and the risk of it not continuing.

is to recognize the direction of the long-term trend and determine the risk of it not continuing. In the course of its existence, a trend will be beset by a number of corrections that are likely to cloud the big picture. The investor should consider all of the evidence possible within the framework to determine whether those corrections threaten the trend's longevity.

The first question addresses the subject of market averages, like the Dow Jones Industrial Average. Suppose the Dow is at 1500. We now know the level of the Dow, but this does not tell us anything about the condition of the market. Is the market fundamentally overvalued or undervalued relative to interest rates (question 2)? If so, then we need to consider a change in the direction of the trend (question 3) and see whether our other indicators confirm such a possibility (questions 4 and 5) or suggest a continuation of the trend.

As we go through the framework, it should become apparent that market analysis is a somewhat negative process. It involves careful consideration of a broad variety of market conditions with one eye searching for chinks in the armor. For the value investor, the market needs to "prove" that its weaknesses can be extremely destructive before they warrant a shift in the portfolio. The following is a relisting of the basic questions along with the types of indicators that can provide the answers:

1. Where is the market now?
   a. Dow Jones Industrial Average
   b. Standard & Poor's 500 Index
   c. Other market averages
   d. Unweighted indexes

2. Is the market overvalued or undervalued?
   a. Earnings and interest rates
   b. Dividends and interest rates
   c. Market value relative to book value

3. What is the direction of the long-term trend?
   a. A value approach to charting

    b. The long-term cyclical perspective

    c. The condition of interest rates and inflation

4. Is the trend healthy (confirmation) or deteriorating (divergence)?

    a. Market averages

    b. Transportation averages and Dow Theory

    c. Advance/decline line

    d. New highs and new lows

    e. Margin debt

5. If healthy, is the trend overbought or oversold?

    a. Mutual fund cash available

    b. Advisor sentiment

    c. Insider selling

    d. Secondary distributions

WHERE IS THE MARKET NOW?

Perhaps the most common question in stock market circles is, "How did the Dow do today?" But while the Dow Jones Industrial Average is the most watched barometer of stock market activity, it is just one of the many market averages available and is often not the most accurate reflection of overall stock market movement. Since the Dow can be misleading, it is important to evaluate the other market averages that are also readily available in your local newspapers. Note the differences among the various averages. These differences will play a key role in the discussion of confirmation and divergence later in this chapter.

The Dow Jones Industrial Average

The Dow Jones Industrial Average is an average of 30 stocks chosen and maintained by the Dow Jones Company. The chosen 30 include some of the largest corporations in the world and represent a fairly good cross section of the U.S. economy. The Dow list as of May 31, 1987 is shown in Table 5-1.

From time to time, the list is updated to rid the index of an old powerhouse that has fallen on hard times and no longer reflects the strength of corporate America. Sometimes a stock will be eliminated from the Dow list because of a merger. The stock that replaces it is usually a mature and proven company, often the leader in an industry that has taken on greater importance in the economy but has not been adequately represented in the Dow. Additions in the past decade of American Express, IBM, McDonald's, Merck, and Philip Morris are evidence of that Dow maintenance strategy.

TABLE 5-1   Stocks Comprising the Dow Jones Industrial, Transportation, and Utility Averages as of May 31, 1987

Dow Jones Industrial Average

Allied-Signal, Inc.
Aluminum Company of America (Alcoa)
American Express
American Telephone & Telegraph
Bethlehem Steel
Boeing Company
Chevron Corp.
Coca-Cola Company
Du Pont (E.I.) de Nemours
Eastman Kodak
Exxon Corp.
General Electric
General Motors
Goodyear Tire & Rubber
International Business Machines
International Paper
McDonald's Corp.
Merck & Company
Minnesota Mining & Manufacturing
Navistar International
Philip Morris Companies
Primerica
Procter & Gamble
Sears, Roebuck & Company

TABLE 5-1 *(Continued)*

Texaco, Inc.
Union Carbide
United Technologies
USX Corp.
Westinghouse Electric
Woolworth (F.W.)

Dow Jones Transportation Average

Allegis Corp.
AMR Corp.
American President Companies
Burlington Northern
Canadian Pacific Limited
Carolina Freight Corp.
Consolidated Freightways
CSX Corp.
Delta Air Lines
Federal Express
Leaseway Transportation Corp.
Norfolk Southern Corp.
NWA
Pan Am Corporation
Piedmont Aviation
Ryder System, Inc.
Santa Fe Southern Pacific
Trans World Arlines
Union Pacific
USAir Group, Inc.

Dow Jones Utility Average

American Electric Power
Centerior Energy
Columbia Gas System
Commonwealth Edison
Consolidated Edison
Consolidated Natural Gas
Detroit Edison
Houston Industries
Niagara Mohawk Power
Pacific Gas & Electric
Panhandle Eastern
Peoples Energy
Philadelphia Electric
Public Service Enterprise
Southern California Edison

Despite efforts to keep the index current, the Dow is still an average of only 30 stocks. Due to that limitation, the Dow has weaknesses as an overall measure of stock market activity. The Dow stock prices are added together to reach a total, and that total is divided by a divisor, which is adjusted for such things as stock splits and stock dividends in order to retain the proportions of each stock. But a stock trading at a very high price will take on a greater importance in the average. For example, in 1986, when IBM traded at 150, it represented 8.8% of the Dow (at 1900). Furthermore, a stock propelled higher by takeover talks will seriously distort the average, which will only be relieved after the stock is removed from the Dow and subsequently replaced.

Nevertheless, the Dow is still an excellent indicator of market activity. The 30 stocks contained in the average make up a substantial amount (often above 25%) of the total value of the stock market. Its movement rarely diverges from the movement of broader indexes containing many more stocks. Of course, when the Dow does diverge from the other indexes, it is a serious warning to evaluate carefully the strength of the current trend.

One can speculate whether the incredible importance attached to the Dow is actually responsible for its remarkable ability to track the market. But whether the tail is wagging the dog or not, the Dow is an indicator to be watched and studied. Because it is the most visible yardstick for the investing public, it is the most likely to mislead the masses and, therefore, sticks out as the standard against how other indicators can be evaluated.

The Standard & Poor's 500 Index

The Standard & Poor's 500 Index (S&P 500) is the most popular alternative to the Dow. Professional portfolio managers often compare their performance against the S&P, because it represents a broad sampling of investment-grade stocks. As the name implies, the S&P 500 is based on the market value of 500 stocks. Market value is computed by multiplying the stock price of each stock by the number of shares outstanding, which determines the relative importance of each stock in the S&P 500 average.

Like the Dow stocks, the 500 stocks are among the leading stocks on the exchange. With its collective market power, the 500 stocks comprise about 90% of the value of the entire New York Stock Exchange. The 500 stocks are split as follows: 400 industrials, 20 transportation companies, 40 utilities, and 40 financial companies. Each of these subgroups form their own indexes which are also available in many newspapers.

An index of 500 stocks may seem broad enough to reflect the entire stock market, but the index does have its failings. Because the index is based on market value, stocks with unusually large capitalizations (e.g., IBM, AT&T, and GM) comprise a great percentage of the index, just as they do in the Dow. In fact, as of the end of 1986, the 10 highest valued stocks accounted for more than 18% of the entire value of the S&P 500. Despite the tendency toward a big stock bias, the S&P has retained its integrity over the years as an excellent barometer of stock market activity.

Since the S&P 500 is based on market value, stocks are frequently added and deleted from the average to retain the S&P as an index of the 500 highest market values. This may cause a certain price advantage for stocks that are in the index, particularly because of the existence of index funds.

The science of indexing began in the 1970s, when portfolio managers were faced with difficult markets and had little success in convincing their clients they were worth their fees. Academicians made the plight of the portfolio manager even worse by claiming that no one could outperform the market averages over the long term because stock market movement was random, the so-called Random Walk Theory.

In response, index funds popped up across the country, with portfolio managers set up by computer to mimic the performance of the S&P 500 by maintaining portfolios identical to the index. These index funds, the stock market's monument to mediocrity, are still very popular today and have a profound influence on stocks that are in the S&P 500.

When a stock is added to the S&P, the index funds are forced to buy the stock in tremendous quantities to achieve the correct proportions of the index in their portfolio. The immediate effect of the change in stocks is to increase the price of the newly added stock and decrease the price of the deleted one. Eventually, the index funds adjust their portfolios and the prices of both added and deleted stocks behave normally. It can be questioned whether the index funds have an ongoing effect, positive or negative, on the valuations of S&P stocks and non-S&P stocks, but this I leave to the researchers.

In the past few years, stocks in the Dow and the S&P 500 have become the focus of even greater market interest because of the new stock index futures and options. Major institutions use these complex instruments for both hedging and portfolio insurance, causing violent up-and-down movements in both the averages and the individual stocks.

This unprecedented volatility has scared thousands of smaller investors out of the stock market, but like any contrarian situation, this actually creates tremendous opportunities for the value investor. Stock index trading results in some of the most advantageous under- and overvalued periods, making the market ripe for a value investor to buy bargains and sell off overpriced issues. Since the long-term value investor is relatively unconcerned with short-term fluctuations, this rollercoaster volatility "is not a problem, it's an opportunity."

Other Market Averages

The New York Composite Index is based on the market value of every stock on the New York Stock Exchange (NYSE). This may seem like the ideal index but, like the S&P, it suffers from the problem of having a small group of powerful stocks (in total market value) comprise a great percentage of its movement. Despite its acceptance of all stocks, the less-powerful stocks are such a minor part of the average that it can also be characterized as an index of the major NYSE stocks.

The American Stock Exchange operates the AMEX Market Value Index as an index of all of the American Stock Exchange stocks based on market value. The over-the-counter markets have the OTC Composite and the National Market Composite indexes. Both the AMEX and the OTC are generally composed of younger, more speculative companies, which can lead to helpful inferences regarding confirmation and divergence of the popular market averages.

The Wilshire 5000 Equity Index is perhaps the broadest market average regularly reported by the popular press. The Wilshire Index represents the total market value index of all stocks listed on the New York Stock Exchange and the American Stock Exchange and includes most stocks actively traded over the counter. Compiled by Wilshire Associates of Santa Monica, California, the Wilshire 5000 is shown daily in the *Wall Street Journal* and weekly in *Barron's*, and is gaining acceptance in many newspapers.

Unweighted Indexes

The more popular market averages, like the Dow, S&P, and NYSE Composite, have been criticized for presenting a skewed image of the stock market that does not reflect the overall price movement of the broad market. The primary complaint is they are too greatly dominated by a relatively small number of large stocks. In recognition of the thousands of smaller stocks that have become very popular among investors, many services have developed unweighted averages which give equal weight to small and large companies alike.

The Value Line Composite Average is an unweighted average covering all of the stocks regularly reviewed in the *Value Line Investment Survey*. Prepared, of course, by Value Line, the index is widely seen in the popular financial press, including the *Wall Street Journal* and *Barron's*. The current list (1987) numbers 1676 stocks, and includes 1505 industrials, 160 utilities, and 11 rails. Although more than 80% of the stocks in the average are from the New York Stock Exchange, the average is considered by many to be an excellent barometer of small stock activity. Every day, the index computes the percentage move for each stock and sums the total. The index is set on a basis of 100 as of June 30, 1961.

Conclusion

Most investors follow the Dow, but they should also have an awareness of what the other market averages are doing as well.

Of course, just knowing where the market is on an index does not tell us whether the investment climate is favorable for stocks or not. For this we have to look at how the stock market is valued relative to competing investments, and later, to take an objective look at the internal condition of the market.

IS THE MARKET OVERVALUED OR UNDERVALUED?

The stock market is not valued in a vacuum, it is a relative value. For example, the value of a basketball player would be difficult to determine if there was no professional league or structure to the sport. But against a limited number of professionals with comparable skills, a player and management can work out a contract that places a definite price on his value to the franchise. In the case of the stock market, fundamental value is elevated to market value by the relationship of stock market returns to interest rates.

Earnings and Interest Rates

The Earnings Value Index (EVI) explained in Chapter 4 is a logical method for determining whether the stock market is more attractive than competing cash alternatives. This is accomplished by comparing the earnings yield for the S&P 500 against the rate on three-month Treasury bills. If the earnings yield for stocks is less than the riskless return of T-bills, then stocks are relatively less attractive and will eventually drop in price to correct the imbalance of value.

Accordingly, an EVI below 0.95 is bearish, particularly when interest rates are rising. A mark between 0.95 and 1.05 is moderately bullish, and an EVI above 1.05 is generally very bullish. Because the stock market is an arena of expectations, the direction of interest rates in conjunction with the EVI will often act as a trigger to changes in trend. In addition, it is far more reassuring to follow an EVI signal with confirmation by the Dividend Value Index (DVI).

Since the p/e ratio serves both as a return and a measure of market perceptions, knowing what level it is relative to in past history can be a helpful indication of value, although not as consistent a guide as the EVI. Over the past 20 years, levels of extreme undervaluation have been registered by a p/e ratio below 8 (1974 and 1982), while overvaluation has occurred with p/e ratios above 17 (1966 and 1972).

All four extremes resulted in tremendous opportunities for profit, but without comparing the p/e ratio to interest rates, you might have bought or sold several more times at other extreme valuations that occurred during the 20-year period. For example, in 1971, stocks rose steadily to new highs even though the average p/e ratio was above 17 for the entire year. In that case, the critical difference was the fact that short-term rates were hovering around 5%, which made the stock market a more attractive investment than riskless alternatives.

Dividends and Interest Rate Value

Dividend distributions give stock market investors an up-front return on their equity investments. While dividends can be canceled, they certainly have greater reliability than expected returns from a stock's price appreciation. For this reason, dividends are somewhat comparable to the rate on three-month Treasury bills, except for their double taxation characteristic. In the DVI, we (imprecisely) eliminate the corporate tax by multiplying the dividend yield by two, thereby placing dividends on more of a parity with T-bills.

However, because T-bills are a riskless asset and stocks contain a great deal of risk, for stocks to be a comparatively better investment, they must provide investors with greater potential returns. When the return on dividends (adjusted for the corporate tax) is less than that of T-bills, then stocks lose their appeal, because the returns are not compensating for the added risk.

This very bearish circumstance is signified by a DVI below 1.00, while a reading above 1.00 shows that stocks can at least successfully compete with riskless assets. Like its companion calculation, EVI, because the stock market is continuously trying to anticipate changes in value, the direction of interest rates adds a great deal of significance to the timing of bullish or bearish signals.

Like the p/e ratio, knowledge of what the dividend yield is on the average S&P 500 stock is helpful, although it can be misleading without relating it to interest rates. Historically, a dividend above 6% has corresponded to important bottoms (1932, 1942, 1949, 1953, barely in 1974, and 1982), while a dividend below 3% has often produced important tops (1929, 1961, 1968, 1972). Over time, dividends have proven themselves to be an excellent indicator of market over- and undervaluation, although I strongly suggest the use of DVI in addition to (or instead of) simply looking at the raw dividend yield.

It is fascinating to see that the difference between over- and undervaluation is a multiple of approximately two (dividends 6%:3%, p/e ratios 17:8). To be able to maintain these 2:1 ratios, the market would have to be very stable in its valuation, much like that of a bond, which is its primary competition for investment money. This propensity for 2:1 relationships between market extremes suggests that stock valuations generally double in bull markets and halve in bear markets, underscoring the importance of market timing.

This multiple of two can be helpful in picking individual stocks too. In Chapter 11, I use this multiple to guide a simulated investment program performed with overvaluation and undervaluation parameters on individual stocks. This makes sense, since the stock market is a market of stocks; what serves as a guide for the whole should be relevant to its individual components.

Market Value Relative to Book Value

We have already discussed the idea that when investors buy stock, they buy a share of equity in a company. Book value is another name for equity. In Part 3, book value is a major topic of discussion in the determination of value in individual stocks, but it can also be used to measure value in the market as a whole.

Barron's occasionally lists the book value of each stock in the Dow Jones Industrial Average and the total book value for the Dow as well. An annual chart of the Dow and its book value is shown in Figure 5-2 for the 1947–1986 period.

Let us set some easy-to-follow guidelines for identifying under- and overvaluation. If the Dow is trading below book value, then the stock market is at a historically attractive valuation for long-term purchase. Since 1936, only 1942, 1949, 1974–1975, and 1978–1982 has seen the Dow fall below its book value; all of which

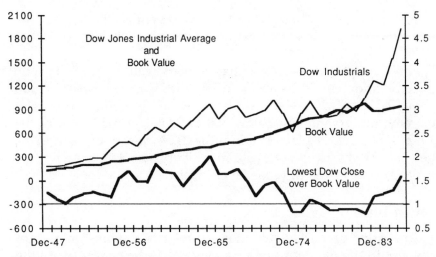

Figure 5-2. A forty-year history of the Dow Jones Industrial Average shows that the stock market is an excellent long-term value when it is priced near or especially below book value.

were wonderful times to buy stocks. Extreme low points in valuation formed at between 80 to 90% of book value.

It is interesting to note that between 1977 and 1982, the Dow fell to low points each year that were 80 to 90% of book value. In each case (except 1981 at 824), the market established a low between 740 and 800, which was a strong technical support level for the Dow. The fact that the Dow was also undervalued on the basis of book value illustrates another instance of the interplay between technical and fundamental value.

As for overvaluation, the runaway aspects of bull market extremes make it difficult to place an intelligent number on the upside potential of market value to book value, but let us use some simple reasoning to hone in on a logical level to expect. Logically, if extremes in overvaluation occur in multiples of two for p/e ratios and dividends, then book values should follow in the approximate 2:1 ratio as well.

Therefore, if undervaluation is below book value, then over-valuation is above twice book value. And since overvaluation should be just as extreme as undervaluation, the 10 to 20% difference between book value and extreme undervaluation can be placed as an upper limit. Thus, twice book value equals 200%, plus the extra 10 to 20%, equals an extreme overvaluation level of 210 to 220% book value.

For example, if the Dow has a book value of 1,000, then overvaluation would be above 2,000, with extreme overvaluation above 2,100 to 2,200. Undervaluation would be below 1,000, with extreme undervaluation below 800 to 900. The 1965 peak of the 1942–1966 cycle registered a high of 232%, just above our 220% benchmark of extreme overvaluation. As this book is being written in 1987, the Dow is at those levels again.

Conclusion

The question of market valuation is probably the most important element in the market timing framework. If the consensus of the three components (earnings, dividends, and book value) is swayed to an extreme, the investor should be on notice to look carefully at his portfolio for making adjustments. If the valuation indicators are neutral (which they should be most of the time), then investors should be happy to sit with their stocks, as long as those stocks are not overvalued.

The answers to the next three questions deal mainly with technical indicators. Again, due to our long-term value approach, technical work should be used primarily as confirmation or warnings to valuation work but not as the primary decision variable. Very often, the technical indicators will send signals a month or more before the valuation gauges, giving us an advance warning that a trend might change. But until the balance of value swings to an extreme, you should leave your positions largely intact. Again, let the market timing framework prove that a change in trend is imminent, rather than letting your predictions prejudice your over-all market outlook.

WHAT IS THE DIRECTION OF THE LONG-TERM TREND?

Throughout our discussion of interest rates, we saw that interest rate trends tend to last for a couple years or more, primarily due to the length of time needed to develop inflationary trends. Because interest rates are such an important determination of stock market value, stock prices tend to remain in a trend as long as interest rates do. Therefore, once the market is in a trend, it is likely to remain trending, obviously making it very helpful to know which way it has been going.

Certainly, anyone who has been around a trading pit has heard the phrase, "the trend is your friend." This is just a way of saying that if you know a trend is in progress, you should stay with it as long as you can, because it is more likely to continue than to end. This is especially important, given our overall strategy of long-term value investing. The longer we can stay with a trend, the more profit we are likely to squeeze from it.

A Realistic View of Charting

To help us in the pursuit of monitoring trends, let us enlist the help of charting, an activity that has been compared with reading tea leaves by many stock market experts. In some ways, I agree with their assessment, but I also believe that charts can be helpful in gaining a perspective as to where the market is and in what direction it might be going. This brief discussion of charting is in no way meant to be a complete treatment of the field; there are a number of books for that purpose. What I am going to try to do is to offer a realistic method of looking at charts, without delving into the fringe areas that have drawn so much criticism.

It is unfortunate that charting has been touted by promoters as the easy way to make big money in the stock market. They suggest that one can read a chart and make an investment decision, totally disregarding such basic considerations as value or corporate qualities. This may work for the short-term trader who is positioned on the trading floor, able to move in and out of stocks on a daily basis as if they were commodities. However, to the normal investor, this is an invitation to disaster, because the trading dynamics are unlikely to continue over the long term. Maybe the chart pattern will dictate an action that is correct for a few weeks, but over many stocks and many years, short-term charting strategies are not likely to show any better performance than a dartboard. Charts offer only a graphic presentation of stock movement; taken by themselves as an investment strategy, they are of little value.

Now that you have a realistic view of charting, let us see what it can do to help you gain a historical perspective and a view of the future in individual stocks and the stock market.

Charts can be viewed in very simple terms. A stock is either going up (*uptrend*), down (*downtrend*), or sideways (*consolidation*). The shorter the perspective of the chart, the less significance it has for long-term investors. For instance, a three-month chart gives too brief a history of price movement to be able to draw any meaningful conclusions. But a longer-term chart of one year in length and preferably more than two years on either a daily or weekly basis, gives a history that can identify important price levels that could become the long-term tops or bottoms of the future. Additionally, long-term charts offer the clearest picture of cyclical price trends.

Support and Resistance

When a stock is undervalued after a long decline, eventually the marketplace realizes it and accumulation takes place. The stock may still be under selling pressure, but value-oriented investors will absorb large supplies of stock offered for sale, leaving a consolidation in stock prices. This creates a floor under the stock that provides support against further price declines in the future. Important market bottoms are marked by massive accumulation by investors at long-term support levels, which actually represent the levels at which the marketplace consistently recognizes undervaluation.

When a stock is overvalued after a long advance, eventually the market realizes it and distribution takes place. The rise will fizzle out and move sideways in a consolidation. This topping consolidation is called resistance, which forms a ceiling against further price advances in the future. Important tops are formed by distribution at resistance levels that signify recognition by the marketplace of overvaluation in a stock.

Support and resistance levels can become psychological barriers to future price movement. The 1,000 level on the Dow stood as an impregnable barrier from 1966 until 1982. Every time the Dow approached 1,000, it either exceeded the level only marginally or failed to break through, soon finding a reason to slip into a bear market. It is interesting to note that although the Dow never progressed, the broader Value Line average made substantial gains during this period (see Figure 2-4, page 40). This should serve as another reminder to always look at the broader market averages, which often tell the truer story.

It is also instructive to note how the 750 level on the Dow served as powerful support for launching rallies in the late 1970s and early 1980s. In that 20-year span, simply by buying stocks when the Dow fell below 800 and selling when the Dow neared 1,000, an investor would have made a lot of money. Of course, that is a simplistic way of investing and would have left you out of the 1982 bull market, but it shows the worth of knowing where long-term support and resistance points lie.

An extremely important tenet of charting is that once resistance is broken, it becomes support for future moves. For example, now that 16 years of resistance at Dow 1,000 has been broken, it is likely to become a superb support level against future declines. This is especially true because the longer it takes to build a support or resistance level and the more times it is successfully tested, the more resilient it should be against future tests. Sixteen years of history built up at 1,000 is pretty tough to beat. Of course, the same goes for support levels which, if broken, become future marks for resistance.

Volume Moves Price

Trading volume moves money flows in and out of the stock market. The building of long-term support levels for market bottoms ordinarily show very low volume, because prices are depressed, which, in turn, depresses investors. Accumulation occurs, but because it is so gradual, it hardly causes a ripple in trading volume. As prices rise off the support level, they show powerful volume as investors rush to invest large pools of available cash in response to the new rally.

Market tops show a very different pattern of volume, almost exactly the opposite of what we saw in the case of a bottom. Volume is very heavy going into a top. Prices churn in a sideways motion, causing the formation of a resistance level. The churning is caused by value investors, who bought at lower levels, selling their stock to speculators who are willing to buy a hot stock at any price. Once the stock is distributed, volume lightens and the price begins to fall.

Thus the basic pattern of volume is that it tends to follow the direction of the trend. This is true for the same reason that interest rates are so vital to stock market performance: because it takes money to move the market. The market will recognize over- and undervaluation by setting support and resistance levels. However, primary changes in trend will not occur unless something triggers a change in the flow of money, either into or out of the stock market. Usually that element is interest rates, but it can be any number of other events as well.

Uptrends begin after a quiet building of support and are ignited with an explosion of trading activity as demand outstrips supplies of stock. Downtrends usually begin after a climactic trading peak accented by heavy volume, signifying that most investible funds have been employed. Trading activity slows and supplies of stock flood the market. Because the buying interest is not there, investors trapped at the top have to accept lower prices and the downtrend snowballs.

The Dow chart (Figure 2-4) shows a series of shorter trends that combined to build a 16-year pattern of consolidation from 1966–1982. Toward the end of 1982, the stock market exploded through the Dow 1,000 resistance mark of this consolidation to record highs. This is known as a *break-out*, which means that a stock has broken through resistance up to new levels. Volume is extremely heavy on break-outs, because to break through resistance, buyers have to overpower investors who have become accustomed to selling at that price level. Since 1,000 was such a well-tested resistance, it took tremendous inflows of capital for buyers to soak up all of the available stock for sale.

If resistance was not broken on heavy volume, then it would probably not be of much significance to the long-term future of the trend, because a new pattern of buying was not established. Heavy volume on break-outs is similar in some ways to the explosive trading seen after long-term bottoms begin their advance. Thus, so many investors bet against the odds of a rally that once the move takes place, they have to first buy stock to reverse their positions, and then quickly buy more to catch the advance.

A Common Sense View of Chart Patterns

The subject of chart patterns has filled many thick books, the ambitious products of analysts diligently cataloging a seemingly endless variety of patterns under a lengthy list of catchy names. Terms like head and shoulders, triangles, and others have miraculously stuck with star-struck neophyte technicians, who believe that each little twist of the chart can be analyzed and turned into instant money. For my money, there is really just one chart pattern, that of the idealized behavioral cycle.

However, for the moment, let us assume that the chartists are right. Rather than overwhelm you with a listing of potential chart patterns, allow me to organize all of those colorful names into four chart patterns that seem to repeat with frequency. (The other patterns that have been cataloged are, to put it kindly, more an act of self-absorption than of any use in analysis.)

1. Triangles
2. Head and shoulders
3. Double tops and bottoms
4. Broadening formations

Triangular chart formations look just like triangles and suggest an uncertain market that is building pressure between support and resistance points. Eventually, the price breaks out of the triangular structure, usually in continuation of the previous trend. Because of the pressure, the effects of the triangle are short-lived, ordinarily lasting as long as the apex of the triangle. Since triangles are rarely involved in primary changes in trend, they have little relevance to long-term value investing.

The other three chart patterns are really just manifestations of the idealized cycle because, as we saw in Chapter 2, the stock market processes the events of the day into an orderly market result. And though the event may be unprecedented, the processed result will take on a familiar pattern, because people are people, and the composition of human reactions has basically remained constant in recent generations (see Figure 5-3).

Now that we understand that all chart patterns (other than the triangle, which is more of a continuation pattern) are really just variations of the idealized cycle, the whole concept of charting makes sense. Charts naturally take the shape of the behavioral

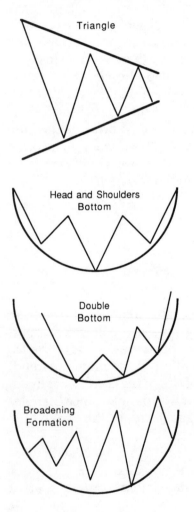

Figure 5-3. The triangle usually occurs in the course of a trend, rather than at a top or a bottom. The other three chart formations are shown to be variations of the same thick-lined idealized cycle. These three are bottom formations; topping patterns are simply the mirror image.

cycle, which makes it difficult to reliably predict short-term movements, but does lend itself to longer-term trends. As time passes, the gradual development of value is further enhanced by increasing confidence by the marketplace, creating a logical progression of value. There will be slips in development and lapses in confidence, but overall, the structure will show an upward progression over the long term.

The interplay between stock market value and market psychology is played out on stock charts in the following ways:

When investors are overpessimistic, they sell stocks down to levels of undervaluation, which causes opportunistic buyers to accumulate stock and build support for future advances in the stock.

When investors are overoptimistic, they push stocks up to levels of overvaluation, which cause opportunistic sellers to distribute stock and create resistance against future advances in the stock.

The Long-Term Cyclical Perspective

The long-term trends on the Value Line chart (Figure 2-4) are very clear. The uptrend line is formed by drawing connecting points underneath the uptrend pointing higher, while the downtrend is denoted by points connected by a line drawn on top of the prices heading lower.

The first move on the Value Line chart is a downtrend, lasting from the beginning of 1969 until the end of 1974. The next is an uptrend, lasting from 1975 through the rest of the chart. On the Dow, the trends are not nearly as clear, with the long-term consolidation building through 1982 and then the advance beyond the resistance. Again, this shows the value of looking at other market averages besides just the Dow.

There were, of course, shorter-term trends. Anyone armed with daily or weekly charts would see tremendous fluctuations within these long-term trends. In hindsight, with the benefit of a 20-year chart, it is easy to see that smaller stocks (as portrayed by the Value Line Average in Figure 2-4) had two basic trends and that the large Dow stocks muddled along for seven years (1975–1982) before breaking to the upside. As an investor caught in the confusing swirl of market movement, it is very difficult to stand back from the commotion and look at the big picture. But it's crucial to your long-term success in the stock market to do so.

The stock market has shown a tendency to move in a series of four-year cycles, generally broken up into about 2½ years of uptrend and 1½ years of downtrend. The four-year cycle can be contracted or stretched by a year or more, but it does give investors a guideline for longer-term investing. In addition, as seen in Figure 2-4, the four-year cycles can be consolidated into cycles of much longer lengths, sometimes of 8-, 12-, or 16-year durations, or even longer. The important point is not to time the cycles down to the day, or even the year, but to realize how the various cycles are fitting together to form either a basically favorable or unfavorable market environment.

The market is going to confuse you, as it confuses everyone, with short bursts of up-and-down activity, running in lengths (shown in the Hurst study in Chapter 2) that span from minutes to days, months, and so on. While there is significance to each of these cycles, to maximize your long-term results in the stock market, you need to accept these shorter-term cycles as the building blocks of the all-important longer-term cycles. By sticking to our long-term framework of market timing, investors should be able to recognize the less-important, shorter-term cycles and let them pass without disrupting their long-term investment positions.

The Condition of Interest Rates and Inflation

As we have seen, market prices are the product of long-term cycles in psychology and interest rates taking effect on fundamental value. None of the three elements can be ignored in understanding the progression of long-term cycles. Since we can assume that our civilization will continue to grow, fundamental value is considered a constant growth element that is not subject to such volatile swings as psychology and interest rates. And because interpretations of market psychology can be too subjective, the most objective alternative to tracking long-term price cycles is to examine the condition of interest rates and their companion, inflation.

Because of the preponderant effect of interest rates on stock market value, the direction of the long-term trend in stocks is often dependent on the long-term trend of interest rates and inflation.

From 1960 through 1965, inflation was virtually nonexistent, with consumer prices showing annual increases of less than 2% per year. From top to bottom, the Dow gained over 70% in those five years. Between 1966 and 1967, the market was topping, as the Consumer Price Index neared a 3% gain. In 1968, when the Consumer Price Index increased by more than 4%, interest rates began rising enough to affect adversely the balance of value in the stock market, putting stocks at a disadvantage with competing investments.

Between 1968 and 1974, the stock market took a nosedive, with money diverted into real estate to take advantage of a powerful inflationary trend. In 1974, the bottom of the 1966–1974 correction, the Consumer Price Index increased by 11% in just one year, due to an increase of over 50% in energy prices. Inflation cooled between 1975 and 1978, which saw stock prices make a modest recovery. But between 1979 and 1981, inflation returned to even higher levels, and stocks could not make any further progress because of competition from high-yielding debt instruments, real estate and other real assets.

The 1982 bull market coincided with the end of the long-term inflationary cycle, making it possible for money to flow from real estate, gold, and other real assets into financial assets, like stocks and bonds. Inflation fell back under the 4% level for the next four years, creating an environment of steadily falling interest rates which gave the competitive advantage among investment vehicles back to the stock and bond markets.

To evaluate the long-term trend properly, investors should look at the overall perspective, which encompasses not only actual stock prices, but also the longer-term cyclical development of interest rates and inflation. Since interest rates move the stock market and inflation moves interest rates, investors should be well-acquainted with inflationary pressures building in the economy and realize that their influence on the diversion of investment capital creates the environment for long-term trends in the stock market.

IS THE TREND HEALTHY OR DETERIORATING?

Once you know the direction of the long-term trend, it is important
to look below the surface of the market averages and evaluate its
condition. If the market is at an extreme valuation, signs of deterioration in the trend should already be showing up. This assessment brings us into the murky waters of technical analysis to
see whether the indicators are confirming the trend or diverging
from it. If the technical indicators are confirming the direction of
the trend, then it is probably healthy and should continue, unless
it is overbought or oversold, which is the next question. If the
indicators are diverging, then perhaps the trend is weaker than
portrayed by the market averages.

Again, remember: Technical analysis should be used as an advance warning system to extreme valuations, but should never
outweigh value considerations. The nine indicators chosen for
discussion below are helpful in recognizing long-term problems
in the market's structure, but no important investing decisions
should be made solely on their strength or weakness.

1. Market averages
2. Advance/decline line
3. New highs and new lows
4. Margin debt
5. Mutual fund cash available
6. Short selling statistics
7. Advisor sentiment
8. Insider selling
9. Secondary distributions

Confirmation and Divergence

The Dow Jones Industrial Average is like a facade. Everyone admires
its beauty, but few bother to examine the building critically to see
how well it is constructed. Trends are built like a building, they
are only as strong as their weakest link. If the foundations for the

trend are strong and secure, then it is likely to continue. But if the trend is losing the support of its various components, then it is likely to deteriorate and give way to a change in direction.

For example, an uptrend is built on the strength of advancing stocks. There are about 2,000 stocks that trade on the NYSE; counting the AMEX and OTC markets, there are over 6,000 stocks. With only 30 stocks in the Dow, all of them NYSE companies, the Dow is hardly representative of the entire stock market.

If the Dow is rising *along with a great majority of the other stocks*, then the uptrend is probably confirmed and healthy. Further confirmation is attained by evaluating the other market averages and indicators composed of statistics that are readily available in local newspapers. But if the Dow makes a new high *and relatively few stocks are following*, this is a divergence, and eventually the Dow will lose the support of its leading stocks. Due to the Dow's construction, it can keep making new highs on the advances of just a few stocks. One by one, however, those few stocks can run into trouble and crack the facade, forcing a change in the Dow's trend, long after many other stocks have already begun serious downtrends. During most of these diverging periods, a diversified portfolio will perform poorly, because it is likely to contain many stocks not found in the Dow, most of which will already be declining.

Confirmation and Divergence—Market Averages

The first source of confirmation should come from the various market averages themselves. A new high in the Dow should be confirmed by new highs in the S&P 500, NYSE Composite, and the other averages. If the Dow reaches a new high without confirmation from broader-based, big board averages like the S&P 500 or NYSE Composite, then the advance can be characterized as narrow and constrained within the blue chip stocks.

Even if the S&P and NYSE do confirm, if the Value Line, Wilshire 5000, AMEX, or OTC averages fail to confirm, then the divergent trend must be looked at suspiciously because the smaller stocks are not participating with the New York issues. The more diverging chinks that can be found in the trend's armor, the more vulnerable it is to changing direction.

Transportation Averages and Dow Theory

The transportation stocks have long been an important part of the stock market. In the early days of the market, transportation stocks meant the railroad companies; in fact, the Dow Transportation Average was known as the Rail Average until 1970. Of course, the Dow Transportation Average now includes a fair representation of airlines, air freight, and trucking companies, as well as railroad stocks.

Charles H. Dow began work on the Dow Theory in 1900 in a series of editorials in the *Wall Street Journal*. His work was expanded on by many authors in the following years, including a 1932 book by Robert Rhea entitled *Dow Theory*. The Dow Theory principles of price and volume trend analysis created the cornerstones of technical analysis as it is known today.

The Dow Theory was perhaps the first attempt to show the importance of confirmation and divergence to stock market trends. The theory dictated that new highs in the Dow Industrials should always be confirmed by new highs in the Dow Transports, and vice versa. In other words, should one average reach a new high, the other average should hit a new high as well, as shown on the left side of Figure 5-4. The same goes for new lows in either average. A bull market would not be confirmed if both averages failed to confirm new upswings in trend, as shown on the right side of Figure 5-4. Should the industrials signal a new bull market without confirmation by the transports, a strict Dow Theorist would still be bearish on the stock market on the belief that the upward move was a "false" break-out that would soon fail to the downside.

The basic principle makes sense even in today's market environment. The industrial stocks are the backbone of the economy, but they need transportation to spread the goods throughout the country for optimum sales to occur. Further credence is gained for the Dow Theory in modern times because of the marked effect of interest rates on most transportation companies. Because economic expansion or changes in interest rates moves stock prices, the transportation stocks often serve as a leading indicator by changing their trend before the industrial stocks. The current list of stocks in the Dow Transportation Average is included in Table 5-1.

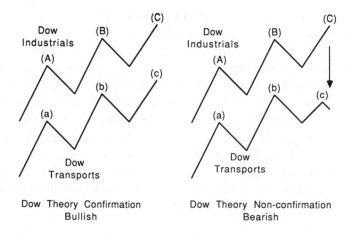

Figure 5-4. The Dow Theory dictates that a change in the primary trend of the stock market must have confirmation by both the Dow Jones Industrial and Transportation Averages. Note how the figure on the left shows each new high confirmed by both averages, while the figure on the right has the last peak in the Industrials unconfirmed by the Transports.

There are many failings to the Dow Theory, some of which have to do with the complexity of today's market. Transportation companies are heavily dependent on the price and availability of oil, making the transports highly sensitive to volatile changes in the oil markets. Sometimes this sensitivity will cause the transports to move counter to the prevailing trend of the rest of the stock market. This could cause strict Dow Theorists to miss important moves in the stock market as they wait for confirmation. Another weakness is the influence of airline stocks, which are subject to an unstable environment of strikes, price wars, and other events which have little relation to the general market trend.

Even if a move in the Dow is eventually confirmed by a move in the transports, the process of waiting for confirmation between the two averages can result in missing much of the move in the primary trend. This runs directly counter to the long-term value strategy espoused in this book. Confirmation by the two averages adds comfort and should be respected for its historical significance. As an investment tool, however, strict adherence to the Dow

Theory is ill-advised, as it often results in entering a rally so late that the risk/reward ratio is no longer favorable.

Whether or not transportation stocks are used for confirmation, they remain an excellent indicator of stock market activity. While the Dow Jones Transportation Average of 20 stocks is by far the most popular transportation index, the New York Transportation Index has the added advantage of containing a broader representation of transportation stocks. It helps to look at the S&P Transportation Index and especially the New York index to confirm that the Dow Transports are not undergoing any special distortions. Most of the time, the three indexes move together and often lead the composite market averages to new trends.

The Advance/Decline Line

Breadth is a term used to describe the degree to which a wide number of stocks are broadly represented in a market trend. The advance/decline line, perhaps the best measure of breadth available, is used to evaluate the sturdiness of the market's technical foundation. The more stocks and groups participating in a market trend, the more likely that trend is to continue. When a trend is not confirmed by breadth, as the trend matures, fewer stocks and groups will participate in the trend, leaving a weak foundation of stocks to maintain its direction. Eventually, the internal structure of the trend gives way, leading to a change in the direction of the primary trend of the market averages.

The advance/decline line (a/d line) is simply the cumulative total of the advancing issues minus the number of declining issues. Since the number of advancing and declining issues is calculated on both a daily and a weekly basis and found in most newspapers, the line can be kept for both time periods.

Advance/Decline line = Cumulative total of:

(number of advancing issues) − (number of declining issues)

To account for the possibility that the line could go negative and therefore ruin some of the possible uses of the gauge, it is common to begin the accumulation of numbers from a large base number, like 100,000. Table 5-2 is an example of the calculation.

This simple addition method makes it difficult to compare one period of time to another because of the steady increase of new issues in the stock market. In 1977, the New York Stock Exchange traded fewer than 1,900 issues per day. In 1986, over 2,000 issues were traded every day. Based on the prior method of calculation, it would be misleading to compare a day where half the issues advanced in 1977 against a day when half the issues advanced in 1986. Even though the days were equally strong, the calculation would show the 1986 day as the more powerful advance.

To solve this problem, we can calculate the a/d line on a net percentage method, which includes the number of unchanged issues in the calculation. From the base of 100,000, simply accumulate the net percentage issues each day and/or week, whichever time period you prefer. It works as follows:

Total issues = Advancing + declining + unchanged issues

$$\frac{\text{Advancing issues}}{\text{Total issues}} - \frac{\text{declining issues}}{\text{total issues}} = \text{Net percentage issues}$$

A/D line = Cumulative total of net percentage issues

TABLE 5-2   An Example of the
Traditional Advance/Decline Line
Computation.

(A)	(B)	(C)	(D)
		(A-B)	(C+D)
Advances	Declines	Net	Cummulative
			100,000
791	717	74	100,074
1,274	366	908	100,982
855	751	104	101,086
770	768	2	101,088
855	652	203	101,291
539	1,008	-469	100,822
913	590	323	101,145
819	684	135	101,280
687	794	-107	101,173
831	642	189	101,362

The first question to ask of the a/d line is, "Is the line moving with the market averages (confirming) or counter to the trend (diverging)?" Many important changes in market trend occur when the a/d line is diverging from the market averages. At each new high or low in the market averages, the a/d line should be checked to see if the average's move has been confirmed by a new high or low in breadth. If not, the investor has good reason to become suspicious of the trend.

One of the more recent examples occurred before the mini-bear market of 1983–1984. The a/d line peaked in May 1983 and slipped progressively lower even as the Dow rose to marginally new highs for several months. The market finally gave way in January 1984, as so few stocks were remaining to carry the market higher that the market structure collapsed (see Figure 5-5). This led to a decline of 200 points in the Dow, about 15%, nearly all of it in less than six weeks. The weakness in the a/d line suggested a much weaker market. Sure enough, the Value Line Index, fell over 20%, and many market leaders fell substantially more.

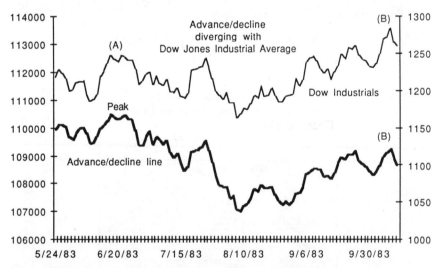

Figure 5-5. The advance/decline line measures the strength of the broad market, which tends to lead moves in the Dow Jones Industrial Average. Before the 1983–1984 mini-bear market, the a/d line peaked several months ahead of the Dow to warn of weakness in the overall market structure. In January 1984, the Dow finally collapsed.

Figure 5-5 is an excellent example of viewing the stock market as a building structure. The strength of the trend is somewhat similar to a political vote, with a similar psychology. The president of the United States is elected by the American people through the electoral college process. Similarly, individual stocks (the American people) "choose" a trend through their industry groups (the electoral college).

The strength of the presidency is often based on the percentage of the vote that the winning candidate received, also called the mandate. The more stocks and industry groups that participate in a trend, the stronger the mandate for that trend. Once the president (the trend) loses some of the support of the people (stocks) and Congress (industry groups), the more difficult it is for him to accomplish his policies (to maintain the direction of the trend).

New Highs and New Lows

When a stock makes a new high or low for a one-year period, it is making a definitive statement of its strength. The total number of all stocks on the NYSE making new highs is an excellent indicator of market strength. The stock market can muddle along and make new highs on the Dow, but if it can show a substantial amount of stocks recording new highs, it must truly be a powerful rally.

Each day, on a daily basis and at the end of each week on a weekly basis, most newspapers report the number of new highs and new lows for the various exchanges. Although the number of issues traded has generally expanded over the years, this should not be a major concern, because for new highs and new lows, we are primarily interested in comparisons during the current market cycle. If new highs are reached in the market averages and higher levels of new highs are reached, then the uptrend is confirmed. But if new highs are continuously slumping while the market sets new highs, then the advance is narrow and less likely to be sustained.

To smooth the movement of the index, many analysts like to take a 10-day moving average of the net highs/lows, an index that is presented in many charting services. To compile a 10-day moving average, simply average the last 10 days of recorded data. The same can be done on a weekly basis. Like most breadth indicators, the net number of new highs is an advance warning indicator that affords plenty of lead time. In the first stages of an advance, there will be a tremendous rush of new highs, because so many stocks either have been in downtrends or have labored in consolidations to build support. But as the advance matures, fewer and fewer stocks will be able to sustain the momentum and new highs will shrink appreciably.

For example, in the powerful 1982–1983 bull market, the 10-day moving average of net new highs peaked in October 1982 at about 430, just 2 months after the advance began. After that, new highs made a steady line of lower peaks, even though the market moved higher. By the January 1984 peak, just before the 200 point slide, the moving average was only about 80. Even though the Dow had reached new highs, 200 points above the October 1982 peak, so few stocks were still advancing that new highs were

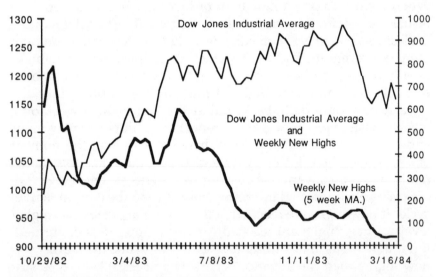

Figure 5-6. The number of stocks registering new highs is often very high in the early portion of an advance because so many stocks have been in downtrends or consolidations. But as the advance wears on, even though the market averages might be rising, fewer stocks are able to record new highs. Eventually, as happened in 1984, the market averages break down.

barely favorable. The deterioration in net new highs and the advance/decline line (discussed above) were two invaluable measures of breadth that were precursors to the 1984 mini-bear market (see Figure 5-6, which uses a five-week moving average to smooth weekly highs and lows).

Margin Debt

When buying stocks, some investors do not like to pay for their entire transaction, choosing instead to put down a minimum amount for the purchase and accept a loan for the balance. While this is normal fare in buying real estate, this practice in the stock market is usually only employed by speculators. This is called buying a stock on margin. Margin debt is the amount of money still owed on margined stock transactions. Money in margin debt can be used by investors to purchase other things, but most often, it represents a ready pool of money that will be used by investors for further transactions in the stock market.

Since heavily margined speculation was a principal cause of the 1929 debacle, the government gave the Federal Reserve control over margin requirements. Like any instrument under control of the Fed, margin debt is carefully monitored for its effects in raising or lowering the amount of money in the financial system. If the Fed believes that rising margin debt is leading to a dangerous environment, it can raise the level of margin required, a signal of tightened money conditions.

Margin debt can be understood as a barometer of investor confidence in the stock market. The stronger investors perceive the stock market to be, the more willing they might be to extend their investible funds to the maximum power by buying stock on margin. Since stock is used as collateral and the transaction includes payment of interest, margined stock is often the first stock sold in an investor's portfolio. This accounts for the quick build-up of margin debt in bull markets and the equally quick decline in margin debt in serious bear markets.

In addition, since stock is used as collateral, the value of the collateral decreases when the stock falls in price, forcing the investor to put up more cash to retain his margined position. As stock prices fall, margin calls encourage investors to liquidate their margined positions rather than put up more collateral. This creates a greater supply of stock on the market, exacerbating the decline. For these reasons, decreases in margin debt should be taken very seriously as signs of a forthcoming bear market.

Margin debt is computed on a monthly basis by the New York Stock Exchange and is reported in *Barron's* toward the back of the paper under the New York Stock Exchange Monthly Figures. The figures are released a few weeks after the close of each month, so the numbers are not quite timely. However, since this is a long-term indicator, the lag time is not terribly crucial.

Since the figures can be volatile, it is helpful to use a six-month moving average to smooth the figures. A rising moving average confirms an advancing market, showing a ready supply of available cash prepared to enter the market. Once the margin debt moving average line falls, margined positions are probably being liquidated as large supplies of stock flood the marketplace, confirming a move to the downside (see Figure 5-7).

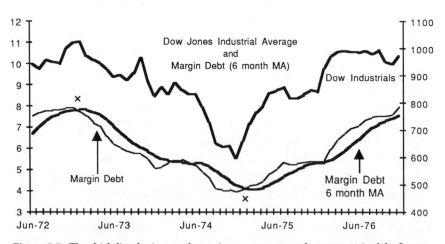

Figure 5-7. The thick-lined, six-month moving average smooths out margin debt figures, which usually confirms long-term stock market movement. When actual data crosses the moving average line (indicated by an ×), a change in trend is indicated for both margin debt and the stock market.

Conclusion

When the bulk of these indicators diverge from the trend of the popular market averages, you should take a very serious look at the valuation of the stock market and the stocks in your portfolio. Since some divergences can be found at any time, it is prudent to recognize their presence, but also to recognize that not all trends follow the textbook. Particularly toward the latter stages of a trend, the market is likely to get ragged, showing plenty of divergences, and yet keep trending until the balance of value is significantly upset.

For example, in the case of an aging uptrend, the divergences will not *cause* a bear market; they are just indications that the structure is breaking down and has potential for collapse. The stock market is still a balance of value between stocks and competing investments. Structural problems can come and go without forcing a change in the primary trend; only a change in the balance of value will break a long-term trend.

IF HEALTHY, IS THE TREND OVERBOUGHT OR OVERSOLD?

Major changes in market trend occur when the market reaches extremes in market valuation, which are accentuated by overoptimism at market tops and overpessimism at market bottoms. The behavioral cycle is always expressed by how the stock market is trading, which makes the use of technical indications like overbought and oversold conditions so valuable to market timing analysis.

At the peak of an advance, the stock market will be overbought on a variety of gauges. Once overbought, the market is likely to continue to rise until it runs out of speculative buying power. Once the overbought condition is relieved, stock prices are vulnerable to a downturn. Of course, on the flip side, once the market reaches extremely oversold conditions after having plunged to the downside, prices will eventually consolidate to alleviate the condition and a rally is likely to begin. Since we are primarily concerned with changes in the primary trend, we will concentrate on gauges indicative of long-term overbought or oversold behavior and not go into the wide variety of momentum-type indicators.

Mutual Fund Cash Available

The Investment Company Institute Research Department of Washington, DC, publishes monthly data on mutual funds, which can be found in the back of *Barron's* under the heading of Monthly Mutual Fund Indicators. These data have a lag time of about one month, but do not hinder the validity of the indicator. Since these institutions account for a tremendous amount of the trading volume on the stock exchanges, the amount of available cash they have on hand, which is called the liquid asset ratio, represents a major pool of money that can flow into the stock market. Mutual fund cash, then, is an excellent long-term indicator of market psychology, reflecting the confidence of large institutions. To smooth fluctuations, take a three-month moving average of the liquid asset ratio.

One problem with this indicator is that mutual fund cash levels tend to move with interest rates. As rates rise, institutions are able to earn a higher rate of return on their money and tend to keep a larger percentage of cash on hand. Some analysts compensate for this by adjusting for interest rates. Norman Fosback, of Market Logic, a newsletter out of Fort Lauderdale, Florida, coined his Fosback Indicator, which subtracts the T-bill rate from the mutual fund cash figure. As long as mutual fund cash exceeds the bill rates, there is a bullish amount of cash available for investment among the institutions. For example, if rates are 8% and the mutual fund cash ratio is 9%, the figure is bullish.

While the Fosback Indicator is superior, the raw mutual fund cash levels can also be analyzed without adjustment. Historically, when mutual fund cash rises above 9.5%, it is usually a sign that institutions are loaded with cash and are overpessimistic. When cash falls below 6%, it usually means that institutions are overoptimistic and fully invested. Once they are fully invested, an important source of available capital to flow into the market has been removed, and it is questionable where money will come from to fuel the rest of the advance.

In recent years, because of the popularity of mutual funds, many funds seem to be holding more cash than the historical norms. One reason could be because of the popularity of switching between mutual funds and money market funds, a topic discussed in Chapter 10. If too many investors panic and order a switch at the same time, the mutual funds could become caught in the ugly situation of having to dump shares on the market without regard to price just to fulfill their investors' requests. The overbought and oversold numbers of 9.5 and 6% might still be valid, but should not be considered as absolute buy and sell signals, just good indications of available cash-on-hand for investment.

Short Selling Statistics

Due to the emergence of stock index options and futures, many of the most reliable indicators of stock market psychology have unfortunately been rendered less useful. While they can still lend insight into market conditions, they no longer adhere to their previous parameters. In view of this, our discussion of overbought and oversold indicators will not include some of my former favorites, such as the Members Short Sales Ratio, Specialist Short Sales Ratio, Odd-Lot Short Sales Ratio, and the venerable Short Interest Ratio. It may take several years to assess the changes wrought by stock index options and futures, but in the meantime these gauges simply do not carry enough reliability to warrant serious consideration.

Advisor Sentiment

Investor's Intelligence of New Rochelle, New York, has been publishing statistics on the market opinion of investment newsletter writers since 1963. The results of their studies suggest that the market timers of investment advisory newsletters are generally *wrong* in their assessment of market trends at important market junctures. They use a 10-week moving average to smooth the fluctuations of the number of bearish advisors. Ten-week readings of bearish opinions below 20% indicate probable market bottoms, while readings above 50% suggest a market top (see Figure 5-8).

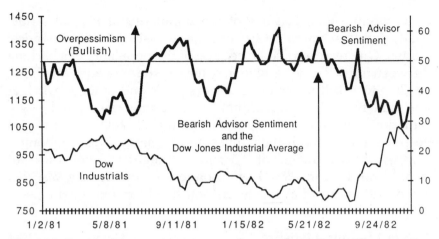

Figure 5-8. Bearish advisor sentiment is an excellent contrary indicator. When more than 50% of advisors are bearish, then sentiment is overpessimistic and likely to form an important bottom (shown by the arrow). Less than 20% in bearish advisor sentiment usually corresponds to market tops.

These results are well in keeping with our behavioral cycle, which dictates that overoptimism is found at market tops, with overpessimism at market bottoms. This index has been remarkably accurate over the years and is also now available through *Investor's Daily*.

Insider Selling

Insiders are those who, directly or indirectly, own more than 10% of any class of stock, or are officers or directors of a corporation. Most transactions by insiders are on the sell side, because they have acquired shares in the company through bonuses or other terms of their employment contract. Insider trading data are released after about a one month lag, so it is always a month or two after the fact. The lag time is not a problem, however, since insider moves are generally months ahead of the market trends.

Unfortunately, these data are not available in newspapers, but can be obtained through several investment services specializing in insider information, such as Vickers Stock Research Corp. in Brookside, New Jersey. Very often, the information will be found in media stories. Therefore, even if you don't subscribe to a service, at least you should know the impact of the data.

$$\text{Insider sales ratio} = \frac{\text{Insider sales}}{\text{Insider purchases}}$$

To smooth out the data, I recommend a 10-week moving average. If the 10-week moving average is less than 1.5, then insiders are selling at a light clip and are considered to be bullish toward their companies. When the moving average moves above 3, then it is bearish and insiders believe their companies are overvalued relative to its future prospects. Even though they are not always familiar with the stock market, the insider knows his company and has information that is sometimes not available to even the most astute analyst.

Insider selling is an excellent long-term market signal. The insider is generally not a motivated seller. In most cases, the insider didn't make an out-of-pocket outlay for the shares, eliminating that "let's get out now to break even" syndrome. Unless strapped for cash, an insider will generally sell only after he feels the company is so overpriced that this is the opportunity of a lifetime to cash in his stock.

Investors can make use of insider buying in individual stocks, too. Stocks which have received substantial buying by three or more insiders within a six-month period are often poised for a sharp run-up in price because of some inside development unknown to the public investor. Of course, insider buying should not outweigh value considerations in making investment decisions.

Secondary Distributions

Secondary distributions are somewhat similar to insider selling. Sometimes, a corporation will take advantage of high stock prices to raise capital by issuing more stock. This is not necessarily management's admission that the stock price is extraordinarily high, but if a large number of companies are issuing secondary distributions week after week, it is definitely a warning signal that stock prices may be fully priced.

Secondary distributions are posted weekly in the back pages of *Barron's*. Since the figures vary a great deal, it is safer to smooth the data over a 10-week period. If secondary distributions number less than 10 over the 10-week period (averaging 1 per week), this is a very bullish sign that few managements believe their stocks are fully priced. If the 10-week number exceeds 50, then the market may be nearing overbought conditions. Once the 10-week total slows below 40, managements have probably finished the collective distribution of their stock and the market is vulnerable to a significant decline.

Conclusion

The overbought and oversold indicators presented here are uniformly of a psychological nature that should reflect under- and overvaluation. Many analysts have a battery of momentum indicators to measure market extremes, but I have not found these reliable enough to warrant serious impact on an investor's long-term investment decisions. The indicators presented have shown a long history of providing advance warning to periods of extreme valuation, and because of their logical nature should continue to provide reliable signals in the future.

STRATEGIC APPLICATIONS

A market timing framework would not be important if the stock market rose without significant damage occurring to prices now and then. But bear markets do happen and remaining fully invested during those periods can cut 50% or more from the value of even the finest portfolio. In light of this danger, technical indicators can be used along with knowledge of how interest rates affect market value to warn of bear markets and suggest a reduction in portfolio risk, as well as a redeployment of capital once the risk of a bear market is diminished to a reasonable level.

The most important piece of our timing framework is the question of whether the stock market is at a point of extreme valuation. The technical indicators presented should give advance warning to extremes in valuation, but should never be used by themselves to make major adjustments in your portfolio. While market psychology will inflate or deflate fundamental value into market value, changes in the primary market trend occur due to extremes in the balance of value. Therefore, although technical indicators may suggest it, I strongly advise you to wait until the balance of value is actually upset before changing the composition of your portfolio.

Part Three
A Value Approach
to Stock Selection

6

Asset Value
Analysis

In Chapter 4 we saw how the stock market can be valued by its returns relative to interest rates and other investment vehicles that compete for the investment dollar. But how are individual stocks valued? What makes one stock worth more than another? To begin answering these questions, let us take a look at the ultimate value investor, the corporate raider, and see what types of things he looks for in a company.

THE ULTIMATE VALUE INVESTOR—THE
CORPORATE RAIDER

Why is the corporate raider the ultimate value investor? He accumulates stock at highly undervalued prices, and sells when the shares have reached a price that he believes represents a fair assessment of the stock's value. Occasionally, the raider does not sell the shares at full value, and instead, decides to run the company. Or maybe the raider will take over the company, but rather than run the operation, he will sell off pieces of it, hoping that the pieces will be worth more than the whole.

However he wishes to exert his influence, the corporate raider injects a competing force into the marketplace that makes it a more efficient valuing mechanism. The existence of the corporate raider, although feared by managements and maligned by the media, is almost a poetic illustration of the translation of fundamental value into market value.

Whether it is recognized by the marketplace or the marketplace is forced to recognize value by work of the corporate raider, value will be recognized.

The corporate raider is not as much a riverboat gambler as the public might think. In fact, there are few investors more deliberate than the corporate raider. He looks for value in assets that the marketplace overlooks. In a tired old steel company, it might be the sheer value of its plant and equipment or the tax benefits piled up after years of losses. In a fast food chain, it could be the real estate on which the restaurants sit. Or, in the case of an oil company, it could be potential oil reserves or other natural resources that have gone unrecognized by the market.

Of course, to the common investor, these hidden assets will usually remain hidden. Getting access to such information about a company is nearly impossible for an outsider, but then again, it is not absolutely necessary for success in the stock market. Because of the volatile nature of stock prices, investors can take advantage of times when stock prices do not accurately reflect a company's assets by employing much simpler methods of valuation.

The corporate raider buys a stock for what it is, a share in a corporation with assets that have potential earnings power. If the assets and earnings power are not reflected in the stock price, the company is a potential takeover candidate. Due to the amount of work and capital that a raider must invest to complete a takeover, he must recognize a significant deficiency in how the market is valuing the stock before he makes his foray. A stock that is only marginally undervalued, the kind that most investors are willing to accept, will not offer enough of a payoff to make it worth his while.

Therefore, the corporate raider is a student of the balance sheet. He will usually first assess the assets he can be sure of, such as cash. If a company has $10 million in cash and one million shares outstanding, then it has $10 in cash per share. If the stock price is only $11, then he can buy the rest of the company for just a dollar per share. This may sound like an extraordinary case, but in extremely undervalued periods, stocks like these exist. Then he will look at the rest of the assets and the liabilities against them, making allowances for the inherent flaws in the balance sheet. From there, he is likely to look at the earning power of the assets, since if he is to hold on to the company, it must be able to generate sufficient earnings from the investment.

As an investor, you do not have to put in as much study or expense as the corporate raider, but you should take the same viewpoint. This chapter takes a brief look at the balance sheet, not from the viewpoint of an accountant, but from that of the strategic value investor—one who, like the businessman/corporate raider, is seeking to buy stock whose assets and earning power are significantly undervalued by the marketplace.

INTRODUCING THE BALANCE SHEET

The balance sheet shows the financial position of a company as of a single date in the year. Corporations issue balance sheets in their quarterly reports, dated at the end of each fiscal quarter, including an annual report showing the balance sheet as of the end of the year (the fourth fiscal quarter). To keep things consistent and simple, for our purposes, we will only consider the balance sheet as of a company's year-end.

The balance sheet shows the historical cost of assets, liabilities, and equity. Because value analysis has traditionally focused on the value of assets, the balance sheet has always been a primary concern of the value-oriented crowd. In the "go-go" 1960s, when stocks were soaring, earnings became the name of the game, and the balance sheet was shoved aside as if it were archaic. The financial difficulties of the 1970s put the balance sheet back into the picture, and the 1980s have seen an increasing emphasis on the fundamental value of the balance sheet.

It would be a serious mistake to discard the balance sheet as an anachronism. The stock investor is still buying a share of the ownership in a company. Even if an investor wishes to concentrate on earnings rather than assets as a measure of investment value, a very important question remains, "How much earnings is the company generating from my investment dollar?" It takes assets to generate those earnings and those earnings add up to share-holder's equity, which is the value that underlies your investment. So, even if you are dedicated to the earnings approach to investment value, the balance sheet tells a story that you should understand.

LIMITATIONS OF THE BALANCE SHEET

The balance sheet does require careful scrutiny for several reasons. First, it is always late. By the time the balance sheet is released, it is old news. At the minimum, a few weeks have passed and some things may have already changed by the time a stockholder receives the report. Besides, the company has probably taken great care to dress up operations near year-end to make the balance sheet look as good as possible. Remember, the balance sheet shows the financial position of a company for one day only, the last day of the fiscal quarter.

Balance sheets are historical records. In this age of inflation, the current value of assets varies over time. For example, an item like a manufacturing plant will be presented at its original cost less the depreciation taken on it, to account for the aging of a tangible asset that might lose value due to wearing out or obso-lescence. However, if, due to wear or obsolescence, the assets are worth far less than the depreciation method indicates, the books should be adjusted to reflect the severe loss in value. In practice, such exactness in record keeping does not always happen.

On the other hand, if an obsolescent plant happens to be located on the Magnificent Mile in Chicago, it might be worth a fortune in real estate, far more than is shown on the books. This type of undervaluation is the thing that takeover artists dream about, because depreciable assets are never adjusted higher in value on the books, despite what they might be worth. Accounting treatment is a double-edged sword that can go both ways to either inflate or deflate the apparent value on the books. And because very few investors will know whether the balance sheet is overstating or understating the underlying asset values, the historical aspect of the balance sheet is a difficult limitation to overcome.

Another limitation is that of accounting treatment. Depending on the objectives of corporate management, Generally Accepted Accounting Principles (GAAP) can offer enough latitude to accountants to dress up the appearance of financial statements. In the case of a manufacturing plant, for instance, there are several different ways in which the company can use depreciation to add to or subtract from both asset values and reported income.

Fortunately, there are strict limitations on changes in accounting methods, so investors are assured that the statements are somewhat consistent from year to year. Although the balance sheet is perhaps less easy to manipulate than the income statement you should be aware that the influential hand of corporate management is involved in the presentation of the statements wherever possible.

If you have an annual report in your hand, the first thing you should do is to check the auditor's opinion. If it says "presents fairly" in the last paragraph, then the CPA firm has given the financial statements a "clean opinion." This means that the corporation's presentation of its financial position is a fair one and is not misleading to investors. (A clean opinion does *not* mean that the auditors have checked every record or agree with every questionable accounting treatment that the corporation made on its books to make them look good. It simply means they are satisfied with the overall fairness of the statements and that the balance sheet does not contain any misstatements that would be so material as to mislead the investor.)

If the auditor's opinion does not say "presents fairly" or something very similar, then the auditor has some reservation about the way the company is presenting its financial statements. Some modification will be given, or an exception will be noted. In the auditor's actual opinion, this modification is likely to be extremely important to the fair presentation of the statements. The auditor and the corporation most assuredly have fought long battles over an exception appearing in the report. In some cases, a corporation will fire its auditor and look for an auditor that will give it a clean opinion. If this blemish is so important to the corporation and the auditor—the people in the know—investors should take it seriously as well.

ANALYZING THE BALANCE SHEET

For ease of discussion, the balance sheet can be broken down into three different areas: assets, liabilities, and equity. Assets are what a company owns, liabilities are what they owe, and equity is what the owners have left after liabilities are subtracted from assets. Assets and liabilities can be broken into two groups: short and long term. Short-term items are those which can be expected to be liquidated into cash within one year, while long-term items are expected to last longer than one year.

The basic relationship to remember is:

$$\text{Assets} - \text{liabilities} = \text{Equity}$$

or

$$\text{Assets} = \text{Liabilities} + \text{equity}$$

However you want to say it, the balance sheet always balances (see Figure 6-1).

CURRENT ASSETS AND LIABILITIES

Current assets are very important to the value investor. As shown in the prior example, long-term assets, like the manufacturing plant, are not always accurately portrayed in the balance sheet. However, current assets, particularly cash, can be counted on to better reflect their worth. Because the current value of long-term assets is so difficult to determine, in the event of a liquidation, analysts primarily use current assets to measure liquidity.

Liquidity tells you how much cash the company could come up with if it had to sell everything immediately. To investors, this

Mark's Dream, Inc.
BALANCE SHEET
December 31, 1987

ASSETS

Current Assets

Cash		40,000
Marketable Securities		30,000
Accounts Receivable (net)	175,000	
Less Doubtful Accounts	-25,000	150,000
Notes Recievable		20,000
Inventories		500,000
Total Current Assets			740,000

Long-Term Assets

Long-Term Investments		260,000
Land		250,000
Plant and Equipment	960,000	
Less Accumulated Depreciation	-260,000	700,000
Intangible Assets		50,000
Total Long-Term Assets			1,260,000

Total Assets	2,000,000
	========

LIABILITIES AND STOCKHOLDER'S EQUITY

Current Liabilities

Accounts Payable		200,000
Notes Payable		100,000
Other		70,000
Total Current Liabilities		370,000

Total Long Term Debt	330,000
Total Liabilities	700,000

Stockholder's Equity

Common Stock	1,000,000	
Additional Paid-in Capital	50,000	
Retained Earnings	250,000	
Total Stockholder's Equity		1,300,000

Total Liabilities and Stockholder's Equity	2,000,000
	========

Figure 6-1. A sample balance sheet shows the basic relationship of total assets equaling total liabilities and stockholder's equity ($2 million each).

represents a strict valuation of net assets, a minimum asset value they can believe in for stock valuation purposes. Current assets and liabilities are those items that can be expected to be liquidated into cash within one year. Current liabilities include accounts payable or the current portions of long-term debt that are due this year. Current assets usually include such items as cash, receivables, and inventory.

Cash is always the most honest item in the balance sheet, it is actually counted dollar by dollar and cannot be creatively valued by those pushing the pencils. Current receivables are amounts that are expected to be received within the year, less any amount that the company does not expect to collect. Receivables do have a measure of uncertainty, because they are an expectation, but this variable can be minimized by applying methods recognized by GAAP.

Inventories can be manipulated in a variety of ways which not only affect the balance sheet, but also have a direct effect on corporate earnings. The higher the inventory valuation, the higher the reported income, and vice versa. Therefore, year after year of higher inventories can be viewed with suspicion, although investors can rarely be sure if it is warranted or not. In practicality, you must assume the auditors will do their job and report, in their auditor's opinion, anything so grossly erroneous that it would mislead investors.

The *current ratio* is one of the most hallowed of all financial ratios, although its applicability to the stock market is somewhat limited. The current ratio is:

Current ratio = Current assets ÷ current liabilities

Healthy balance sheets are traditionally characterized by a current ratio of at least 2:1. The object is to invest in companies which can meet their obligations through the year without having to sell productive assets or incur long-term debt. The basic assumption is that current assets would be used to pay off current liabilities. Assuming that a company does not want to use up all of its current assets to pay next year's expenses or that some of the assets will not readily become cash, a cushion of 2:1 is generally considered sufficient to handle unusual difficulties that might occur.

Of course, different industries have different demands on their funds. Some industries have current ratios below 1, but are still quite healthy. It is very important here, as in most facets of fundamental analysis, to compare companies against those in the same industry, as each industry has its share of financial quirks that distinguish it from other types of businesses. If a company has a much lower current ratio than others in its industry, you should be aware that its financial and operating abilities might be strained.

WORKING CAPITAL

Working capital is another way of showing the liquidity of a company. Very similar to the current ratio, it is simply the difference between current assets and current liabilities.

Working capital = Current assets − current liabilities

Working capital is supposed to represent the free amount of liquid assets in a company. Due to the difficulty of judging whether some current asset items are actually going to become liquid cash within one year, working capital is not a perfectly accurate name. Nevertheless, various ways of using the working capital calculation can be very effective in determining stock valuations, as we will soon see.

Working capital as a measure of stock value was perhaps made famous by that dynamic duo of financial analysis Benjamin Graham and David Dodd, who showcased the technique in their classic textbook entitled *Security Analysis*. One objective they had was to find stocks that were trading at less than their working capital (they called it "net current assets") per share. This would provide a "margin of safety" (limited downside risk) in case the market went against their positions.

A more severe test that Graham and his disciples have used with great success is to subtract long-term liabilities from working capital. This is called net-net working capital. By doing this, an investor has subtracted all of a company's liabilities from its current assets, placing no value whatsoever on long-term assets. In this case, the objective is to buy a stock for an amount equal to or less than its net-net working capital, thereby receiving the long-term assets like plant and equipment for free. Net-net working capital should approximate the amount of money that would be received in a very hurried liquidation of a company.

Net-net working capital = Current assets − total liabilities

This is still a popular goal among value investors and should be pursued by investors as long as the company is not in a hopeless business situation. These net-net stocks—stocks trading at or below their net-net working capital—are few and far between, depending on the status of overall market valuation. In very strong markets, where stocks are receiving generous valuations, only the very weakest stocks will show up as a net-net situation. In very weak markets, particularly after a prolonged decline, even some very good companies may appear as net-net stocks.

Investors should not assume that a net-net stock is a stock that cannot lose. These stocks are often burdened with severe problems that frighten investors away. Many times, these problems are worth avoiding, often placing a company into a desperate situation. Perhaps it is a one-product company that cannot generate sales due to its one product rapidly becoming obsolete. Or maybe the company is bankrupt due to years of frivolous business practices and overwhelming competition.

But sometimes, a good company will receive a great deal of bad press about a problem in the company, depressing the stock to unrealistic levels, maybe even to a net-net situation—something like a product liability lawsuit or the failing of an unusually visible division of the company; a story that grabs the headlines, but is not enough to seriously injure the long-term prospects of the company. Emotional sell-offs in quality companies to net-net levels offer superb opportunities to buy undervalued companies.

Value Line offers a list of companies from among the 1,700 companies they survey that are trading below their net-net working capital (referred to as "liquidating value" in their text) each week in their Summary & Index section. This list can also be used as a proxy for the entire market. If their list only has a handful or less of names on it, then the market is probably fully valued. But if there are two or three dozen names listed, the market is likely to be undervalued. (This is a subjective test of market value; I have not been able to collect numbers over a long enough period to give any strict guidelines. But since Value Line is an excellent research service offered to the public and can often be found in public libraries, investors should make use of this information.)

MODIFIED NET-NET WORKING CAPITAL

Buying a company for its net-net working capital is a pretty good deal, unless its inventory is ridiculously overstated or the company's problems are insolvable. It is rather like buying tires at an automobile showroom and having the dealer say to you, "Here, I'll throw in the Chevy with those tires." Chances are the Chevy can be sold for something. Regardless of my taste in cars, or its working condition, I would take the car. Eventually, someone would buy the whole car for more than the cost of the new tires.

The unfortunate truth is that net-net stocks of any quality are very difficult to find, unless the stock market is extremely depressed after a severe decline. Maybe a more realistic approach to liquidity and working capital is to assign a reasonable amount for long-term assets held by the corporation. If cash needs to be raised immediately, long-term assets, such as plant and equipment, should be able to provide some liquidity. Of course, the assets would have to be sold too quickly to get a good deal and many of the assets might prove to be worth much less than is shown on the balance sheet.

To compensate for the downside risk in long-term asset valuation, a fair percentage can be assigned to approximate the value received in a desperate sale. A modified working capital equation would look like this:

Modified net-net
working capital = Current assets − total liabilities

+ 25% of plant and equipment

The same type of decision-making methods as used with net-net stocks can be applied to the modified net-net stocks. If the stock price is lower than modified net-net, then the stock is undervalued relative to what the owner might reasonably expect to receive on a desperate liquidation.

THE DEBT:EQUITY RATIO

As we have seen, long-term assets and liabilities are those items that have a life of one year or more. Long-term assets include plant and equipment and any other asset of a long-term nature, such as a receivable that may take several years to collect, or a patent with a long life of potential earning power. As discussed previously, despite all of the rules attendant to them, long-term assets are rarely shown accurately on the balance sheet. This can arise because of problems in accounting for depreciating or obsolete assets, as well as those reasons which might make the asset worth far more than the books reflect.

Long-term liabilities include various items of long-term debt, an important figure because heavy interest costs can become a drag on a company's earnings performance. Ideally, investors would like a company that can finance its operations through its own earnings, thereby growing at the cost of its internal funds, a subject elaborated on in Chapter 7. A company that must continually go into the debt markets to sustain its operations is at the mercy of interest rates and borrowing conditions. Should interest rates rise when borrowing needs arise, the company could be locked into a situation that could be unfavorable for several years to come.

The debt:equity ratio is a well-known ratio of financial health. Just as the name implies, it is caluculated as follows:

Debt:Equity ratio = Long-term debt ÷ common stockholder's
equity

A ratio of more than 50% traditionally indicates that perhaps too much debt is outstanding. Again, this ratio should be analyzed within the context of each industry as some industries regularly operate with substantially more or less debt than others.

The amount of debt will become an important subject in Chapter 7, when we include the figure in assessing the ability of a company to generate earnings from its total invested capital. In other words, because debt is a source of invested capital and is potentially damaging to a business operation, I consider the return on capital (earnings generated by equity plus long-term debt) a more telling measure of investment performance than the return on equity.

BOOK VALUE

Stockholders' equity is the amount left to the owners after liabilities are subtracted from assets. When an investor buys stock, he is actually purchasing equity in a company—a share of its net worth. The most common expression of worth in a stock is its book value per share. Book value is simply the stockholder's equity divided by the number of common stock shares outstanding.

$$\text{Book value} = \frac{\text{Common stockholders' equity}}{\text{Number of common stock shares outstanding}}$$

In a sense, book value can be understood as the net amount of assets after subtracting liabilities. Generally, a stock will trade above its book value, because the market has given the stock a premium for having value greater than the historical cost of its net assets. This premium value may be for expected earnings power or for goodwill recognized in the marketplace. It may also be because the historical cost of the assets shown in the balance sheet does not account for extra value hidden in the assets, such as valuable natural resources or unique technologies.

A stock that trades at less than its book value is valued by the market at less than its historical cost. In other words, a share in this company would not be worth as much as what the company originally paid for its assets. Surprisingly, there are many stocks available on the stock market with these credentials. The assets may be overvalued on the balance sheet, due to obsolescence; or contingent liabilities like lawsuits that threaten the future of the company. Perhaps the company is so weak that its assets no longer have the power to generate future earnings.

Very often, these are just unpopular stocks that have been undervalued by the stock market, either by speculative dumping or outright neglect. Some stocks trade below book value for several years in a row, because their operations are of questionable potential or because of quirks in the accounting or operating practices of their industries. Most quality corporations that have good earnings power will trade below book value only after a sharp drop in the stock market or a spate of bad news. These out-of-favor stocks can require much greater patience than stocks coveted by the public, but the rewards are usually greater and the risks far less than with stocks trading well above book value.

TRACKING BOOK VALUE

Since the long-term price of a stock should shadow the movement of book value or a multiple of book value, investors should monitor the growth of book value much as they do the growth of earnings. The same stock might sell at book value when it is out of favor and three times book value when in favor. The long-term investor will want to see how book value is growing and what multiple of book value a stock is likely to top or bottom at.

If a stock can be purchased at book value, and book value has been rising at 20% per year over the last five years, then over the long-term, the stock price can be expected to rise with book value on a nice growth trend. The continued growth of book value is not guaranteed—nothing is—but if the company is financially healthy, the odds are with the long-term investor.

Buying a quality stock below book value is like getting a conceptual insurance policy. As we saw with the universal concept, over the long run, the value of a stock should equal the value of its net worth. Also, the rotation of stocks from favored status to unfavored status is a dynamic process. Eventually, a quality stock's discount to book value will be recognized by the marketplace and as long as the underlying assets are still productive, the investor will be rewarded.

The composition of a company's assets generally does not change very much over time. Even a company that has a great deal of hidden assets will usually maintain approximately the same ratio of hidden assets to book assets. Based on this rough assumption, investors can watch the multiple of book value against the stock price over a long period of time (10 to 15 years) as a general guide of valuation.

A simple way is to look at a Value Line sheet of stock XYZ, taking the high stock price of a market cycle and dividing it by the book value for that year to get a general level of peak valuation. Later peaks for the stock should approximate the same multiple of book value. Do the same for the low stock price to get a low valuation level. This can serve as a basic guide for stock valuation.

A comparison of book value of stock XYZ can also be made against its industry members. Corporate acquisition experts often do this when one company in an industry is acquired in order to value the rest of the members of that industry. The basic premise is that most companies in one industry will maintain a similar asset mix.

If company ABC was taken over at a stock price of three times book value, then it can be assumed that the approximate market value of the other companies in the industry should be around three times book value as well. It should be noted that some companies trade at a higher multiple of book value than others for several years on end, but this tendency can also be factored into your analysis. In Chapter 7, we will see that earnings efficiency, as suggested by a higher return on shareholders' equity, is usually accorded a higher multiple of book value.

The opportunity to find stocks trading below book value is much greater in depressed market periods than in high-flying bull markets. Again, Value Line offers a screen in their Summary & Index section of about 100 stocks from their survey which are trading at the widest discount from book value. Although many of these stocks will not meet your minimum specifications for an investment in the stock market, some might, and it could be worth your while to investigate this handy guide.

Buying stocks at or below book value or at low multiples of book value has become very popular, but, like buying net-net stocks, it is certainly not a surefire road to riches. In fact, book value can be misleading. It is very possible for a company to trade at a high multiple of book value and still be undervalued because of the earnings power of its assets. Book value is, at best, a crude measure of the equity value. But it can be used as a guide for stock valuation against a stock's past history and against other members of its industry group.

STRATEGIC APPLICATIONS

The balance sheet is a record of a company's historical cost of assets, liabilities, and equity as of one single day (the last day of a fiscal quarter) in a year. Despite its limitations as a historical record and a measure of current value, the balance sheet can give a fairly accurate account of the value of a company. Investors should approach the purchase of stock as if they were actually purchasing the company as a business. In this sense, they are purchasing the value of the assets less the liabilities—an amount equal to the equity.

The balance sheet offers two main forms of value: working capital (and its variations) and book value. Modified net-net working capital values a company on the assumption of a liquidation, by valuing the long-term assets at a percentage (around 25%) to allow for a desperation sale. Book value can be measured against a stock's history of book value multiples or against the other members of its industry group.

The basic objective for both methods is to purchase stocks at points of undervaluation—specifically, at or below the value determined by the working capital or book value calculation. This gives the investor a margin of safety, in case the market turns against his positions. An investor using these methods, who buys stock at a price approximately equal to or less than its fundamental value, can feel more secure in a downturn because the intrinsic value of the investment will act as a level of natural price support. Based on that premise, such an investment would probably have relatively less downside risk and greater upside potential.

7

Earnings Value Analysis

The income statement shows the progress of the balance sheet. If the assets in the balance sheet do not have the ability to generate earnings, the balance sheet will remain somewhat static, especially in the shareholders' equity section. Cash flow will be poor, making it difficult to replace assets that are too old to be productive. But, on the other hand, if earnings are strong enough, the company can fuel expansion with internally generated funds, thereby avoiding the assumption of excessive debt that can be crippling in the long term.

EARNINGS AND EQUITY GROWTH

Since earnings increase equity, and equity increases investor value in the form of stock prices, we now have a pretty good formula for making money in the stock market: find a company that earns money. Throughout this book I have stressed the viewpoint of the businessman who buys companies to add to his financial empire. Let us simulate the purchase of a company. For starters, let us begin small. I hear that Mini-bucks is selling their entire operation for just a hundred bucks in stock. That sounds fair, since its book value is also $100; we are not paying any premium above the historical asset cost of the company.

Our goal is to make money on the investment. But we are not going to do it by just selling the net assets, since they are also worth $100, giving us a break-even situation. Instead, we need to see earnings generated by the assets to increase the value of the equity. In the first year, we earn $20 in profit. The equity now is $120, and if the market perfectly recognized equity in its stock prices (which it does not), we would have a 20% profit on the sale of our stock.

In other words, *equity plus earnings equals more equity*. If you cannot get the earnings machine going, the value of your equity investment is not going to increase. This is the type of business viewpoint we are going to pursue in this chapter. We are buying an equity share of a business. We know that we will make money on the investment if we can buy the company's net assets (equity) for less than they will be worth in the future. To accomplish that objective, we must buy companies with at least one of the following two characteristics:

1. The assets are so undervalued right now that we can make a substantial profit on their immediate sale, or
2. The assets are generating sufficient earnings growth to eventually build the value of the assets substantially beyond their current market value.

The first possibility is difficult to find because there are so many people looking for significantly undervalued assets. The second kind is easier to find since many companies are earning money. But what makes one earning company better than another? And after we decide which company is better at earning money, is that necessarily the better stock to buy? Neither question has an obvious answer, but both are critical to answer and both comprise the subject matter of this chapter and the analysis for Chapter 8.

EARNINGS PER SHARE

Earnings per share (EPS), is at the center of our analysis. We use it for measuring corporate performance and the valuation of stocks. Simply calculated, EPS is:

$$\text{Earnings per share} = \frac{\text{Net income}}{\text{Number of common stock shares outstanding}}$$

Accepting the EPS figure without looking behind the numbers can get you into a lot of trouble. Without going into so many potential problems that the discussion would rival an accounting book, let us look at just one area: the importance of eliminating nonrecurring (extraordinary) items.

Extraordinary items are nonrecurring charges that are the result of an event that is not a part of normal operations. A lawsuit might be pending for several years and then decided in a judgment against the company. EPS before the suit might be up 20% to $6. Suppose the judgment cost the company the equivalent of $2 per share. EPS would be shown as only $4. Just looking at the bottom line of $4, this would appear to be a poor year for the company, as earnings seemed to have dropped 20% from $5 to $4 per share. Is this really a poor year, considering that operating income is up 20%? The EPS figure used in your analysis should reflect the growth in income from continuing operations: $6.

Similar distortions can occur on the other side of the coin, with an extraordinary item causing a large increase in earnings. Suppose a company sold off a division, resulting in a huge gain in earnings. It cannot be assumed that the company will be able to sell a large division of its operations every year to maintain this high level of earnings. This is an example of an extraordinary gain, a gain that will inflate earnings for one year, but is not a part of operations and cannot be expected to occur again or with any regularity.

Looking for these extraordinary, nonrecurring items is very important to understanding the EPS figure. The number on which you would ideally like to focus your analysis is operating earnings, without the addition of extraordinary items. Other items, like foreign currency transactions, that occur within the scope of operations but are likely to swing heavily from year to year based on factors outside of the company's operations should be evaluated with care as well.

There is another side to extraordinary items that most investors tend to overlook. Suppose Black Hole Corporation earned $1 per share this year, but reported an extraordinary loss of $4 per share from the sale of an unprofitable division. Our first reaction is to add back the loss to the $1 to equal $5 of operating earnings, and use the $5 figure in our investment calculations. Normally, this is correct, since it more accurately reflects continuing operations. However, adding back that loss should only be done with knowledge of the company's big picture, and it might be a mistake to do so, particularly if we failed to notice that over the past two years, Black Hole sold other divisions for a total of $6 in extraordinary losses.

When a company takes an extraordinary loss of this nature, perhaps it is because their method of reporting earnings is not accurately reflecting the results of the enterprise. Black Hole's losses are so large compared with operating earnings that perhaps some of the losses should have been included in operating earnings. Moreover, in this case, the losses occurred three years in a row, another indication that maybe the losses were more a part of regular operations than an extraordinary occurrence. While it is admirable to shed losing divisions, corporate management must also bear responsibility for going into losing ventures, too many of which should not be ignored.

In this age of heated competition for the investment dollar, the reporting of EPS is a major event for a company. This number is not just arrived at by adding up all of the income and printing the figure in the annual statement. Most corporations have refined the reporting of income to an art form, carefully considering the likely reactions from the investment community.

Of course, there are limitations in the flexibility that management is allowed with respect to GAAP and the enforcement of those rules by the independent auditor. If the independent auditor believes that any aspect of the income statement may be materially misleading to investors, a statement will be made in the auditor's opinion in the annual report.

THE PRICE-EARNINGS RATIO

The p/e ratio is perhaps the most recognized ratio in fundamental analysis. It is a measure of value and of market perceptions. It is calculated as follows:

$$\text{Price-earnings ratio} = \frac{\text{Stock price}}{\text{Earnings per share}}$$

In general, a stock with a high p/e ratio has been recognized by the marketplace as one with potential superior to other stocks. The market is willing to pay more money for each dollar per share of earnings than for other stocks. A low p/e ratio would indicate the opposite; the stock is recognized as having less price appreciation potential than other stocks on the exchange, and the market is less willing to pay for a share of those earnings.

Sometimes market perceptions take on extremes due to some event that bids a stock up to an unrealistic p/e or plunges a stock to a very low p/e. Other times, a stock is simply not recognized by the market for its underlying potential and is temporarily accorded a low p/e ratio. These are situations that we will discuss later. For now, let us just say that market valuations are not always hindsight perfect.

What constitutes a high or low p/e ratio? This question can be answered in many ways. The first way is to compare the p/e of a stock to the average p/e of the entire stock market. The p/e for the Standard & Poor's 500 and the Dow Jones Industrial Average is printed weekly in *Barron's*. The p/e for the S&P 500 is preferable, as it is a much broader average and therefore is more representative of the entire stock market.

Another way to assess the p/e ratio of a stock is to see how it compares with others in its industry. Stock market services like Value Line arrange their stock listings by industry groups, making it easy to compare the p/e ratio of one stock with others in the same industry. As stocks in the same industry generally move together, so do p/e ratios. You can even create your own industry average to follow the relative attractiveness of one industry to another industry, or to the entire stock market.

A stock with a p/e ratio far above the average is viewed very favorably by the stock market, while a below-average p/e is viewed cautiously. This, of course, is a generalization which does not recognize companies with an unusual earnings period, either much higher or lower than is commonly reported for that particular company. For these companies, the market sizes up the earnings change, making a judgment of whether to discount it as a turn that is unlikely to continue, or accept it as a new trend in earnings and accord it a p/e ratio that fits the new company profile.

In Chapter 8, we will look at the stock of Polaroid, a well-known leader with several years of superior corporate performance that stumbled through a decade of weak earnings. The newspapers showed the stock trading at a p/e above 100 in September 1985, but it was not overvalued. In fact, it was quite undervalued, because earnings were minimal and its assets still had substantial earnings potential. The stock built a strong technical price base while the turnaround was developing, and a year later, earnings rose, re-storing the p/e ratio to more normal levels.

The flip side might happen to a stock that has a big earnings year but has a history of erratic earnings. The market might only give the stock a p/e of 5, while the rest of the market is trading at a p/e of 15, because market participants are expecting earnings to fall back to lower levels. Both of these examples illustrate the virtues of *consistent* earnings performance, which gives the market greater incentive to price stocks with a more fitting p/e ratio.

Since the p/e ratio is a measure of perceptions, we must consider what attracts confidence in investors. An unstable company that shows wild earnings fluctuations will lose the trust of investors and will usually have a lower p/e than other stocks, even when things are going well. Because of the loss of trust in the marketplace, the company will not be accorded the respect (and therefore, the p/e ratio) that is given to more stable stocks.

A company that turns in strong earnings performances year in and year out will generally be accorded a high p/e ratio, because investors have faith that earnings will come through. And even if the company has an off year, the stock will not decline so greatly because of the goodwill it has built in the marketplace. This is just the type of company that we are looking for. It will not result in the big kill as taking a chance on a high flyer might, but over time, a portfolio of steady performers will yield superb growth in your investment assets.

THE CASH FLOW ALTERNATIVE

Since earnings can be influenced by income items that are not a part of operations, cash flow can be a helpful alternative way of measuring how a company is doing. Cash flow has been misconstrued as the actual flow of cash in a company. This is definitely a misnomer. It is simply the net income (earnings) with noncash expenditures (such as depreciation and deferred taxes) added back.

Noncash expenditures might not sound like much, but to a manufacturing company, depreciation can add back as much as one-third or more to earnings. Thus, if earnings were $4 per share and depreciation amounted to $1, the cash flow would be $5 per share. Depreciation does not involve an actual outlay of cash, it is really just an entry in the books to represent the approximate loss in value of tangible long-term assets. Cash flow excludes depreciation as an expense against income, leaving only the supposed cash outlays.

GAAP allows income to be counted without actual cash receipt or cash outflows occurring. Therefore, net income is not a simple adding up of cash earned over the year, nor is cash flow a measure of income flowing through a corporation. Cash flow is subject to the same distortions that net income is, except for the noncash adjustments. In light of these distortions, GAAP strongly recommends against the presentation of cash flow per share on an annual report for fear that it will be misleading to investors.

$$\text{Cash flow per share} = \frac{\text{Net income} + \text{noncash adjustments}}{\text{Common stock shares outstanding}}$$

(Noncash adjustments: usually just depreciation and deferred taxes)

Cash flow can be an easier figure to work with than earnings per share. Earnings per share are sometimes in a deficit, making it impossible to come up with a multiple for the p/e ratio. But even if earnings are negative, cash flow per share might still be positive because of the depreciation add-back, making price as a multiple of cash flow easy to calculate. Just like the p/e ratio, the price/cash flow per share is a valuation of how much the market-place is willing to pay for each dollar of cash flow.

$$\text{Price/cash flow per share} = \frac{\text{Price of the common stock}}{\text{Cash flow per share}}$$

Cash flow can be analyzed in the same way as the p/e ratio, but has some special advantages. Fluctuations in depreciation can force wide swings in net income which will not impact cash flow because depreciation is not considered a cash flow. Sometimes depreciation will be so heavy that it will make earnings appear as a loss, while cash flow will show operations in good shape. For these reasons, cash flow is a far more stable number and sometimes yields more reliable results for comparison purposes. The Value Line service often places a price-per-cash-flow line on a stock chart to show the relationship between stock prices and cash flows (see Figure 7-1).

Free cash flow is a term loosely used to describe the amount of cash remaining after a corporation makes its capital expenditures and pays its dividends. A company that can meet those obligations and still has cash flow remaining is thought to be one that can finance all of its operations through internal funds. Such a cash-rich company has many options. It can expand operations whenever it wishes without regard to interest rates or it can use the funds to acquire new companies. A company with plenty of cash is often a target of takeovers, which also serves to raise its stock price.

$$\frac{\text{Free cash}}{\text{flow}} = \frac{\text{Cash flow } - \text{ capital expenditures } - \text{ dividends}}{\text{Common stock shares outstanding}}$$

Free cash flow is one of the most desirable attributes a stock can have because it depicts a company that is growing within its

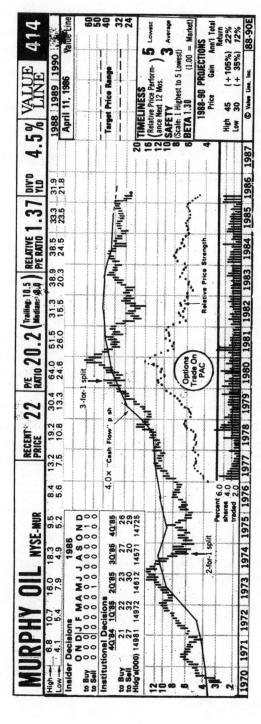

Figure 7-1. An example of a Value Line chart showing the relationship between a company's stock price and its cash flow per share. *Courtesy:* Value Line, 711 Third Avenue, New York, NY 10017.

means. It is surprising how few companies have free cash flow and how many of them continue to pay their dividends. As I said earlier, cash flow is not a precise calculation, and therefore, neither is free cash flow. However, a company that does not have free cash flow has a greater probability of feeling some strain to pay for their dividends or expansion plans. Some highly regarded commentators have questioned this common deficiency and wonder whether those companies would not be better off eliminating their dividend or canceling expansion plans. A company that has free cash flow has such an edge over others that I am often reluctant to invest in a company that doesn't show the attribute.

SALES

Earnings growth does not happen by accident, it occurs through a growth in sales. Sales are the lifeblood of any company. As long as sales are increasing, there is hope that profits can be increased in the future. A successful sales organization can usually be turned into a financial success.

Ideally, a company begins with a product, increases its sales, increases its income through its sales organization, and then as the company matures, is able to improve its profits through steady sales and intelligent finances. A company that is not able to improve its sales steadily, faces an uncertain future, as financial controls can only go so far to improve income. After a while, financial streamlining will inhibit the operations of a company. If it cannot generate sales, the company does not have a future.

From an analytic viewpoint, sales is a relatively problem-free number. As we have seen, EPS can be affected in many ways due to quirks of accounting rather than the results of operations. Cash flows take out the controversies of depreciation allocations but are still laden with the same conceptual problems of timing transactions for income. By contrast, sales are actually net sales—sales of the product less an allowance for returns. While the return allowance number can be more subjective than we might like, the effects on the sales figure are usually minimal and will rarely affect the meaning of the number.

For comparing year-to-year results, sales are ideal in that they are always positive. A company may be reporting negative earnings each year, but sales will always be positive. Negative earnings raise several questions. Are the lower earnings the subject of weak sales or poor finances, or are they the by-product of an aggressive sales expansion that may pay off in future years? Sales per share can be looked at in the same ways as earnings per share and will yield more consistent results, particularly with younger or faster-growing companies.

$$\text{Sales per share} = \frac{\text{Sales}}{\text{Common shares outstanding}}$$

Kenneth L. Fisher, in his excellent book *Super Stocks*, popularized the Price Sales Ratio, which used sales in place of earnings in a p/e ratio-type equation. The premise was that earnings are subject to too much variation in methods of presentation, but that sales is a purer figure showing the internal growth of a company. This was applied, in particular, to newer technology companies, which might show poor earnings because of rapid expansion, but because of sales, were growing quite rapidly and would show earnings in the future. Furthermore, since Wall Street is so obsessed with earnings and often neglects sales, the market price of their stocks would not reflect their tremendous growth.

$$\text{Price Sales Ratio} = \frac{\text{Stock price}}{\text{Sales per share}}$$

I agree with this logic, but investors should be careful in comparing one company with another on the basis of the Price Sales Ratio. For technology companies, the Price Sales Ratio is excellent, because they can earn a high profit margin on each sale once the company is up and running. A grocery chain, however, is quite a different story. It would always show extremely high sales relative to its earnings because it earns a low profit margin on each sale. In this case, the market price of its stock is accurately reflecting the earnings potential of the company because earnings will always be a tiny percentage of sales. This makes it critical to compare members of the same industry group against another when using the Price Sales Ratio.

Since we are taking the position of a long-term investor, a declining year of earnings should not be too upsetting. True, the stock price may take a dip, since earnings are closely tied to stock prices. But as long as sales are chugging along, we can remain faithful to the company on the assumption that some exogenous event occurred that year to stall earnings growth that will not affect the long-term future of the company. Eventually, earnings will catch up to sales and the stock price will reflect the growing equity valuations.

A company, however, that is having difficulty showing sales growth is simply not a desirable company. It may be able to maintain earnings growth by cutting back operations, but unless the streamlined version can build sales growth, what kind of a future does a company that is getting smaller and smaller have? Eventually, they are going to get down to the bone and find themselves with a skeleton of a company that cannot compete.

Sales growth is a almost a necessity for successful long-term investments. If a company shows more than one decline in sales over a 10-year period, I may not even consider it for investment, since there are plenty of other productive companies to choose from. A company with a spotty sales growth record is usually one which requires favorable business conditions to prosper. Since the economy is cyclical, with ups and downs occurring regularly, this would ordinarily not be a company that is suitable for long-term investment.

THE DIVIDEND YIELD

A company's earnings can be either retained in equity and plowed back into the business or paid out to shareholders in the form of dividends. This might make it seem that a company which pays out dividends does not have anything better to do with its money. If they would just use that money in their operations they would grow faster and increase the value of the shareholders' equity position faster over the long-term—or so some analysts argue.

There is some merit in that argument, and some famous chief executives adhere to it, offering no dividends to investors while running extremely successful companies. But to the long-term investor, receiving a dividend is very desirable, particularly if it is from a company that has strong free cash flow. Such a company often produces so much free cash from its operations that it is able to increase its dividend year after year.

Dividend increases can really add up to a windfall for investors. Suppose you buy a stock for $100 per share. In the first year, it is has a dividend of $4 per share. This would give it a dividend yield of 4%.

$$\text{Dividend yield } = \frac{\text{Dividends per share}}{\text{Stock price}}$$

Four percent is a fairly average yield, but suppose this company is able to generate tremendous cash flow by earning high rates of return on its investment. It is so strong, in fact, that dividends are raised by about 10% each year. After seven years, the dividend is $8 per share. Now the stock is yielding 8% on the original investment each year, a level that makes holding the investment extremely attractive and might even double again over the next seven years. Moreover, the shareholder has already received a good portion of his original investment back in dividends (before taxes) before even thinking of selling the company.

Of course, not many companies show such outstanding dividend growth, but they do exist among companies that are able to generate strong earnings and free cash flow from their base of capital. In general, companies pay dividends according to how much their shareholders will benefit from deployments of available cash. Fast-growing companies usually pay a small dividend or no dividend at all because they need all of the available funds to build their operations to an optimum level. Perhaps they are positioned in expanding markets that can produce a high return on investment, making it best in the shareholders' interests to keep plowing money back into the business.

More mature companies do not need all of their earnings reinvested in the business because their operations are at a more stable level. They may be in slower growth industries which do not require huge injections of capital, but rather a gradual building of a strategic position. These companies pay a higher dividend to investors because the marginal benefits of expansion with every available dollar are not as attractive to shareholders as receiving a return on their investment.

Therefore, a company that pays high dividends is generally safer because much of the return is up front in the form of dividends. The price-earnings ratios are usually lower for these companies, because a higher percentage of earnings is used to pay for dividends rather than being plowed back into operations. In weaker companies, dividends are a diversion of available funds that strain a company's finances and could be better used in operations. But in the type of company we will be looking for, earnings and free cash flow are so strong that dividends are no strain at all and can be expected to show meaningful growth in the future.

RETURN ON EQUITY

The return on shareholders' equity shows the income earned by a company on each dollar of a shareholders' investment. In a sense, it is a calculation of earnings efficiency. The higher the return the better. The common stockholders' return on equity is simply the net income divided by the common stockholders' equity. The proper way to compute the return on equity is to average this year's ending equity and the equity at the beginning of the year on the premise that earnings were produced evenly throughout the year.

$$\text{Return on equity} = \frac{\text{Net income}}{\text{Average stockholders' equity}}$$

The return on equity capsulizes the relationship between the most important items of the income statement and the balance sheet by dividing net income by the book value (shareholder's equity). The company able to maximize its earnings on its base of shareholders' equity is maximizing the value of its shareholders' resources. This would seem to be the ideal indicator of corporate performance for shareholder benefit, but it neglects the existence of long-term debt.

Let us say you bought a business for $60, which became your total shareholders' equity. After the first year of break-even operations, you realized that to get things rolling at an optimum level, the company needed to assume $40 of long-term debt, and did so. In the next year, the company earned $6, to give you a return of 10% on equity. But is this the total amount of your investment in the company? Not really; the total amount of invested capital is $100—the equity plus the long-term debt. Therefore, the return on total invested capital is really just 6%.

RETURN ON TOTAL INVESTED CAPITAL

The return on total invested capital (return on capital) is a more realistic indication of investment return. Invested capital equals shareholders' equity plus long-term debt. Long-term debt takes on a similar function as stock; it finances operations for extended periods of time. Choosing debt financing or stock financing is a management decision that is usually unrelated to the purpose of the financing. In either case, the company is receiving the desired money; the difference is in how it will affect the company's total capital structure. In this sense, stock and long-term debt are each forms of invested capital and both should be considered when evaluating return from investment calculations.

$$\frac{\text{Return on total}}{\text{invested capital}} = \frac{\text{Net income}}{\text{Average total invested capital}}$$

Total invested capital = Average stockholder's equity + average long-term debt

It should be noted that the proper way to compute the return on total invested capital (return on capital) is to average the ending balance and beginning balance for the year, just as was done for the return on equity. This is not an absolute necessity; the differences in the results are usually not going to be large enough to seriously hinder the accuracy of the calculation.

The return on capital equation takes into account the amount of long-term debt assumed by the company, an important consideration for long-term investors. A company burdened by a heavy debt load can be vulnerable to changing economic conditions. If business conditions worsen and sales revenue slips, a company laden with debt can be damaged by having to pay out precious income to service the debt.

This can do long-term damage to the company, restricting development of operations in markets that demand immediate attention while limiting the ability to capitalize on new opportunities. A company with little or no debt service lives within its means and is not faced with these kinds of concerns in the inevitable weaker years. It may have to adjust its plans now and then, but long-term strategies will ordinarily not be affected.

Both the return on capital and the return on shareholders' equity are excellent indicators of how well a company is performing. It is not surprising that companies with outstanding earnings records have high returns on equity and capital. High performance companies like Merck regularly earn returns in the neighborhood of 20% on capital and equity. In Chapter 8, we will do a quick profile of Merck, a company that has put together several favorable corporate characteristics well enough to earn the title of "America's most admired corporation" in a recent *Fortune* magazine poll.

An above-average company might earn only 10% on capital, while a mediocre company would earn closer to the 5% level. Cull from the stock market a list of companies that earn the highest return on invested capital and you probably have compiled a listing of most of the finest companies on the exchange. The Value Line Investment Service does something similar to that, by performing a weekly screen of companies with high returns on invested capital, although this list sometimes contains some companies that have experienced one or two big years in a series of lesser years and are not suitable for long-term investors.

In fact, I will go out on a limb and say that it is unnecessary for investors to even consider companies that have not proven the ability year after year to earn at least 10% on capital. This point will be amplified in great detail in Chapter 11, but it is worth considering at this early point.

If stock prices are based on equity value and equity value is increased by generating earnings, why bother with a company that has not proven itself as an efficient generator of earnings? Just by considering the best earnings generators—say, those that consistently earn above 12% on capital—you have eliminated about 80% of all companies, leaving you the cream of the crop on which to concentrate your analysis. Except for stocks that are extremely undervalued according to assets and potential earnings power, why spend time on mediocre companies?

THE RETURN VALUE RATIO

The Return Value Ratio (RVR) is a calculation that I created to cull from the stock market companies that earn efficient rates on capital and are selling at a reasonable price. The basic objective is to receive the highest return for the lowest price.

Let us invert the equation for value stated in Chapter 1:

$$\text{Value} = \frac{\text{Reality}}{\text{Perception}}$$

In this case, to find value in the stock market, the reality of a stock's worth should be higher than what the market perceives. A stock is worth only as much as what the investor can receive in the form of returns from his investment. And market perceptions take the form of stock market valuations of earnings. In other words:

$$\text{Investment value} = \frac{\text{Actual investor returns}}{\text{Market valuation of returns}}$$

Since the investor actually receives a stream of earnings from his total investment, the top part of the equation should be the return on invested capital. And since the market values that stream of earnings, the most logical figure to use for the bottom is the p/e ratio. This results in the following equation for measuring value:

$$\text{Investment value} = \frac{\text{Return on invested capital}}{\text{Price-Earnings Ratio}}$$

As you have probably guessed by now, I have a preference for stocks that show an immediate return on capital—in other words, companies that pay dividends. Remember, the decision to pay dividends is a diversion of earnings away from reinvestment in the corporation in favor of direct payment to the shareholders. Unfortunately, adding the dividend yield to the equation effectively results in double counting the dividend, once in earnings and again in the dividend. This makes the equation less correct theoretically and may place a priority on instant returns rather than long-term capital appreciation, but I think it adds a valuable component to the equation.

$$\frac{\text{Return Value}}{\text{Ratio}} = \frac{\text{Return on capital} + \text{After-tax dividend yield}}{\text{Price-Earnings Ratio}}$$

The after-tax dividend yield is based on the most common tax rate for individuals, which is assumed to be the maximum income tax rate. Before the Tax Reform Act of 1986, that rate was 46%. So, if a stock yielded 5%, the after tax dividend yield would be 2.7% (5 × (1 − .46)). In 1987, with the maximum tax rate moving to 38%, the after-tax dividend rate would increase to 3.1% (5 × (1 − .38)). This accounts for the tremendous increase in the value of stocks that paid high dividends immediately after the tax reform act passed. In fact, within a few months after the act's passage, the Dow Jones Utility Average rose about the same as the average after-tax dividend (shown above: 3.1 ÷ 2.7 = 14% gain).

The instant response of the market to a change in the value of after-tax dividends, plus the superb record of the Dividend Value Index from Chapter 4, should underscore the importance of dividends to stock prices. As I have said so many times before, there is nothing precise about the calculation of earnings, so the goal of this equation is not to come down to a precise measure of investment value. In truth, no such precision can possibly exist, because stock market values are produced by a conglomeration of intrinsic value, interest rates, and market psychology.

Precision does not really matter—it is the logic that counts. Granted, there is faulty logic in the double counting of dividends, but paying a dividend *is* of some extra value to the shareholder. Dividends add a measure of safety by offering an instant return and usually reflect a company that has cash to spare. A company that never cuts its dividend and can consistently raise the payments is usually one that can be counted on to prosper in the future. The investor not only receives an instant return, he also receives an extra vote of confidence, which is an important component (market psychology) of stock price valuation. Of course, if theoretical correctness is important to you, feel free to subtract dividends from earnings when computing the return on capital component of the Return Value Ratio (RVR).

The RVR places stocks on a fair and uniform basis for comparison. It can be used to cull quickly from the market stocks that may appeal to you on a value basis, leaving you a solid group of values to choose from. Of course, it is important to make sure that you choose consistently growing companies, since an erratic company can show one good year of return on capital and then falter in the periods following.

As a guideline, I try to buy only companies with an RVR above 1.5, preferably above 1.75, and with reasonably good sales growth. An RVR above 2.0 is a very good value; an RVR above 2.5 is a superb value. If you choose to eliminate dividends for theoretical correctness, you can reduce those guidelines by about one-third.

The RVR is not a perfect method for choosing growth stocks— no method is—but it does a pretty good job. One obvious drawback is that it excludes those stocks that have a high price-earnings ratio. A stock that regularly carries a p/e of 30 is unlikely ever to qualify under this type of screen. This is an unfortunate by-product of any investment discipline—that certain companies simply will not fit in to one's investment strategy. If this seems too big a sacrifice, perhaps you should reconsider the relevance of the discipline. A stock with a p/e of 30 does not belong in the portfolio of a strategic value investor because the market price already reflects most of its value. Such a lofty p/e usually limits the upside potential of a stock and raises the vulnerability of the stock price to subsequent disappointments. Purchasing a stock with an excessive p/e ratio generally exposes you to an unfavorable amount of risk relative to potential reward.

Another potential discipline problem with the RVR calculation occurs when p/e ratios for the entire market rise to very high levels. This has the effect of reducing the number of stocks that can qualify under the screen. It might be tempting to allow for this change in market valuation by easing up on the qualifications. But this may be a good problem to have, as it can serve as an excellent overall market indicator that prices have risen too high without the support of earnings. When RVR is showing very few buying opportunities, it is often a sign that the market is overvalued and is approaching a long-term top.

Conversely, when p/e ratios for the entire stock market are very low, a great many stocks will qualify under the RVR method. While it may seem frustrating to try to differentiate between the relative merits of the various stocks, this can be a market indicator that stocks are greatly undervalued. When stocks are so undervalued, the market is likely to eventually respond with a powerful bull market that will push nearly all of the low-RVR stocks to much higher levels. Similar to the book value and working capital calculations, market screens with RVR can be used as a very effective fundamental tool for market timing.

QUALIFYING THE RETURN VALUE RATIO

There are some young growth companies that earn very high rates of return on invested capital, some even ranging from 50 to 70%. This would allow companies with p/e ratios of 25 or 30 to qualify easily under the RVR, levels which ordinarily reflect too much optimism already in stock prices, and therefore, too much risk and too little upside potential. A good way to restrict the qualifications of the RVR is to implement a variation of the Earnings Value Index (EVI), discussed in Chapter 5.

With the EVI, we saw how the stock market as a whole was undervalued when the earnings yield (the inverse of the p/e ratio) for the average stock in the S&P 500 was greater than the rate on three-month T-bills.

$$\text{Earnings Value Index} = \frac{\text{Earnings yield}}{\text{Rate on three-month T-bills}}$$

where

$$\text{Earnings yield} = \frac{1}{\text{p/e ratio}}$$

Because the market is cheap when its earnings yield exceeds the rate on three-month T-bills, we can use this as a qualification for the RVR. In other words, stock should not be bought with an earnings yield less than the rate on three-month T-bills.

For instance, if a stock has a p/e of 20, then its earnings yield is 5% (1/20). If the rate on three-month T-bills is currently 6%, then the stock's earnings yield is too low compared with interest rates. Despite the fact that the company might have a return on invested capital of 40%, buying a stock with an earnings yield below the riskless rate of return means that you are buying a stock with less upside potential than the riskless rate of return (three-month T-bills), and assuming, of course, greater risk.

The only exception to this qualification would be a rare stock like ServiceMaster, which has been able to earn extraordinarily high rates of return on capital (above 30%) for over 10 years, the equivalent of more than 2 economic cycles. Such a company will almost always carry a higher p/e ratio than the general market, but it is justified, since it has proven itself to be a consistently superior company.

Most companies earning such high rates of return are young companies that have not been in existence long enough to be tested over more than two market cycles and a variety of economic conditions. When conditions become difficult or their product receives greater competition or loses its appeal, rates of return can plummet quickly. These high-p/e stocks have not proven enough to warrant investment consideration by a value investor, even though the market may find them very appealing. Once the bubble bursts on these companies, the stock market is often terribly unforgiving in driving their stock prices lower.

STRATEGIC APPLICATIONS

Stock price valuations reflect the equity position of a company. To increase equity, the corporation has to produce earnings, which can be reinvested into the company to build more equity for shareholders. Some companies may decide that a portion of the earnings can be remitted to shareholders in the form of dividends, which will provide them with an instant return on their investment.

In light of this, the ideal company to buy is one that is able to generate the greatest amount of earnings from its entire base of investment capital. Since long-term debt is an alternative to equity, it is important to include debt in this calculation, hence the return on total invested capital equation. Most companies already have the bulk of their value reflected in their stock price, as suggested by the p/e ratio. This makes it important to consider the amount of investor returns as a function of market valuation as portrayed in the RVR. By investing only in companies that show a high RVR, we can maintain a portfolio of undervalued stocks that should prosper over the long-term.

8

Winning Stock Investments

Executing consistently profitable stock transactions is a matter of buying the right stock at the right price, then selling it once it is fully valued and recycling the proceeds back into other "right stocks." Over the course of the past seven chapters, we have talked about under- and overvaluation for both stocks and the stock market, but we have not discussed the more intangible qualities of individual stocks that often contribute to winning stock investments. Let us now discuss some of the more conspicuous qualities that make companies good investments, and then look at four real-life investment examples that proved successful.

MERCK AND THE *FORTUNE* POLL

Toward the end of 1986, *Fortune* magazine held a poll among 8,200 senior executives, outside directors, and financial analysis to "rate the companies in their own industry on eight key measures of reputation." Their January 19, 1987 cover story named Merck as "America's most admired corporation." Of course, market participants do not always think like businesspeople, but as I have insisted, they should. In view of this, the background behind Merck's popularity among people in the know is instructive for what might make companies a winner among shareholders.

Whether rightly or wrongly, few things are admired more than the ability to make money, so it was no surprise to see *Fortune* specifically note in the fifth paragraph of a 46-page story:

> The ten most admired companies have made lots of money for their stockholders. Their median return on equity for 1985 was 19.75%, and every one bested the Fortune 500's median ROE of 11.6%. The most admired list's 1985 median total return to investors—stock price appreciation plus dividends—was an outstanding 49.9%, vs. 26.3% for the 500.

The relationship between popularity, profit performance, and stock price movement might be a coincidence, but I doubt it; the ability to generate earnings for shareholders efficiently is perhaps the best determinant of a winning stock.

Merck's outstanding corporate performance was certainly noted by Wall Street. At the time of this writing (January 1987), Merck was trading at a p/e of 28, a whopping 65% higher than the 17 p/e of the average stock in the S&P 500. Priced at 129 with its 28 multiple, the stock was heavily recommended by most of the major brokerages. The stock had already more than tripled from the low of 39¼ reached in 1984, when it traded at a more reasonable p/e of 12 and sported an attractive RVR of 1.67.

Merck scored among the top three companies in six of the eight categories. Here are the six attributes that boosted Merck's score to number one:

1. Long-term investment value—first.
2. Use of corporate assets—second.
3. Financial soundness—third.
4. Ability to attract, develop, and keep talented people—first.
5. Quality of products or services—second.
6. Community and environmental responsibility—third.

Merck placed within the top five in two other categories: "quality of management" and "innovativeness."

ATTRIBUTES OF A WINNING STOCK

Let us review the list of Merck's six key winning attributes, using Merck as an example of qualities desired by the value investor.

1. *Increasing Shareholder Value.* The ability to earn money is admired, and therefore, it is no surprise that Merck, the most admired company, was also voted the best long-term investment value. It drew a second place for its use of corporate assets, which is another way of saying that the company makes excellent use of its investment capital. Over the past 10 years, Merck averaged an 18% return on capital and 20% on equity, including a 25% return on equity for 1985, about twice that of the average company.

Merck was third in financial soundness, which is a measure of how much those polled trusted the company's finances. Merck almost always shows a current ratio above 2:1 and long-term debt is a measly 6% of total capital. Over the past 10 years, earnings, cash flow, and book value per share have risen every year and dividends have been raised in all but one year. Finally, free cash flow was about $2 per share, leaving the company enormous amounts of money to cultivate existing and future businesses.

Impressive earnings statements catch the eye of the investment public, but there is a lot to be said also for the *consistent* performance Merck has displayed over the years. Consistency builds trust, and in the topsy-turvy world of the stock market, that means stronger stock valuations. The state of the economy has become so difficult to assess that wildly erroneous predictions by prestigious institutions (and especially, the federal government) make good material for humorous stores in the *Wall Street Journal*.

A company that is able to turn in consistently superior performance will be rewarded with a high p/e that will be more resilient than most in a market decline. Regardless of the condition of the economy, the consistent performer will be able to increase shareholder value at a steady rate, value that will eventually be recognized in a strong stock market. The long-term value investor can bank on emotional sell-offs to bring the stock down to undervalued levels, where he can pluck the bargain and hold it with a large measure of confidence through the next bull market.

2. *Market Niche Leadership.* The ability to get and keep talented people (first place) is a reflection of power, which comes, in part, from having a leading position in its market niche. A company does not have to be the largest in its industry, like IBM, but a company that has a leading position in its particular market niche has better control of its destiny. Of course, if a company does have the dominant stake in the field, it has the advantage of being able to muscle into markets by the sheer size of its operating budget.

In Merck's case, it closed down a number of operations saddled by low returns to concentrate its resources in the biotechnology field, where it was able to throw several more times the amount of money into research than its competitors. Although it was not the first to enter the new field, it built an overall lead in technology through the strategic deployment of its enormous financial resources. By virtue of overwhelming research expertise and financial power, Merck has become the leader of an attractive market niche and is able to attract, develop, and keep the most talented people.

3. *Sales Growth with Enduring Products.* In most cases, an investor would not know whether a company produced a good product, unless it was a consumer-type company selling products to the general public. But a strong marketing organization creates the reputation of a quality product (second place), boosting sales and increasing shareholder awareness. Over the past 10 years, Merck increased its sales per share every year (actual sales were flat one year), with actual sales rising 125% in 10 years.

Merck's products address genuine problems that need continual solutions. For instance, Merck produces drugs for hypertension and ulcers. While the drugs themselves are not fads, the very composition of a technology company makes its products similar to fads, because it is only as good as its last product breakthrough. A large part of Merck's number one rating overall in the poll can be attributed to their leadership in biotechnology, a field that is currently enjoying a sort of cult-worship on Wall Street.

Technology, however, can be a double-edged sword. When it produces, profits roll in at a rate thrilling to shareholders, but just fast enough for corporate managers to recycle into new technologies.

Like the gunslingers of the Old West, there is always another gunfighter around who is faster off the draw—or who uses a machine gun. Keeping ahead in the technology game requires a great deal of research, which in turn, requires spending huge sums of money with a relatively low probability of its paying off. Once the product comes on the market, which can take a number of years, new technologies can make it obsolete while it is barely on the shelf.

Merck has made technology work for them, but there are not many Mercks around. They may have achieved their top rating by success in a hot field, but before their foray into high-tech, they built a sturdy record of consistent performance in less-thrilling businesses. As its products age, it will be interesting to see whether Merck still heads the list. A comparable case is that of SmithKline Beckman, which ranked eighth in the 1983 Fortune poll with the help of their blockbuster Tagamet™ drug. By 1986, SmithKline was midway down the list at 135, by far the worst drop of any company among the top 10 companies of 1983.

It can be said that IBM, unofficially the most admired corporation for many years (and leader of the Fortune poll for four years prior to Merck), is not really a technology company, but a marketing company. Their products are not always on the cutting edge, but through their well-developed sales organization and overwhelming financial power, they are able to dominate the vast computer market.

Unfortunately, IBM is in a technology-based industry, and with Digital Equipment being able to exploit technological advantages in certain specialties during the mid-1980s, IBM's dominance in the computer market has become less certain. This could force IBM to commit to being more of a technology company, making it a less attractive long-term investment, because it will more susceptible to the inherent problems of competitive technology.

Companies that rely on fads or breakthrough technologies to put products on the market are inherently riskier, since the likelihood of rejection by the marketplace due to nonacceptance or obsolescence is much higher. Companies that produce products with a longer shelf life are more likely to produce a steady stream of sales growth over the long term. It takes sales to power earnings, and Wall Street will generally reward predictable sales and earnings growth with a higher stock price-earnings multiple.

4. *Freedom to Grow.* Ranking third in community and environmental responsibility may not seem important to most investors, but such a ranking is also reflective of the movement toward nonregulation in the drug industry. In the 1970s, the regulatory climate in this country toward the drug industry (and others) was so strict that few new products could be introduced. In those days, drug companies were not so glamorous because of the inability to market new products.

The lack of freedom to grow not only hampers the ability of a company to progress but also has a deadening effect on stock prices, which depend on optimism to inflate fundamental value into high market values. If regulations make it impossible to get a product out of the laboratory, what positive breaking news is there to anticipate? In the beginning of 1973, Merck hit a high of 50, a level it failed to exceed for a full 10 years, when the regulations were finally eased. It is interesting to note that during this period of suffocating regulation pervasive in several industrial arenas, the country was in a general malaise and the stock market (as measured by the Dow) stumbled in a narrow range without making any upside progress.

Companies beset by regulations are likely to be stagnant stocks, but can really perk up once the regulations are lifted. This has been seen over and over, by the deregulation of the phone companies, airlines, utilities, and so on. Once the regulations were lightened or lifted entirely, the stocks responded with unusual vigor. This does not mean that investors should completely avoid regulated companies, but unless you are primarily interested in dividend income, it is a good idea not to let heavily regulated companies comprise a sizable part of your portfolio.

Another quality to be concerned with is a company's dependence on government business for a meaningful proportion of its sales and earnings. These companies can go through long periods of stagnation because of exogenous factors like federal budget cuts or political blocks posed by the voting public. The most obvious example in recent years was the boom of defense stocks in the early Reagan years, followed by their lackluster performance in his latter years, when the public tired of the defense build-up and its effect on threatening budget deficits.

5. *More Unpopular—More Potential.* Merck is obviously not an unpopular stock, particularly now, as "America's most admired corporation." With its current title and 28 p/e, it might not be a very good investment either. How much upside potential can Merck have? Can it triple, as it did two years ago, when it was a little less popular and had a p/e of 12? Sure, it can triple, but *only* if everything goes absolutely right with the company and the rest of the stock market. I might not sell the stock right now, but I would rather buy a stock that was less recognized as a superstar, because the more popular a stock, the more efficiently the market has priced the stock, which significantly reduces the upside potential.

Smaller companies are most likely to be less popular, because it is harder for institutions (like mutual funds or large pension plans) to invest in them because of a lack of liquidity. To gain a meaningful representation in their portfolio, they would have to buy significant percentages of the company's entire outstanding stock, a difficult and bothersome process which causes them to pay high prices for large blocks of stock and sell at lower than market prices. This liquidity problem is so acute that most institutions do not even consider stocks with under $100 million in market value, effectively shutting them out from small stocks and leaving the spoils for the individual investor.

Companies that are recognized by large institutions as potential investments receive tremendous coverage by analysts, while small stocks receive minimal or no coverage at all. Because institutions comprise over 80% of all trading executed on the NYSE, they are the market, and their opinions are often instantly translated into market prices. Therefore, because of such close scrutiny, institutional-type stocks are more often fully priced relative to their current prospects. For all of these reasons, smaller stocks are usually less efficiently priced than larger stocks and can offer more attractive valuations and greater profit potential.

Finally, a smaller company is more likely to get taken over than a large one. Takeovers are one unexpected payoff from long-term investing. It is simple Adam Smith (the real one) economics. Once a company is making too much money in a field, it is bound to attract competition. Since it sometimes costs more to start up a new division than to buy the competition, smaller companies with a strong market share in their particular niche are prime prospects for takeover attempts.

The so-called smaller companies dominate the OTC and AMEX exchanges, but there are, of course, hundreds of them on the NYSE. And smaller stocks are not the only unpopular stocks. Larger stocks can be unpopular too, resulting in pricing inefficiencies.

For example, Exxon, one of the largest companies in the world, was very unpopular early in 1986 while the stock market was making spectacular gains. Oil prices and their stocks were down sharply, and the industry's future seemed precarious. When Exxon was priced at 55, I was criticized for recommending it, because it was "too dangerous." At 90, 12 months and a 60% increase later, Exxon became known as a popular stock to own, suitable for even the "safest" retirement accounts.

My personal feeling was that Exxon was a lot safer at 55 than at the inflated price of 90. At 55, it had a p/e of 7 and a dividend yield of 6.3%, less than half the p/e and twice the dividend of the average stock on the S&P 500. With a return of capital of 17% for several years running, the Return Value Ratio was about 2.90, one of the highest RVR's around at the time.

True, by the time Exxon was being touted, the desperate oil situation was looking a lot less uncertain. But at 90, the stock price reflected that new optimism. Even though the stock still contained upside potential, it certainly had less upside potential and more downside risk than at 55. Granted, oil prices were a bit scary at $9 a barrel, having dropped from $35 in a matter of months—but how low could oil go? Eventually, the oil price situation would stabilize and return to normalized levels, at least well above the emotional panic-induced mark of $9.

The worst seemed to be over from a fundamental standpoint, and technically, there appeared to be major accumulation of the shares occurring in the low 50s. From the viewpoint of a value investor, I was comforted by a number of factors: the low p/e, the secure 6%+ dividend, a powerful balance sheet with only 14%

debt, and the simple fact that Exxon was one of the most powerful companies in the world. In time, the emotional scare regarding oil prices would probably dissipate, making Exxon an excellent investment over the long term. Until then, I would be content to sit with a generous dividend yield that rivaled money market instruments.

Now, let us summarize the desirable characteristics discussed in the past few pages:

1. *Increasing Shareholder Value.* A company should consistently prove its ability to earn high rates of return of capital for its shareholders. If a company achieves this year in and year out, the market is more likely to price the stock at a higher multiple of earnings during upswings and maintain its price better during downswings.

2. *Market Niche Leadership.* The company should be a leader in its specific market niche and do whatever it does very well. It is also helpful if the company's finances are such that it can put together a stronger campaign to accomplish its objectives than its competitors without straining finances.

3. *Sales Growth with Enduring Products.* Sales growth powers earnings, so the company's primary products should not be a response to a fad, but rather provide solutions that are actually needed, so that sales growth can be sustained. Product lines that demand intensive technology are less favorable, because of high development costs and quick obsolescence.

4. *Freedom to Grow.* It is better to have a company that is operating in an unencumbered environment than one beset by regulations or subject to the whims of the federal government's budget policies. A company with the freedom to grow will be more dynamically priced by the marketplace.

5. *More Unpopular—More Potential.* Less popular stocks, usually smaller companies or larger ones saddled by temporary problems, are less likely to be efficiently priced and have greater profit potential. The more popular stocks are more likely to be recognized for their upside potential by the marketplace and be more efficiently priced.

FOUR EXAMPLES OF STOCK SELECTION

Now, to put the last few chapters in perspective, let us look at four examples of how I used these principles of undervalued assets and earnings to select the right stock at the right price. The kind of analysis illustrated here can be applied by any investor to find the right stocks of today and tomorrow.

Polaroid—Undervalued Assets

I recommended Polaroid on September 27, 1985 at a price of 31⅜. By March 1986, the stock had already reached a high of 72⅞, representing a gain of over 130% in less than six months. By March 1987, Polaroid sold as high as 85, a gain of over 170% in 18 months.

Background. Polaroid is the leading manufacturer of instant photographic cameras and films. The company was in the limelight back in 1972, when it introduced its SX-70 camera. At that time, the stock sold near 150. A decade following its peak in popularity (and hence, stock price), Polaroid was viewed as a has-been company.

Late in 1985, new investor interest appeared in Polaroid because of the potential settlement of a major lawsuit with Eastman Kodak, who had invaded their instant camera market. In January 1986, the suit was, in fact, settled in favor of Polaroid.

It is interesting to note the action of Kodak after the suit was settled against them. Kodak stock plunged from 51 to 46 in the first couple of days. But after three weeks of basebuilding, Kodak rose 39% to 64 over the next two months. By 1987, the once-unpopular Kodak had become a market leader.

Fundamentals. On the surface (at the time I recommended it) Polaroid had very little in the way of attractive fundamentals (see Figure 8-1). It still looked like the same lumbering has-been of the past decade. Sales were flat, showing no improvement since 1978. Earnings were erratic. The financial papers showed a p/e ratio of 121 due to weak earnings.

First-quarter earnings were in deficit, but the second quarter was slightly higher. Third-quarter earnings were to be reported

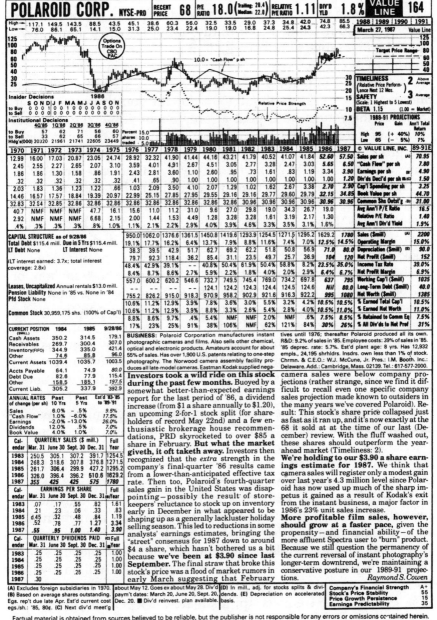

Figure 8-1. A Value Line evaluation of Polaroid eighteen months after it was recommended. An entire Value Line sheet is shown as an example of the service; all other illustrations show just the historical financial information. *Courtesy*: Value Line, 711 Third Avenue, New York, NY 10017.

quite soon, and the stock seemed to be acting pretty well in advance of the release. It seemed as if third-quarter earnings might come out to be favorable, at least compared to the previous year's third quarter of 6¢.

As it turned out, third quarter earnings came out at 48 cents and earnings were up about 150% for the fourth quarter. Still, that put the return on capital at only about 4.5%, certainly not worthy of a stock selling at a high earnings multiple. As an earnings and growth machine, the company seemed to be going nowhere. The yield was a fair 3.2%, with no dividend increase since 1979.

There were two things that attracted me to Polaroid on a fundamental basis: (1) the prospect of a decline in the dollar and (2) the company's assets. Polaroid was selling at about book value. This was really nothing new; the stock had traded at or below book value for the past six years. Still, this was encouraging.

The company's net current assets added up to $689 million, or $22 per share. Furthermore, even after subtracting long-term debt, the net-net working capital (without adding any percentage for long-term assets) came to $18 per share. In other words, in an instant liquidation, without *any* value given to long-term assets, the company would receive about $18 per share. With our purchase price of 31⅜, the downside risk in a worst-case situation was about a 42% loss.

But realistically, in the case of a liquidation, the company would be able to get something for the long-term assets. A reasonable percentage for recovery of value in a hurried liquidation would be 25%, so let us add back an extra 25% for gross plant and equipment to reach a modified net-net working capital.

To arrive at gross plant and equipment, we see that the depreciation rate for 1984 was 5.6%. Assuming no change in that number and taking Value Line's estimate of $57 million for depreciation, the gross plant and equipment equals about $1,018 million for 1985. This was computed by taking $57 million divided by .056. On a per-share basis, $1,018 million equals $32.84. Taking 25% of the $32.84 equals approximately $8 per share. So, the modified net-net working capital equals $26 per share (18 + 8), just about $5 below my recommended price of 31⅜ for the stock.

Let us review exactly what all of this means. The net working capital (current assets minus current liabilities) is equal to $22 per share. Long-term debt was relatively low, just $4 per share. By subtracting out the long-term debt, we get $18. This is the worst-case liquidation value supposing that all of the long-term assets of Polaroid are totally worthless and all of the debts of the company are paid, leaving $18 left over for the stockholders.

But usually, the plant and equipment of a company can be sold for something. To arrive at a realistic liquidation figure, take 25% of total depreciable assets. This comes to $8 per share. Adding $8 to the $18 gives $26 per share, which is the amount of money that would probably be received if the company liquidated itself under a situation of extreme duress.

It is very reassuring to know that you are buying a company for a price approximately equal to its liquidation value. Even if Polaroid liquidated the day after it was purchased, you would have probably lost only about 5 points, just 16%, not bad for a case in which *everything* has gone wrong. Even if several things do go wrong with the company over the long term, you will probably come out reasonably well, particularly with a top-notch operation like Polaroid.

Now for the most fascinating part. Look at the monthly chart on the Value Line sheet (Figure 8-1). Between 1983 and 1985, the low price (technical support) was between 24 and 25, *about the same as the liquidating value of the company*! Do you get the idea that all of this fundamental value stuff might be worthwhile? And does this not heavily suggest the existence of a link between fundamental and technical value?

Prospects of a decline in the U.S. dollar made Polaroid a timely stock. Because of its extensive exposure in foreign markets, Polaroid's earnings are very sensitive to movements in the U.S. dollar. Most of the product is manufactured in the United States, so that a drop in the dollar would boost earnings to the company without affecting its costs. This was another reason that Polaroid came to my attention.

In 1985, the U.S. dollar was rising on a speculative binge to unrealistic highs, reaching levels that could have a disastrous effect on the global economy. I felt that the speculation to the upside had been overdone, and so I was looking for companies that would benefit from a drop in the dollar. (Ford, the next stock to be discussed, was one of the other companies that fit this criteria.) In the following week, five major industrial powers (The Group of Five) agreed to make a concerted effort to lower the dollar, attracting tremendous new buying interest to Polaroid.

Polaroid was not the type of company that I generally look for, in that sales growth and earnings were stagnant for so long. But the asset valuation coupled with the prospects for the dollar made it a worthwhile investment. Earnings would increase markedly with a decline in the dollar, which would restore the company to respectability as an earnings machine. In fact, by the end of the next year (1986), earnings would triple and the stock market would anticipate the increase by more than doubling the stock's value. In retrospect, the stock was purchased for less than a p/e of 10 on 1986 earnings, far cheaper than the rest of the market.

Industry leaders that fall on hard times often make very attractive investments. Because public and institutional investors are so involved with such famous companies, when things go awry, prices are often driven to unrealistically low levels. As long as the fundamental growth or assets are still intact, these fallen giants make excellent long-term investments. The problem is to hold onto them until some catalyst comes along to clear the uncertainty and push the stock to higher levels. For Polaroid, that catalyst was the decline in the dollar and the settlement of the Kodak suit.

Technical Indications. Polaroid had a wonderful long-term basing formation, coupled with some explosive trading activity. Looking at the long-term monthly chart in Figure 8-1, the base of 24-25 (the approximate liquidation value) held over several tests during a one-year time span between 1984 and 1985. This points out a charting nuance that is quite common, the tendency of a stock to correct half of a previous gain. In this case, the 24-25 support was about halfway (exactly would be 27) in between the 16⅞ low of 1982 and the 37⅜ high of 1983.

I also liked the fact that the high of 37 in 1983 exceeded the 32-33 resistance of 1980–1981. This formed a sturdy six-year base that was sloping upward. The formation was edging higher, suggesting that the long-term base was under accumulation. The long-term perspective had limited downside risk, since the approximate liquidation value of 26 was just a few points below the purchase price of 31⅜ and corresponded to a full year's support at 24-25.

Volume is often the first statistic to catch my eye. Every day, as well as every weekend, I scan the most actives list for stocks with unusually high volume. Some stocks, like IBM, appear in the most actives list with regularity, nearly every day. But when Polaroid appeared repeatedly in the most actives in January 1985, a few times in April, and again in May, I really took notice, because it had not happened for a long time (see Figure 8-2).

The first explosion in volume in January (left side of Figure 8-2) was accompanied by a sharp decline in price, dropping from 28 to 25 in just a few days. During that selling climax, Polaroid touched its 24-25 base and held there for a couple of weeks. Then

Figure 8-2. A daily chart of Polaroid for 1985, which was recommended on September 27, 1985. *Courtesy*: Daily Graphs, P.O. Box 24933, Los Angeles, CA 90024.

strong volume pushed it back up to 27, creating a small gap at 26. This suggested heavy buying with an absence of sellers, a very bullish characteristic. Gaps are usually covered, and Polaroid followed suit, fluctuating between 25 and 27 for over two months, creating an excellent intermediate-term base on top of the long-term base.

The breakout from that 24–27 base occurred in March, on a string of heavy trading days. Another gap was created, this time, right at the point of breakout—very bullish. The first run was to 30⅝, all of it on very strong volume. The breakout gap was covered too, on a dip back to 27 on very light volume. The following move back up was on very heavy volume again, showing an obvious change in trend. Yet another gap was created at 30 in June, which was filled within two months.

The technical story of sharply rising prices on strong volume indicated significant accumulation taking place that would eventually result in higher stock prices. After lying dormant for a long time, Polaroid seemed ready to move. Two weeks before this recommendation, another rise occurred on the heavy volume. Polaroid presented as good a technical case as could be: limited downside risk and impressive buying interest (see Figure 8-3).

Polaroid did not have the sales and earnings growth that I normally consider a prerequisite for investment, but the fundamental asset value offered very little downside risk. The technical case was very strong, suggesting that perhaps something was brewing in Polaroid that the public did not know about. Remember, *the stock market is a better predictor of a company's fortunes than a company's fortunes are a predictor of stock prices.* Sales and earnings began to rise impressively, new products were introduced, the dollar fell sharply to boost earnings, and Polaroid won its decision against Kodak.

Like most investors, I did not know that any of these things would happen, although I did have a clue about the decline in the dollar. But the technical action of the stock was telling me that something good was in the works. Given the estimated liquidation value of 26 and superb technical support at 24-25, Polaroid seemed to be an excellent value with very limited downside risk.

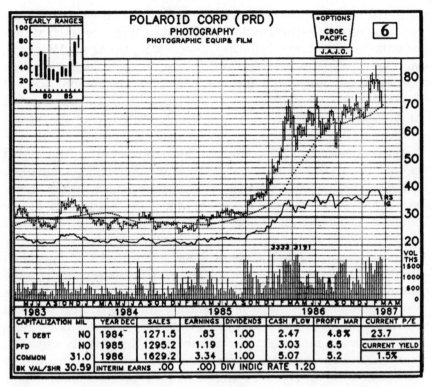

Figure 8-3. A weekly chart of Polaroid 18 months after the recommendation. Note the 1984–1985 base between 24 and 32, the breaking of which led to much higher prices. *Courtesy*: Trendline, 25 Broadway, New York, NY 10004.

Ford Motor—Undervalued Assets and Earnings

I recommended Ford Motor on October 11, 1985 when it was 46¾. By April 1986, Ford had reached a high of 85⅛, an 82% gain in about six months. The stock split three for two in June and rose to 100 by May 1987, for a gain of over 220% (from a split-adjusted cost of 31¼) in 18 months.

Background. In 1981, Ford's ability to continue as a going concern was in serious jeopardy, but by 1985, it had returned to respectability by emphasizing quality workmanship and smaller cars. After three years of languishing with deficit earnings, Ford reported strong earnings in 1983 and kept building on that momentum. The Japanese automakers were still gaining market share, but the new patriotism spurred by the Reagan Administration brought a growing enthusiasm for U.S. cars. Maybe Ford was not going to run General Motors or the Japanese automakers out of town, but they seemed fairly well situated to grow for the future.

Fundamentals. In 1981, at the nadir of its dilemma, Ford traded as low as 10½. It participated strongly in the 1982–1983 bull market, rising to a high of 46¾. But even at 47, Ford was very undervalued, as is obvious by looking at the Value Line sheet (Figure 8-4). Please note that the Value Line sheet shown here was released on March 27, 1987, some eighteen months after the recommendation.

The stock was trading below book value, but this had been going on for about a dozen years, since 1973. However, given the relatively high valuation of the stock market at the time, finding a stock below book value was unusual. With a book value of about $67 per share, Ford was trading at only 70% of book. Long-term debt was very manageable, only about 18% of net worth. The assets had been undervalued for some time, but now the company was beginning to come to life, with new products and a new public image. All of a sudden, those sleepy assets began to mean some-

At 47, the p/e ratio was only 3.4, one of the lowest on the entire NYSE. Apparently, the market was discounting the possibility that Ford would not be able to sustain such high earnings. The market was correct, but it appeared that earnings would not fall to the point where the p/e would be very high. Even if earnings fell 50%, the p/e would be just 6.8, still only a little more than half of the average stock.

The factor of currency valuations also attracted me to Ford. Ford is the leading U.S. manufacturer of cars in Europe. I remembered that when I visited Europe in 1978, I was amazed to see large numbers of Fords on the streets, small cars that seemed to be much nicer than those currently available in the United States. It is often innocuous observations like this one that present investors with potentially rewarding investment ideas.

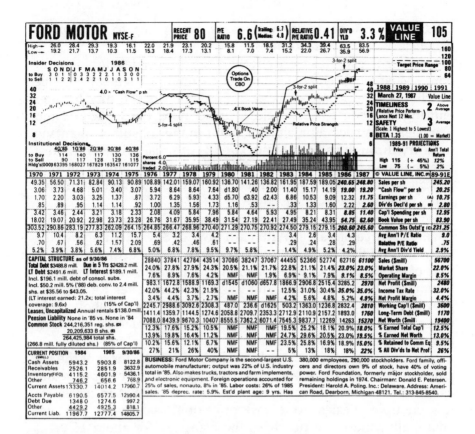

Figure 8-4. A Value Line evaluation of Ford Motor, eighteen months after it was recommended and adjusted for a 3:2 split. *Courtesy*: Value Line, 711 Third Avenue, New York, NY 10017.

By the time I recommended Ford, the so-called Group of Five had already agreed in late September 1985 to push the dollar lower to alleviate the U.S. trade crisis, making investments in companies like Polaroid and Ford with foreign exposure especially attractive. As the U.S. dollar declined, the earnings of these companies would increase as a function of their gains in currency transactions. Furthermore, a lower dollar would increase the attractiveness of U.S. products relative to foreign competitors—including the Japanese.

Ford, with 25% of its sales overseas, was going to be a prime beneficiary of a lower dollar.

Lower interest rates were another very bullish development for Ford. Most car buyers need loans to finance their automobile purchases. The lower rates gave Ford the opportunity to offer enticing financing to boost sales. Furthermore, Ford, like GM and Chrysler, was becoming a major factor in the consumer financing industry through its Ford Motor Credit subsidiary. Lower interest rates boosted the profitability of this increasingly important subsidiary, which made a substantial contribution to the bottom-line gains in Ford's overall earnings.

With earnings improving so rapidly, cash flow was another obvious source of value. With cash flow of $21.80 per share, the stock was trading at about two times cash flow! Furthermore, the total of dividends and capital spending was only $16.10 per share, leaving $5.70 per share of free cash flow left over for internal growth next year. In other words, Ford was trading at about eight times free cash flow, an unusually favorable margin of safety against future disappointments.

Sales were going pretty well, although by 1985, most of the big gains in sales recovery were probably behind the company. But as a function of market price, the stock was trading at an extremely low multiple of sales. At a stock price of 47, sales were $290 per share, allowing us to purchase the company for about 16 cents per dollar of sales, particularly cheap at an operating margin of about 8%. It is interesting to note that in 1972, when Ford traded as high as 42, the sales per share were only $107, giving a ratio of 0.39, 150% higher than the current price-sales ratio of 0.16.

Now, the best part. Let us see how Ford does on a valuation level. Ford was earning a return on capital of 18%. The two previous years averaged over 20%, so the 18% figure was reasonable. At 47, the dividend yield was 5.1%. The Return Value Ratio would equal:

$$\frac{18(\text{return on capital}) + (.54 \times 5.1)}{3.4(\text{p/e ratio})} = 6.10$$

(with "(current dividend yield)" labeling the numerator term)

An RVR above 2.5 represents a tremendous buying opportunity. An RVR of 6.10 was as high as I had ever seen, leaving a great margin of safety for earnings disappointments or panics in market psychology. Especially considering the prospects of a lower dollar, Ford appeared to be a superb buy on the basis of assets and earnings.

Technical Indications. Ford did not really participate in the boom in stock prices in the first half of 1985. In January, the stock equaled its peak of 51 set in October 1984. As Figure 8-5 shows, Ford was in a base-building process for the first nine months of 1985.

Trading volume began to build in September, becoming much heavier after the Group of Five meeting. The stock appeared on the most actives traded list, a group of stocks that should always be monitored for emerging opportunities, since those are the stocks receiving the most attention by the market. Relative strength began to rise as well, meaning that the stock was acting stronger than the average stock on the market. The automobile industry group was emerging as a new leader in the stock market, gaining relative strength during the July to September correction as others fell behind. Ford seemed unusually well-positioned to take advantage of a strong stock market, the falling dollar, and growing interest in the autos (see Figure 8-6).

The breakout on heavy volume (seen in Figure 8-5) from a narrow 43-45 range in early October helped push me into Ford. Prior to that breakout, Ford traded in a narrow 43-45 range for about three months. Ford broke through 45 and 46 on extremely heavy volume, setting up a perfect upside breakout that suggested tremendous long-term potential. In retrospect, due to the unusually cheap valuations, there was no reason to wait for a breakout from the trading range, but in the case of a cyclical stock, like Ford, it gave me greater comfort.

Figure 8-6 shows the superb base of support built by Ford from 1984 to 1985 at 26–31 (40–46 before the split). Once a surge of volume advanced Ford beyond the 31 resistance area of the base, no more resistance remained and the stock spurted higher. Quality

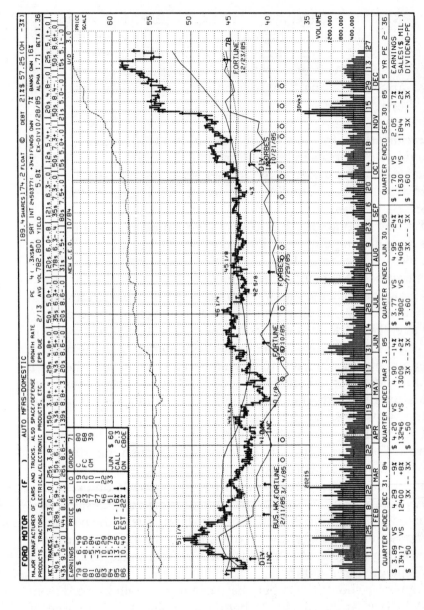

Figure 8-5. A daily chart of Ford Motor for 1985, two months after the recommendation. Note the powerful volume that catapulted Ford from the narrow nine-month base of 40–46. *Courtesy: Daily Graphs,* P.O. Box 24933, Los Angeles, CA 90024.

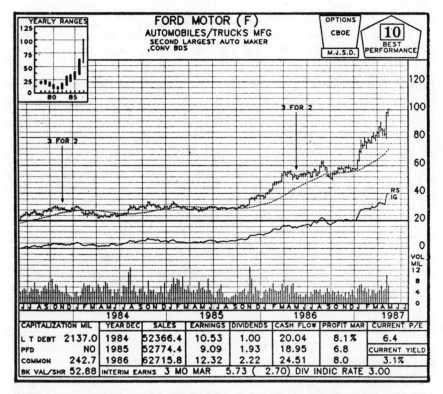

Figure 8-6. A weekly chart of Ford Motor 18 months after the recommendation to show the market action leading up to the buy date in October 1985 and how the stock price progressed. Note: these prices are adjusted for a 3:2 split. *Courtesy*: Trendline, 25 Broadway, New York, NY 10004.

companies with improving earnings prospects that show such a powerful long-term base make excellent investments. The longer the base and the stronger the liftoff from that base, the more powerful the advance could expect to be.

In accordance with my belief that the technical patterns are the result of market psychology interacting with fundamental value, the building of a long-term base is often indicative of a very important change occurring in the investment value of a company. In the case of Ford, it signified the building of a new product line that could successfully compete with Japan and GM. The development took several years of research and investment, but the accumulation at the long-term base and the tremendous volume on breakouts suggested superior long-term upside potential.

Ford represented a tremendous value on the basis of its assets as well as its earnings value. It was one of the cheapest stocks available in a highly priced market. Given that fact alone, money was bound to flow to it on the basis of value. The attractive technical elements of the stock expressed this appealing value, suggesting excellent long-term potential well beyond that of other stocks.

Overnite Transportation—Undervalued Earnings

On January 11, 1985, I recommended Overnite Transportation at 28, adjusted later to 14 following a two-for-one split. In September 1986, the stock was taken over at 43, a gain of 207% in 20 months.

Background. Overnite Transportation was a leading trucking company, operating primarily in the eastern half of the United States. Other truckers were driven out of business by sharply higher oil prices, but Overnite's excellent growth record continued largely undisturbed. Overnite weathered those storms admirably, emerging in excellent shape to take advantage of the new lower fuel prices that would attract significant interest in the transportation companies—so much interest that Overnite itself was taken over within two years of my recommendation.

Fundamentals. In early 1985, Overnite was one of the fastest-growing trucking companies and was equipped with a strong balance sheet to support it. The current ratio was 2:1, with cash alone almost equaling all of the current liabilities. Since there was no long-term debt, cash nearly equaled both short- and long-term liabilities, an exceptional quality for a growth stock.

Earnings had risen steadily, with only one down year in the past decade. Sales had shown a similar steady growth trend. Dividends also rose every year except one in the past decade. Operating margins were an impressive 17 to 20% throughout the entire decade, despite the volatile jumps in the price of oil. In short, Overnite was a consistent growth stock (see Figure 8-7).

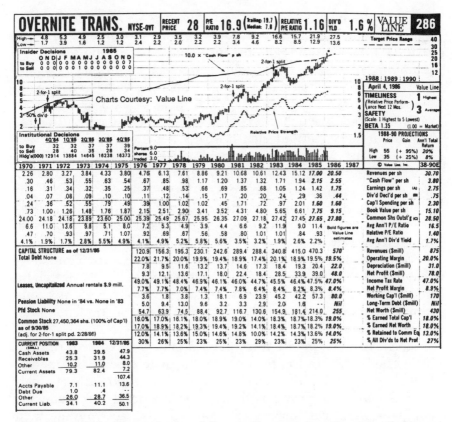

Figure 8-7. A Value Line evaluation of Overnite Transportation; 15 months after it was recommended. *Courtesy*: Value Line, 711 Third Avenue, New York, NY 10017.

At a price of 14 (adjusted for a 2:1 split), the stock was trading at only 10 times earnings and was yielding 2.6%. Cash flow was 2.15 per share. Subtracting 1.60 for capital spending and .36 for dividends, this left over 19 cents per share of free cash flow available for internal growth. Free cash flow was very common for Overnite and certainly one reason that they were able to raise the dividend so often.

Such predictable performance is very soothing to Wall Street and usually results in the marketplace according a higher than average earnings multiple. In this case, Overnite's p/e of 10 was about equal to the average for the entire S&P 500, relatively cheap for a top-notch growth stock.

The return on shareholders' equity was 18.3% for 1985. Overnite had a very consistent and impressive record of returning about 18 to 19% on equity. Again, because there was no long-term debt, return on equity equaled the return on capital. Achieving its superb growth record without any long-term debt showed excellent management and strong finances. All of those years of free internal cash flow had obviously paid off, resulting in the wonderful ability to grow rapidly without incurring any debt.

The Return Value Ratio worked out to 1.97 [(18.3 + (2.6 × .54))/10], representing a very attractive value. The timeliness of the stock was enhanced by weak oil prices, one of the vital raw materials of a trucking company. Oil prices had been sluggish over the past few years and were to collapse later in 1985, resulting in tremendous savings for the trucking companies. When oil stock prices are weak, it often pays to invest in the companies that use oil as a raw material, such as trucking, airlines, air freight, and petrochemicals. This advice, of course, also goes for any companies that use a raw material that is about to undergo price weakness.

Stocks like Overnite Transportation make an excellent case for the virtues of investing in consistent growth stocks. Companies that show several years of steadily rising sales and earnings, particularly when achieved with internal financing, are generally companies that can survive difficult periods and continue their growth. Stocks with these qualities are fine building blocks for a long-term portfolio.

Technical Indications. Overnite Transportation had been in a strong long-term uptrend since 1980. Figure 8-7 showed that Overnite had built a four-year base between 2 and 3, adjusted for two 2:1 stock splits. The actual range was approximately between 8 and 14. In 1980, Overnite broke through that narrow trading channel and continued higher thereafter (see Figure 8-8).

Over the more recent months, Overnite seemed to have a pretty boring chart, but boring charts can be very appealing, in that they can represent a strong base of support and accumulation. From March to July 1984, the stock traded in a narrow channel between 17 and 21. The breakout from this channel in late July occurred on tremendous volume, accompanied by a tiny gap that would

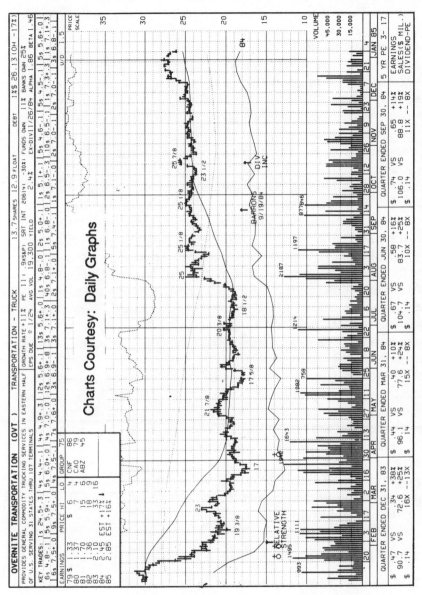

Figure 8-8. A daily chart of Overnite Transportation at the time it was recommended on January 11, 1985. *Courtesy:* Daily Graphs, P.O. Box 24933, Los Angeles, CA 90024.

not be filled immediately. This led to a new and even narrower trading range, from 22 to 25, with a quick spike to 26.

For nearly five months, Overnite marked time at that level along with the rest of the stock market, building support for a major rally. It is difficult to guess the outcome of such a narrow trading range, but this is really unimportant to a long-term value investor. Given the excellent fundamentals of Overnite as well as the rest of the stock market, such a trading range can be viewed as an opportunity to pluck a good value stemming from strong technical support.

Figure 8-9 shows that Overnite rallied to 33 in the first month of holding the stock and soon fell to 26, a couple of points below the original recommendation price. The decline was certainly no reason to sell; in fact, from a value standpoint, it only increased the attractiveness of the stock as a long-term purchase. To a patient investor, this minor decline was of little signficance. Overnite was an excellent value, with strong fundamentals and excellent technical support, both of which were still well intact. With limited downside risk and a bright fundamental future, Overnite represented excellent value for superb long term performance, as the chart in Figure 8-10 clearly shows.

Overnite Transportation was an excellent company selling at an average price-earnings multiple. The fact that oil prices were falling made it an especially timely purchase. The takeover might have accelerated the market's realization of its earnings value, but even if it had not been taken over, the stock would have probably risen to similar lofty levels. A portfolio of consistent growth stocks like Overnite, purchased at cheap valuations and held over the long term, is perhaps the easiest strategy an investor can implement with great success.

Philips Industries—Undervalued Earnings

I recommended Philips Industries on January 11, 1985 at 18. By March 1987, the stock reached 44, a gain of 144% in about 26 months.

Background. Philips Industries is a leader in producing components for the building industry. Philips is commonly believed

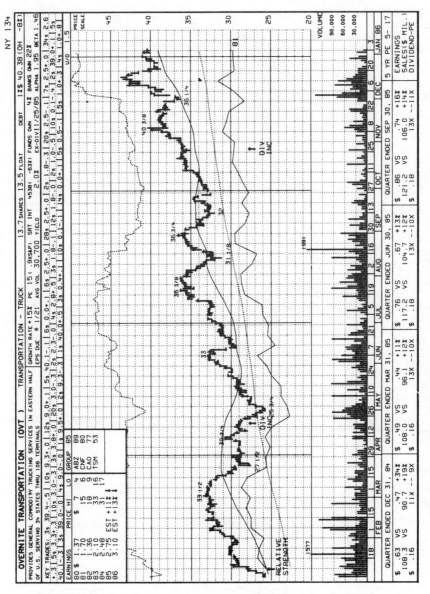

Figure 8-9. A daily chart of Overnite Transportation a year after the recommendation, a few months before it split 2:1. *Courtesy:* Daily Graphs, P.O. Box 24933, Los Angeles, CA 90024.

215

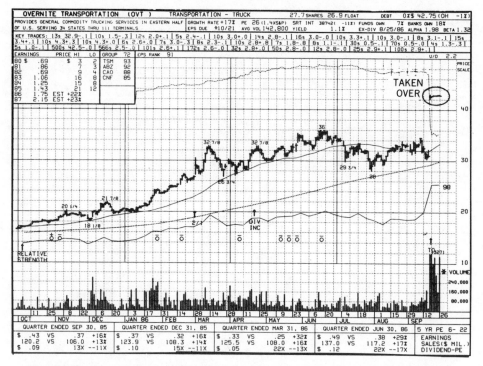

Figure 8-10. Overnite Transportation was taken over at 43, tripling the split-adjusted price of 14 within two years of its recommendation. *Courtesy*: Daily Graphs, P.O. Box 24933, Los Angeles, CA 90024.

to be involved exclusively in the manufactured (or mobile) home industry, but in truth, this accounts for about only 38% of its sales. The remainder of its work is in housing, commercial building, and air handling and treatment equipment.

Fundamentals. Many companies in the mobile homes industry have had phenomenal runs in stock price over short periods in their history, but perhaps no company in the field has put together the long history of consistent sales, earnings, and dividends that Philips has. For the last decade, earnings and dividends have increased every year, with sales taking only minor dips in 2 of the 10 years (see Figure 8-11).

Adjusted for a 2:1 split, earnings were 92 cents for 1984, a better comparison year because of its March 31, 1985 year-end, just two months before the date of the recommendation. Earnings on capital were 17.4% in 1984, higher than in the past, but not terribly out of line. With a dividend yield of 2.6% and a p/e on 1984 earnings of 10, the Return Value Ratio equaled 1.88 [(17.4 + (2.6 × .54) ÷ 10)], certainly a strong enough score to warrant investment consideration.

Cash flow was also very good. At $1.46 a share of cash flow, subtracting dividends of 23 cents and capital spending of 78 cents

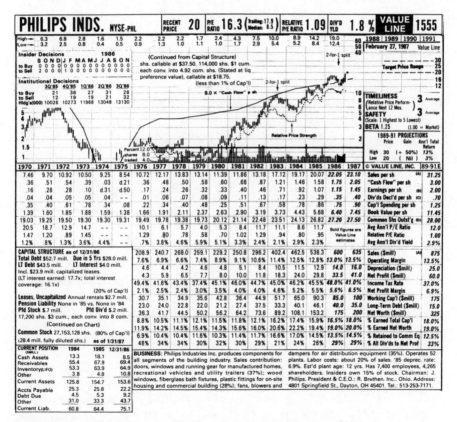

Figure 8-11. A Value Line evaluation of Philips Industries; 15 months after it was recommended and adjusted for a 2:1 split. *Courtesy*: Value Line, 711 Third Avenue, New York, NY 10017.

leaves 44 cents of free cash flow per share left for internal growth and further increases in the dividend. This enabled Philips to grow rapidly while maintaining only a moderate amount of long-term debt. The stock was trading at a 2:1 ratio of price to book value, which seemed very reasonable with respect to its impressive record of growth.

There was nothing phenomenal in the growth record of Philips, just a wonderful consistency in the face of volatile industry conditions. This type of steadiness is especially attractive when industry conditions favor the company. For Philips, this occurs when interest rates fall to levels that encourage more building and lower oil prices bring back buyers of gas-guzzling recreational vehicles.

Companies that have achieved consistent long-term growth records make value investing a lot less worrisome. When the marketplace values a consistent growth stock at unusually low levels, there is great comfort in knowing that the low value is more probably the result of stock market weakness and pessimism than a reflection of internal problems within the company.

This is not to discard the notion that any stock is beyond a careful review of its fundmantals. Every prospective investment must prove its worth. Once you are assured that the foundations of the company are intact, greater confidence can be placed in the continuity of such quality growth, enabling investors to buy aggressively on any price weakness.

Technical Indications. Philips Industries was not a technical bargain at 18. In fact, the stock was near its record high of 20 set in mid-1983, and up nearly 80% already from its low of 10⅜, set just 6 months ago. This was a case of buying strong relative strength, catching a stock midway through a long-term uptrend. Although this is not preferable to placing the purchase at a long-term base (11-13 for Philips), the price was still very attractive on a fundamental value basis (see Figure 8-12).

Despite the price being near record highs, Philips had a good technical background. Between February and July 1984, the stock built a slightly downsloping base at 10½, with a channel between 10½ and 13½. In the big boom of late July 1984, Philips rose over 50% to 16 on very strong volume in just two weeks. Following

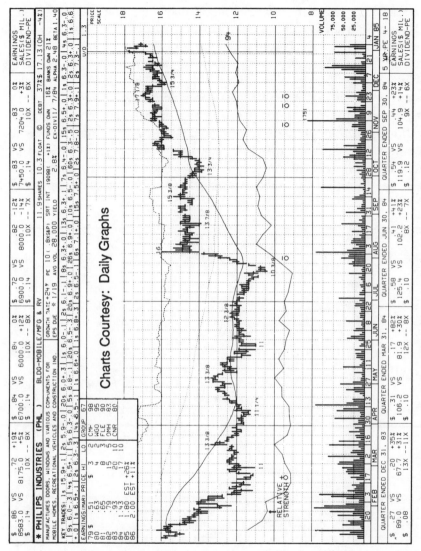

Figure 8-12. A daily chart of Philips Industries when it was recommended on January 11, 1985. *Courtesy:* Daily Graphs, P.O. Box 24933, Los Angeles, CA 90024.

this sharp rise, a 2½-month consolidation of narrow price movement between 14 and 15 built more support for future advances. Finally, in October, the stock began a new ascent, powered by a gap that occurred on very heavy volume.

This series of powerful jumps off price plateaus on strong volume was very encouraging, setting successive levels of good support that would limit downside risk. The recommendation came after breaking another plateau, this time a two-month range between 15½ and 17. Eighteen was a higher than ideal price, but Philips was still well within the parameters of attractive fundamental value, had limited downside risk because of its series of technical

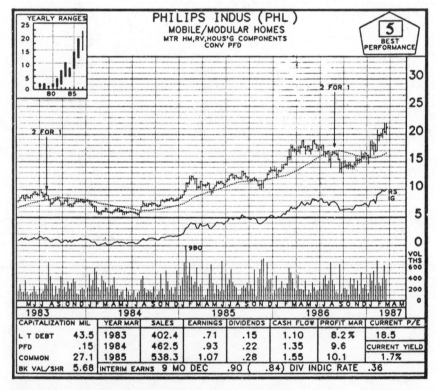

Figure 8-13. A weekly chart of Philips Industries two years (now split 2:1) after the recommendation. Note how the 10 price level was important resistance from mid-1983 to 1984, but became the key support level for future advances when it was broken in 1985. *Courtesy*: Trendline, 25 Broadway, New York, NY 10004.

support levels, and was well positioned for a rise that I anticipated in the stock market (see Figure 8-13).

Philips rose immediately to 25 within a month, but retreated to 18⅜, wiping out the entire profit by May. Again, a minor correction like this is no reason to sell a stock. Philips was not overvalued or facing difficulties that would alter the fundamentals of the company; it was just undergoing profit taking. The stock made another new high of 26¾ in late August, but then fell back again to 19¾ by early November.

This series of higher highs and higher lows defined a nice uptrend, as can be seen by the monthly chart in Figure 8-11. With the stock market still very healthy and the stock not overvalued, holding on through these irritating zigzag corrections was justified. The next run nearly doubled the price of Philips to 38 by April 1986, on expectations that lower interest rates and lower oil prices would encourage the purchase of mobile homes and recreational vehicles. Yet another sharp dip occurred in the fall 1986, down to 26 (split-adjusted to 13), but Philips quickly recovered to rise all the way to 44 (split-adjusted to 22).

In conclusion, Philips was a leader in its field and boasted a superb track record of growing sales and earnings. The price had risen quite a bit before the recommendation, but the stock still represented excellent fundamental value and was well positioned to benefit from further declines in interest rates and the price of oil.

STRATEGIC APPLICATIONS

Winning stock investments are a combination of buying the right stock at the right price. Look at a stock the way you would approach the purchase of a business. Once a company is adjudged to have the right stuff, it is a good investment only if it is purchased at a price that allows for significant upside potential and limited downside risk. Consistent growth stocks like Overnite Transportation and Philips make the most logical candidates for a growth portfolio, since their performance is so well proven that any undervaluation is more likely to be due to an emotional sell-off than a serious long-term problem in operations.

Part Four
The Strategic Value Investor

9

Identifying Important Market Tops and Bottoms

Bull and bear markets are not made by accident. They are a cyclical confluence of psychology and interest rates that fit together in perfect gear. Since the stock market repeats its behavior in cyclical patterns, previous bull markets can serve as models for better identifying future bull markets. Later in this chapter, we will take a step-by-step look at how the market timing framework, discussed in Chapter 6, would have applied to the 1982 bull market. But first, let us delve a bit deeper into cyclical benchmarks, a subject introduced in Chapter 3, that can be of great benefit to you for several bull markets to come.

CYCLICAL BENCHMARKS

Much of this book has been spent discussing cyclical benchmarks. In Part 1, we saw how the stock market moves in a series of cycles, both up and down, but ever building into a larger and more complex network. Due to its cyclical nature, even though specific events may be unprecedented, reactions by market participants that ignite major market moves tend to repeat themselves, because, despite the passage of time, people are still people.

In Part 2, we saw how effective market timing is based on a realization that investment money gravitates to the best value among the various investment markets. When the stock market is yielding returns greater than those available in the credit markets, investors will move money into the stock market, eventually raising the prices of stocks. The framework for market timing identifies some of the more reliable cyclical benchmarks, touching on fundamental value, interest rates, market psychology, and market structure.

While Part 3 focused on individual stocks and not the market as a whole, we came to understand the wisdom of buying undervalued stocks and avoiding overvalued ones, which is the essence of using cyclical benchmarks. Some basic qualities of each point in the behavior cycle were listed in Chapter 3. Let us quickly review these basic characteristics.

Bottoms: Overpessimism creates tremendous selling pressure, causing oversold conditions to a point where stock prices become unrealistically undervalued because of falling interest rates. Buying surfaces, creating support for a future advance in stock prices.

Tops: Overoptimism creates tremendous buying pressure, causing overbought conditions to a point where stock prices become unrealistically overvalued because of rising interest rates. Selling surfaces, creating resistance for a future decline in stock prices.

Now, let us take a more detailed look at the basic characteristics of market tops and bottoms. Keep in mind, not every characteristic will appear at each top or bottom, but enough qualities should appear to help you identify important junctures in the market. To make it easier to see that cyclical benchmarks of a top are simply the flip side of a bottom, the two discussions are presented in almost identical form.

SPECIFIC CYCLICAL BENCHMARKS—MARKET BOTTOMS

Market Bottoms—Interest Rate Conditions

Prior to the bottom, interest rates will have been rising for several months or more as the Federal Reserve responds to threatening inflationary pressures, ordinarily brought on by a previously overheated economy. By the time the stock market nears a bottom, these pressures will have been subdued by the rise in rates and a weakening economy.

Toward the latter stages of the bottom building process, interest rates will begin to fall, but the news will not register as bullish to the investment public. Prospects for the economy may appear so bleak that confidence will be destroyed, leading the consensus to rationalize that the drop in rates is a last-ditch measure to avoid dire economic consequences. The economy may be in the throes of a recession, but the plunge in rates will eventually make the stock market a better value compared to competing investments. When this realization takes hold, the bull market will be ready to begin.

The first indicator to watch is the Federal funds rate. During the prior period of rising rates, Federal funds will be higher than the discount rate. As the Federal Reserve loosens its grip, Federal funds will fall below the discount rate, soon followed by the yield on three-month Treasury bills, which will also dip below the discount rate. The yield curve will become bullish again, with Treasury bill rates falling back below long-term Treasury bond yields. Free Reserves will move above -500 million and perhaps rise to positive levels, and M2 money supply growth will accelerate. The icing on the cake is a cut in the discount rate, probably the first cut in several months, confirmed by a series of additional cuts in the discount and other rates.

Market Bottoms—Fundamental Conditions

Prior to market bottoms, stocks are severely undervalued relative to the past couple of years, but because of high interest rates, they are still not competitively undervalued compared to other investments. Once interest rates fall, because fundamental values are already so depressed, the stock market becomes undervalued and is ready to assume a leadership role in popularity among the various investment instruments.

To create the bottom, stock prices will have been pushed near or below book value on the Dow. P/e ratios on the Standard & Poor's 500 usually fall near eight, often down to the seven mark.

Dividend yields rise near the 6% level, sometimes close to 7%. Of course, the transition to undervaluation is only confirmed when p/e ratios and dividend yields are undervalued compared to interest rates using the Earnings Value Index and the Dividend Value Index.

The p/e ratio and dividend yield, taken by themselves without reference to interest rates, can identify likely bottoms, but these conditions can persist for several months (or years) without triggering a rally unless they are ignited by some call to action. In other words, something has to happen to ignite the transfer of money out of other investments and into the stock market; usually, that something is a decline in interest rates.

The transition from panic to bull market can occur very quickly once lower rates affect the balance of value. In both 1974 and 1982, once rates fell sharply enough to tilt the scales of value in favor of the stock market, major rallies followed within a matter of weeks. This makes it extremely important to monitor both market values and interest rates and the relative value of the two on a weekly basis.

Market Bottoms—Technical Conditions

Market bottoms coincide with the maximum point of overpessimism reached by market participants. When fear is the greatest, stock prices will be the lowest, because market psychology inflates or deflates fundamental value into market values. This panic will be expressed in high percentages of bearish market advisors (more than 50%) and mutual fund cash available (above 9.5%). While the investment public is driven into a frenzy, corporate insiders are relatively cool, showing a very low ratio of insider selling to buying (below 1.5:1) and averaging one or less secondary distributions per week.

The stock market may be deeply oversold with no end in sight, but divergences will often appear in the market structure to suggest a bullish case. The first indication will usually be the diminished number of new lows being recorded, even though the Dow might be breaking to new lows itself. After this occurs, other divergences might follow. Perhaps some market average has not reached a new low with the Dow, especially if it is a transportation index or an interest rate-oriented index, like the utility or financial averages. Maybe the advance/decline line is slowing its descent or building a series of higher troughs. Once the bull market begins, margin debt will confirm the advance by rising out of its previous slump within a month or two.

On a cyclical basis, the possibility of a four-year cyclical low occurring can add to market awareness, but should not be used by itself without concurrence with other benchmarks. Sometimes, logical points for future bottoms can be identified by inspecting the charts of market averages for previous levels of support or resistance. The market averages might fall through the support temporarily to foster more panic in the market, but if the market is fundamentally undervalued, the plunge is not likely to last long. Volume will slow to a trickle as selling pressure dries up and then increase significantly on subsequent rallies. Once the bull market is unleashed, trading volume can be expected to near record levels, and soon break records as the rally gains more followers.

SPECIFIC CYCLICAL BENCHMARKS—MARKET TOPS

Market Tops—Interest Rate Conditions

Prior to the top, interest rates will have been falling for several months or more as the Federal Reserve responds to threatening recessionary expectations. By the time the stock market nears a top, these expectations will have been subdued by the decline in rates and an improving economy.

Toward the latter stages of the top-building process, interest rates will begin to rise, but the news will not register as bearish to the investment public. Prospects for the economy may appear so positive that confidence is overwhelming, leading the consensus to rationalize that the rise in rates is a cursory measure to control potential upticks in inflation. The economy may be in the midst of a growth spurt, but the rise in rates will eventually make the stock market a worse value than competing investments. When this realization takes hold, the market will be ready to begin a bear market.

The first indicator to watch is the Federal funds rate. During the prior period of falling rates, Federal funds will be lower than the discount rate. As the Federal Reserve tightens its grip, Federal funds will move above the discount rate, soon followed by the yield on three-month Treasury bills, which will also rise above the discount rate. The yield curve will become bearish again, with Treasury bill rates rising above long-term Treasury bond yields. Free Reserves will edge below below −500 million and M2 money supply growth will decelerate. The icing on the cake is a rise in the discount rate, probably the first rise in several months, confirmed by a series of further upward moves in the discount and other rates.

Market Tops—Fundamental Conditions

Prior to market tops, stocks are severely overvalued relative to the past couple of years, but because of low interest rates, they are still not competitively overvalued compared to other investments. Once interest rates rise, because fundamental values are already so inflated, the stock market becomes overvalued and is ready to decline in popularity relative to the various other investment instruments.

To create the top, stock prices will have been pushed well above book value on the Dow, perhaps even twice as high or more. P/e ratios on the Standard & Poor's 500 usually rise above 17, often near the 20 mark. Dividend yields fall near the 3% level, sometimes below. Of course, the transition to overvaluation is only confirmed when p/e ratios and dividend yields are overvalued compared to interest rates using the Earnings Value Index and the Dividend Value Index.

The p/e ratio and dividend yield, taken by themselves without reference to interest rates, can identify likely tops, but these conditions can persist for several months (or years) without triggering a decline unless they are ignited by some call to action. In other words, something has to happen to ignite the transfer of money out of the stock market and into other investments; usually, that something is a rise in interest rates.

The transition from overoptimism to bear market can occur very quickly once higher rates affect the balance of value. In both 1973 and 1980, once rates rose sharply enough to tilt the scales of value against the stock market, major declines soon followed. This makes it extremely important to monitor both market values and interest rates and the relative value of the two on a weekly basis.

Market Tops—Technical Conditions

Market tops coincide with the maximum point of overoptimism reached by market participants. When confidence is the greatest, stock prices will be the highest, because market psychology inflates or deflates fundamental value into market values. This optimism will be expressed in low percentages of bearish market advisors (below 20%) and mutual fund cash available (below 6%). While the investment public is very bullish, corporate insiders are taking profits, showing a very high ratio of insider selling to buying (above 3:1) and averaging five or more secondary distributions per week.

The stock market may be deeply overbought with no end in sight, but divergences will often appear in the market structure to suggest a bearsh case. The first indication will usually be the diminished number of new highs being recorded, even though the Dow might be breaking to new highs itself. After this occurs, other divergences might follow. Perhaps some market average has not reached a new high with the Dow, especially if it is a transportation index or an interest rate-oriented index, like the utility or financial averages. Maybe the advance/decline line is slowing its ascent or building a series of lower troughs. Once the bear market begins, margin debt will confirm the decline by falling out of its previous uptrend within a month or two.

On a cyclical basis, the possibility of a four-year cyclical high occurring can add to market awareness, but should not be used by itself without concurrence with other benchmarks. Sometimes, logical points for future tops can be identified by inspecting the charts of market averages for previous levels of resistance. The market averages might advance through the resistance temporarily to foster more optimism in the market, but if the market is fundamentally overvalued, the rally is not likely to last long. Volume will be extremely powerful on the rise to the top, but slow a bit as buying pressure dries up and the market churns to form a top.

Once the bear market is unleashed, trading volume can be expected to get weaker and weaker, as investors become doubtful over the market's prospects and eventually lose interest in its movement.

Now that we have gone through the characteristics of market tops and bottoms, we can see how that knowledge would apply to the real-life case of the 1982 bull market, one of the most powerful in history. But first, to better understand its creation, let us take a brief look at the foundations of its past. Like all bull markets, the powerful bull market of 1982 was not an isolated event, but rather the logical outgrowth of previous market cycles. A long-term historical cyclical perspective helps us understand where the market has been, giving us a much better chance of understanding where it might go.

1929: THE GREAT BEGINNING

The Great Depression of 1929 serves as a readily identifiable benchmark to spot the beginning of modern-day stock market history. From the ashes of the 1929–1932 debacle rose the current long-term cycle, traveling the behavioral cycle from overpessimism to the current March 1987 climate of heavy optimism.

The events of the 1929 crash are well documented and certainly need no detailed explanation in these pages. On a technical level, stocks had reached dangerous levels of speculation. Prices were so extended on the upside that they no longer reflected the reality of business conditions. The speculative excesses, both psychological, economic, and in actual stock prices, needed to be corrected. The result was a depression in the stock market that accurately predicted the forthcoming depression in the economy.

The 1929 crash signaled the end of a long-term cycle that began in 1859. For 70 years, the stock market mounted a tremendous upward move, reflecting remarkable advances in our civilization, as well as the economy. The Dow Jones Industrial Average rose from about 8 to nearly 400, a fiftyfold advance. The depression plunged stock prices all the way down to about 41.50 in 1932, nearly one-tenth of their previous high just three years before. In accordance with the behavioral cycle, the 1859–1929 bull market

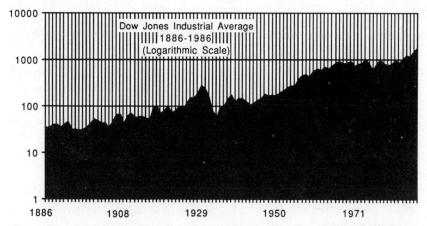

Figure 9-1. A yearly chart of the Dow Jones Industrial Average from 1886 to 1986 shows the end of the 1859–1932 cycle and the beginning of the 1932–current cycle. The chart is shown on a logarithmic scale to more accurately depict the percentage movement. It is interesting to note how both 100 and 1,000 proved to be formidable resistance points that led to tremendous rallies in the 1920s and 1980s, respectively.

began with overpessimism, peaked with overoptimism, and ended in overpessimism, setting up the 1932–current long-term cycle (see Figure 9-1).

The present long-term cycle has also followed the path of the behavioral cycle so far, building with three major advances. As mentioned, the 1929–1932 period formed the overpessimistic phase, which set up the beginning of the long-term cycle. The reconstruction phase lasted from 1932–1937, when the economy was trying to get back on its feet. The growth phase raged from 1942–1966, when the world witnessed the emergence of the United States as the preeminent economic superpower. The current cycle began in either 1974 or 1982, a raging debate whose answer depends on a number of factors and who you talk to.

1974 OR 1982: WHEN DID THE ADVANCE BEGIN?

To the casual observer, this seems to be a question of minor consequence. However, to the serious investor, tracking the progression of cycles can lead to some worthwhile conclusions regarding downside risk and upside potential. Suppose the current date was 1983. A major cycle that began in 1974 would have a much greater risk of ending than a cycle that began in 1982, because it would be highly unlikely that a long-term cycle would last just one year.

The purpose of the following discussion is not only to shed some light on the matter, but, through the consideration of the various elements to offer some insights that may prove helpful in identifying future long-term cycles.

The 1974 versus 1982 debate can be fought on many fronts, some more relevant than others. Clearly, going by price alone, 1974 marks the bottom of the 1966 correction in the Dow. The Dow bottomed at 577.60 in 1974 and reached a much higher low point in 1982 at 776.92. During the 1974–1982 period, the Value Line Average (of mostly smaller stocks) tripled, again making 1974 the logical bottom.

However, price alone does not mark the bottom of a long-term cycle. Since stock market cycles parallel the growth cycles of civilization, major cyclical shifts are perhaps better marked by changes in the economic and sociological strata. In many ways, the 1982 bottom coincided with several pivotal turning points in U.S. life.

The year 1982 marked the acknowledged decline of U.S. industry, relegating former blue chip industries like steel to backyard pieces of scrap. High-tech was no longer on the drawing board—it was a reality. Computers became personal and service industries dominated economic growth. A new service and technology age was born as the old industrial structure was scrapped, a landmark changing-of-the-guard that often marks the emergence of new long-term cycles.

On the social front, the malaise of the 1970s was being replaced by the optimism of the 1980s, with an emphasis on conservative social and economic values. The peace movement disintegrated into the "yuppie" movement, a popular term to describe young urban professionals bent on elevating capitalism into a gusto-grabbing lifestyle. Networking replaced political caucuses and corporate raiders supplanted rock stars as cult heroes. Jane Fonda was no longer protesting the war, she was protesting fat as an exercise guru of the "me" generation. The United States turned off its social conscience and turned on an insatiable lust for money, the perfect environment for a prosperous stock market and a fitting backdrop for the emergence of the optimistic cycle.

Back to the stock market, the optimistic period of the growth cycle peaked in 1966 and wavered for a few years. This led to an overoptimistic period in 1972, when institutions bought a group of growth stocks called the *nifty fifty* to the exclusion of all other stocks. These stocks routinely carried p/e ratios between 30 and 70, while the rest of the market languished. This two-tiered market signaled serious divergences by the broad market against the Dow. Such divergences are a classic benchmark of an overoptimistic phase which, in this case, spelled the demise of the 1942–1966 growth cycle.

In retrospect, the growth cycle peaked in 1966, but became drenched in overoptimism in 1972, and did not begin its decline phase until 1973, when the nifty fifty stocks peaked and the Dow began a brutal plunge. To consider 1974 as the bottom would not make sense, since that would mean a 24-year bull market would spend just 2 years in a decline phase before the next (optimistic) cycle began.

In fact, the 1974 bottom coincided with the emergence of OPEC, which ushered in a vicious inflationary cycle. Inflation is the friend of real assets, not financial assets. Money flowed out of stocks into tax shelters and a new speculative instrument—the home. The peak of inflationary assets like oil, gold, and real estate in 1980 logically preceded the beginning of a new disinflationary cycle that beckoned for financial assets in 1982. By the same logic, the inflationary cycle peaked in 1980, leading one to believe the succeeding disinflationary cycle would last for several years, pushing financial assets into a long-term bull market.

On a cyclical basis, the 16-year correction of a 24-year advance was perfectly acceptable, since it was within the one-third to two-thirds (exactly two-thirds) generalized limits for a correction. Small stocks performed well, but the bulk of the United States' value in stock, particularly adjusted for inflation, did poorly from 1974 through 1982, making 1974 an unlikely bottom.

By the time the 1966–1982 correction was over, a malaise would so engulf Wall Street that *BusinessWeek* magazine printed a front cover that read "The Death of Equities." If the handwriting was not on the wall, at least it was on the front cover of *BusinessWeek*. Overpessimism was driven deep into the soul of the stock market, creating a depressionlike atmosphere that is so essential to major bear market bottoms.

In conclusion, even though it is obvious that the market made price improvement during the 1974–1982 years, the new upward cycle appears to have started in 1982. The intuitive arguments are too compelling to argue otherwise.

Economically, it would be illogical to begin a new long-term cycle in 1974 with the worst possible environment (high inflation) for financial assets, especially since the 1980s provided the perfect mix of low inflation and low interest rates. Sociologically, money was considered an evil in the 1970s, becoming a panacea in the 1980s. This makes sense according to our behavioral model as well. As this would be the stage of optimism (following reconstruction 1932–1937 and growth 1942–1966), the last upward cycle should begin with relatively good circumstances, so that optimism can build quickly.

SETTING UP THE EXPLOSION

The period from 1966–1982 was an ideal time for real assets, and consequently, a terrible time for financial assets. Inflation was high, leading to booms in real estate and gold. The rise in inflation caused interest rates to rise, lowering the value of stocks. In the 1950s and 1960s, Americans were proud to invest in the stock market; by the 1970s, the stock market was regarded as an archaic form of investment.

As the 1970s came to a close, the future of the stock market did not appear promising. Interest rates were in the midst of a three-year uptrend that began in early 1977. Inflation was running at very high levels without an end in sight. Continuous pressure from OPEC pushed estimates of future oil prices up to $70 a barrel, $100 by some accounts, double and triple the already new high of $35. Given this scenario, high inflation seemed to have reserved itself a permanent place in the economy.

On the strength of rampant inflation, gold was on one of the greatest speculative binges in market history, completing an over-optimistic cycle of its own. In May 1979, gold was only $250 an ounce. By the end of 1979, gold had broken the $500 level and seemed destined for $1,000 an ounce. The future of high inflation and real assets seemed secure at the expense of financial assets like the bond and stock markets.

ENTERING THE 1980s

The 1980s began with more bad news. Gold continued to soar on the strength of runaway oil prices. By January 1980, gold reached $850, completing a rise from $103.50 in August 1976. To combat inflation, the decision was made to raise interest rates, in the hopes that eventually the high rates would choke off the rise in prices. It would be a painful experiment, but the unprecedented rise in interest rates in 1980 would prove successful, ushering in a new era of low inflation to the U.S. economy.

Between February 19 and April 2, the prime rate was raised by half-point increments every single week, sometimes twice in one week. The inexorable climb to 20% saw the prime increased a total of 4% in two months. The inevitable crowd of gloom and doomers talked of 25% rates. They argued that the recent era of low interest rates was a historical aberration. The future was foreseen as a continuation of high interest rates, well into the double digits at even their low points.

Gold peaked in January 1980 at $850 an ounce, falling to $500 an ounce by April. But the uptrend was not quite finished. Gold would make one last rush to the $700 level by September 1980, bolstered by soaring oil prices. The stock market responded by pushing up the prices of oil and gold stocks by as much as four- and fivefold in a matter of six months in one of the greatest speculative rampages in stock market history.

Rising interest rates choked off the rally, with the prime rate grabbing daily newspaper headlines in its rise to levels even higher than the "unthinkable" 20% of early 1980. By the end of 1980, the prime rose to 21½%, as the Federal Reserve did its best to strangle the last vestiges of inflation. This extreme cyclical point in interest rates set the stage for one of the greatest stock market rallies of all time. Over the next couple of years, rates would weave their way lower, eventually creating an extremely undervalued stock market environment relative to competing interest rates.

APPLYING THE MARKET TIMING FRAMEWORK: AUGUST 6, 1982

To get a better feel for market analysis, let us first go through the market timing framework suggested in Chapter 5 and answer each question for Friday, August 6, 1982, less than two weeks before the upside explosion on August 17.

1. Where Is the Market Now?

The Dow Jones Industrial Average had built a series of bottoms between 750 and 800 from 1975 through June 1982. Although this formed excellent support, the mood of the market was so negative that it was widely feared that the Dow might crash through the 750 level and reach 600, perhaps even 400. The Dow closed at 784.34 on August 6, breaking through short-term supports to reach the lowest mark of the year, but still above the 750 long-term support (see Figure 9-2).

The S&P 500 had good support in the 100–110 range, but the 103.71 close on August 6 brought the S&P to a new low for the year, crashing below the crucial 105 support and heading toward the 100 level. Like the resistance of 1000 on the Dow, the round number of 100 on the S&P was as much a benchmark of psychological importance as one of technical support. The NYSE Composite had long-term support at 57-60 and closed the day below 60 for the first time in 2 years at 59.69, but still at good support.

Although the short term looked bleak and support levels were being broken with casual disregard, longer-term support levels were all in place for the market averages. Several years of support had been built and successfully tested so far without any breaks in the foundation. This underscores the importance of taking a

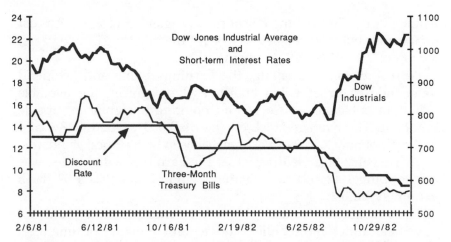

Figure 9-2. The Dow Jones Industrial Average is shown with the rates on three-month Treasury bills and the discount rate. The August 1982 bull market was sparked by lower interest rates, as evidenced by the bullish condition of Treasury bill rates dipping below the discount rate.

long-term perspective to the stock market. Without it, you are very likely to get caught up in the trees and miss the overall significance of the market's message. This time, the message was: although the popular short-term support levels had been broken, the longer, more important support levels were still intact.

2. Is the Market Overvalued or Undervalued?

In 1980 and 1981, the Federal Reserve had used interest rates very effectively to choke off inflation. Now they would use rates to rescue the economy from one of the worst recessions since the Depression. Rates edged up through late June, but now the Fed was letting the reins go, setting monetary policy on an accommodative swing for years to come.

On July 9, the Federal funds rate was 14.47%. Two weeks later, by July 20, the funds rate neared 12% and Treasury bills fell more than a half-point below the discount rate for the first time in seven months. The Fed lowered the discount rate a half-point to 11.5%, the first discount rate cut in nine months. Two weeks later, on

August 2, the Fed cut the discount rate again to 11%. By August 6, Treasury bill rates fell below 10% for the first time in two years, a drop of more than 4% in six months.

With interest rates falling, the Earnings Value and Dividend Value indexes turned wildly bullish, each recognizing the favorable valuation imbalance in stocks and pointing to significant upside potential. The average stock on the S&P 500 yielded 6.48% and had a p/e of only 7.16, both extremely cheap by historical standards. With Treasury bills yielding 9.8%, the Earnings Value Index was a whopping 1.42 and the Dividend Value Index was 1.32, both extremely bullish.

The interest rate and stock market value situation could not have been much more bullish. It was only a matter of time until money poured into the stock market, pushing stock prices into a more rational balance of value. In truth, since earnings had not really increased since 1979, the decline in interest rates accounted for the entire 1,200 point gain in the Dow from 1982 to 1986. By the end of 1986, Treasury bills were about 5.5%, popularizing the stock market as the "only game in town," because inflation was too weak to propel gold and real estate prices, rates were too low to draw income investors, and aggressive tax shelters were effectively legislated out of existence by the Tax Reform Act of 1986.

On a book value basis, the book value for the Dow at the beginning of 1982 was 975.59. With the Dow closing at 784.34 on August 6th, the Dow was selling for only 80% of book value, even lower than the 84% registered at the bottom of the 1974 bear market at 577.60 and lower than at any period in post-World War II history. Since stocks are a bargain when the Dow sells for less than book value, a level 20% below represents extreme undervaluation. In conclusion, it would be difficult to find a time since the 1929 Depression when the stock market was more undervalued than it was before the beginning of the 1982 bull market.

3. What Is the Direction of the Long-Term Trend?

Over the past 16 months, the trend was clearly bearish, with a series of lower highs and lower lows dotting the charts. But from a very long-term investment perspective, the trend seemed to have minimal downside risk. The Dow was at 784, with superb long-term support in the 750–800 range, well above the 577 low of 1974 (see Figure 9-3). The S&P 500, 103 at the time, was in a clearer long-term uptrend, building a series of higher lows since the 1974 bottom, with excellent support at 90 and 100.

While the financial media were bemoaning the death of equities, the long-term value investor was thrilled to take advantage of excellent buying opportunities near long-term support. This is the value of studying stock market history and understanding where the market currently is within a long-term cyclical perspective. As any novice chartist could recognize, the Dow had formed a very long-term cyclical bottom. The fact that the various levels of support and resistance were several years apart only increased their importance, because they had proven themselves over an extended period of time.

From a cyclical viewpoint, in recent years, the market had reached important bottoms every four years like clockwork: 1962, 1966, 1970, 1974, and 1978. Obviously, the possibility of a bottom in 1982 made a lot of sense. Moreover, the long-term cycle of strong inflation and high interest rates seemed to be broken, raising the possibility that money would be diverted from real assets to financial assets to begin a new long-term cycle of low inflation. Cyclically, particularly with the break in inflation, the long-term trend could not have been better positioned.

In conclusion, although the near-term action appeared dangerous, the long-term trend was shaping up nicely. The popular averages depicting major stocks, like the Dow and S&P 500, were falling sharply, but were at excellent long-term support. Market averages portraying smaller stocks, like the Value Line average, were in strong uptrends, providing a positive long-term divergence for stock prices. The presence of such superb long-term support, the expected bottom of the four-year cycle, and potential new cycles in inflation and interest rates, coupled with extreme fundamental undervaluations, minimized the potential downside risk and made the August 6 point in the long-term trend an excellent time for investment.

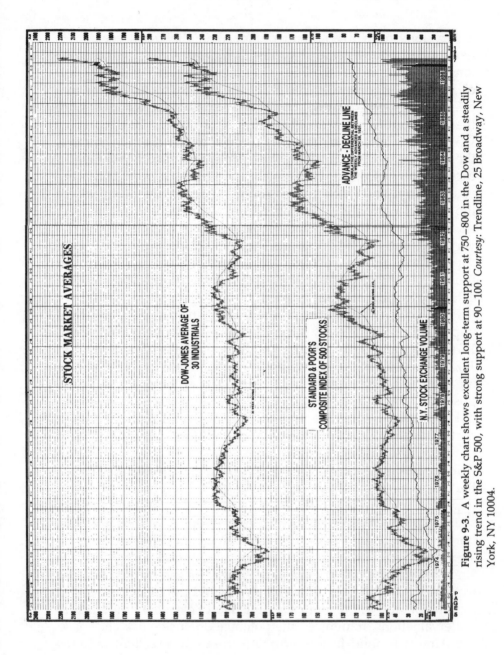

Figure 9-3. A weekly chart shows excellent long-term support at 750–800 in the Dow and a steadily rising trend in the S&P 500, with strong support at 90–100. *Courtesy:* Trendline, 25 Broadway, New York, NY 10004.

242

4. Is the Trend Healthy (Confirmation) or Deteriorating (Divergence)?

The market averages were clearly bearish, all falling to new lows to confirm the sixteen-month downtrend. The Dow Jones Transportation Average broke below its important support at 300, proving bearish confirmation of the Dow Theory. The Dow Jones Utility Average was also bearish, but held above support at 101 set in September 1981. To round out the averages, the New York Financial Index was also bearish, falling to its lowest levels since April 1980.

The advance/decline line was very weak, falling to its lowest levels in quite a few years on a daily basis. Since September 1980, the a/d line had shown a steady downtrend—a cyclically pertinent fact—since it marked two years of downward movement, about half of the ordinary four-year cycle. On a weekly basis, the advance/decline line was entirely different. The weekly line was near the support levels set up in September 1981 and March 1982, while still well above the April 1980 bottom. In conclusion, the weekly picture showed a positive divergence, but the daily picture was still a bit too ominous to be ignored. The diverging advance/decline shows a basic stock market truism:

The short-term is often a confusing influence compared to the more reliable long-term picture.

New highs were virtually nonexistent over the past 2 weeks, averaging about 10 per day over a 10-day period to confirm the bearish trend over the past 16 months. Despite the weak performance, this was still a bit of an improvement over recent months. Furthermore, just one month before, new highs had jumped impressively on a minor rally. Finally, it was encouraging that new lows were in the process of forming their third successive lower peak since September 1981. Overall, the worst seemed to be over for new highs, particularly with fewer new lows being recorded on each new plunge.

Margin debt, one of the slowest indicators to react to changes in trend, dutifully confirmed the downtrend in effect since it topped in July 1981, with the Dow in the 960 trading area. In retrospect, margin debt would actually fall again in September, rise meekly in October, and finally break into a new uptrend by November after the market had already advanced by more than 25%. Margin debt should be used only for long-term confirmation. Once the trend of margin debt flattens out, it is a warning of a possible change in market direction. When the trend in margin debt actually changes, it is confirmation that the market is likely to continue in that direction for several months or more.

In conclusion, the downtrend was well confirmed by the majority of indicators, but the stability in the weekly advance/decline line, the firming of new highs, and the slumping amount of stocks reaching new lows suggested that a turnaround was possible. Nevertheless, based on overall evidence, there were not enough divergences to warrant any belief that the downside market structure was ready to give way in favor of a new uptrend. If there was to be any technical rationale for a new bull market, it would have to come from the oversold indicators.

5. If Healthy, Is the Trend Overbought or Oversold?

Mutual fund cash was deeply oversold, with cash levels nearing 12%, the highest level since the April 1980 rally. This meant that the mighty institutions were overflowing with investible cash itching to find a home. Given the sharp decline in interest rates, it could be assumed that a fair portion of that 12% would find its way into the stock market. If it did, the market would receive a tremendous inflow of buying demand that would soak up available supplies of stock rather quickly and force stock prices higher.

Advisor sentiment was extremely bearish. On June 11, 1982, the percentage of bearish advisors as measured by Investor's Intelligence was a whopping 57.6%, the highest since just before the September 1981 bottom. Market bottoms are usually reached when the percentage tops 50%, so this certainly qualified as an oversold condition. The July rally brought the number of bears down to 41% by August 5, but since it was so close to the mid-June oversold condition, the signal was still in effect. Just before the bull market began two weeks later, the number of bears rose back above the 50% level to 53.9%.

Insider selling was very light, which is indicative of an oversold condition. In fact, an eight-week average of the Insider Sales/

Purchase Ratio fell below 1.0 in April, an extremely low reading. By August 6, the ratio was still oversold below 1.5. Finally, secondary distributions were very low, averaging about one per week, a very oversold pace. Both suggested the belief by corporate managements that their stocks were driven down to levels where they were no longer attractive candidates for further sales—essentially, the fundamental definition of the technical oversold term.

In conclusion, the stock market was very oversold, setting off every possible buy signal. This observation, coupled with the overwhelming evidence from market support levels, undervaluation, and cyclical positioning, made the stock market a phenomenal buy on August 6, 1982. True, there was plenty of fear running through the market, but this was really a terrific psychological positive and the long-term value investor would be comforted by the minimal downside risk posed by this cadre of indicators.

THE STOCK MARKET TAKES OFF

Ten days later, on August 16, the Federal Reserve dropped the discount rate another half-point to 10½ percent, its third such drop in five weeks. The banks followed suit throughout the rate declines, and dropped their prime rate to 14½% on the 16th as well. On August 16, the Dow closed up four points to 792, after having broken 800 to the upside earlier that day.

The next day (August 17) made market history, with the Dow soaring 39 points (about a 5% gain) on volume that was nearly twice that of the previous month's average. On the 18th, volume swelled to 132 million, about three times the average volume of recent months. Within a month, the Dow soared 180 points on an intra-day basis, a gain of about 23%, touching 950. By November 3, the Dow broke its all-time record, closing at 1065.

The stock market was well on its way to one of the greatest rallies of all time. From this explanation, the building process of a major bull market should seem quite logical. Additionally, one should recognize how neatly the fundamental, technical, and interest rate factors fit into the system of cyclical benchmarks. An extreme fundamental undervaluation caused by a cyclical decline in inflation and interest rates set up a technically supported and oversold market for a new long-term cycle. The stage was set for two years of uninterrupted declines in rates and an advance in the stock market that pushed the Dow over 2400 by April 1987.

Major bull markets tend to carry almost every stock higher, with clusters of industry groups rotating in and out of leadership. Even former laggards come to life to take their day in the sun. One group, the food industry, one of the most boring of all stock industries in the 1970s, came to life as one of the most glamorous takeover plays of the entire bull market.

Did something happen to transform the food industry from laggard to larger-than-life status, or was it just a matter of recognizing good value? Since stocks tend to move together in industry groups, if we can understand what makes one group of stocks one of the finest performers in the 1982 bull market, we then have a blueprint for finding leaders in other bull markets. Moreover, by examining a food stock that led the group and a food stock that lagged behind the group, we can better differentiate between attributes that make winning stocks.

FOOD STOCKS—GLAMOUR GROUP OR GOOD VALUE?

The food processing industry is normally a prime beneficiary of low inflation. When commodity prices are high, raw materials for food processors are more expensive, raising costs and reducing profit margins. With low inflation, raw materials are cheap, and the food companies expand their profit margins by maintaining their pricing structure. Prosperous times also help the industry by raising the level of consumer spending.

Additionally, in the 1980s, a new sentiment grew among consumers regarding food quality. When it came to their stomachs, price became less of a concern than quality, boosting sales of high-priced (and high-profit-margined-) prepared dinners for the growing ranks of busy young professionals. Finally, the fitness revolution contributed by ushering in droves of "healthy" and diet-prepared foods in the grocery stores. Let us take a closer look at the food industry phenomenon of the 1980s by examining a winner, H. J. Heinz, and a relative loser, Archer Daniels Midland.

A WINNER: H. J. HEINZ

During the 1970s, Heinz had been one of the sleepier stocks on the NYSE. Adjusted for splits, Heinz rose from a 1971 high of 5.4 to a high of 7.8 in 1980, a gain of just 44% over a 10-year period. Heinz was a good company, but despite its very well-known products, the value of its stock was not recognized by Wall Street. Perhaps the move to lower inflation grabbed the attention of the market, but to the value investor, Heinz would have been a wonderful long-term investment well before the break in inflation (see Figure 9-4).

In 1971, Heinz commanded a p/e ratio above 17, earning 31 cents a share on $8.52 sales per share. Ten years later, in 1980, Heinz was earning $1.21 on sales of $25.58. The stock price had barely moved, yet Heinz had quadrupled its earnings and tripled its sales in just 10 years. Dividends had also been raised fourfold. At its low that year, the p/e ratio was 4.8, a one-third discount from the rest of the stock market at the time. The stock was selling at a market price of just 23 cents per dollar of sales, yet the operating margin was an impressive 11%.

Let us review how undevalued Heinz really was. In 1980, at a price of 6, the Return Value Ratio (RVR) equaled a whopping 3.79:

$$\frac{15.2 \text{ return on capital } + [6.67 \text{ dividend yield } \times (.54 \text{ after tax})]}{4.96 \text{ p/e ratio}} = 3.79 \text{ RVR}$$

The book value was 6.88, so the stock was trading at just 85% of book value. Sales and earnings had risen every year for the entire decade, and yet the stock traded at a 15% discount to the price earnings ratio of the average stock. Dividends were raised nearly every year in the 1970s too. Long-term debt was less than 20% of total capital.

Taking plant and equipment at about 25% of their stated values, the stock was trading just barely above the company's estimated liquidation value. Cash flow was strong, with 30 cents of free cash flow (after dividends and capital spending). The stock was trading at only 3.7 times cash flow and 20 times free cash flow.

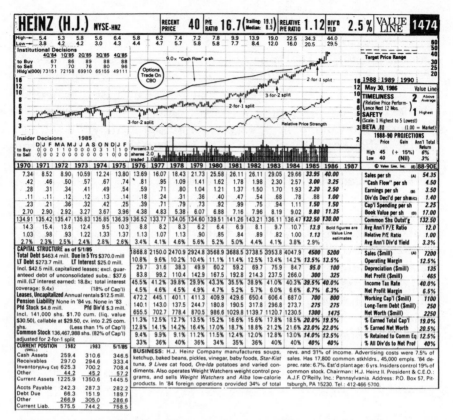

Figure 9-4. A Value Line evaluation of H. J. Heinz on May 30, 1986, offering the benefit of hindsight to the factors behind its powerful advance. *Courtesy*: Value Line, 711 Third Avenue, New York, NY 10017.

With such a phenomenal growth record, it was just a matter of time until the market recognized how undervalued the stock was. Heinz began climbing in earnest in 1981, rising to a split-adjusted 48 in July 1986. The investor who paid $7,200 for 100 shares of Heinz at 72 (6 after splits) in 1980, would have 1,200 shares at 48 worth $57,600 in 1986, an eightfold increase in seven years. The dividend yield on the original $6 split-adjusted share price would be over 16%, making it a good investment for growth and income investors alike.

It would not be difficult to find other stocks that gained as much, or even more, in the 1980 to 1986 period. But this is not the point of the Heinz example. Heinz was a quality company that was ignored by the marketplace. Most investors ignore companies in unfashionable industries, fearing they will never be rewarded.

But the long-term value investor understands that eventually a bull market will produce a catalyst to bring the value discrepancy into the spotlight, leading to worthwhile gains in share prices.

Naturally, it would be a rare event to buy a stock just before it took off. Let us say an investor bought Heinz at 6 in 1978, right near its 1977 high. The stock was somewhat undervalued then, but he would have to wait for three years before seeing any real increase in price. During that time, the stock would become even more undervalued and it would have been very frustrating to hold, since it remained in a tight range for all three years.

But the investor would have enjoyed a substantial dividend yield that rose from 5% to 7% during that period, making the wait a little easier. As long as Heinz remained a healthy company, which it did, it was an excellent investment and should have been held until it matured into a fully valued stock. This, of course, did happen, with the bull market recognizing the deeply undervalued situation, turning this common laggard into a courted leader.

A LOSER: ARCHER DANIELS MIDLAND

In 1980, while Heinz was dozing at a p/e of 5, Archer Daniels Midland flashed a p/e of 15, about twice the value of the average stock. If the food group had a glamour stock, Archer was it, as rising beef costs popularized Archer's huge soybean production as a viable food substitute. Soybeans would be blended into soyburgers, providing a cheaper and healthier food staple.

Perhaps even more exciting was the potential of turning Archer's vast corn resources into gasohol as an alternative to skyrocketing gasoline costs. Visions of gasohol replacing gas as the primary fuel of automobiles nearly quadrupled its stock price between 1978 and 1980. But although gasohol was indeed produced, dreams of Archer Daniels Midland replacing OPEC never materialized. Cars would still run on gas and corn would be relegated to its traditional purpose of feeding man and beast. Soyburgers proved to be a fad that fizzled soon after it was launched (see Figure 9-5).

In 1980, when Heinz sported a 3.79 RVR, Archer's was calculated as follows:

$$\frac{12.6 \text{ return on capital} + [0.5 \text{ dividend yield} \times (.54 \text{ after-tax})]}{15 \text{ p/e ratio}} = 0.86 \text{ RVR}$$

While Heinz seemed to be stuck in the same doldrums in which it had labored for the past decade, Archer appeared exciting, at least to the marketplace. Earnings had just doubled and capital spending was quadrupled to prepare for the unlimited future. The market rewarded Archer with a fully priced stock, valuing its prospects handsomely with an inflated p/e ratio. While Heinz was laboring with a p/e of 5, neglected by the market and therefore a superb investment value, Archer was one of the darlings of the stock market, fully priced and therefore a poor investment value.

Within a couple of years, the luster had worn off. New products flopped. Rising capital spending and debt starved the company. The market accepted its job of mercilessly punishing the stock price with its usual panache, driving the stock from a high of 15 in 1980 to a low of less than seven in 1982 (adjusted for splits), a decline of more than 50%.

The stock did not rise above the 15 level reached in 1980 until late in 1985, well after Heinz and its compatriots were doubling and tripling. By 1986, the stock reached a high of 21, showing just a 40% rise, a mere fraction of the 700% gain of the tortoiselike Heinz. Even though its industry group led the bull market, Archer was so overvalued in 1980 compared with the rest of the food stocks that it did not participate in the advance.

This comparison illustrates the importance of long-term investing in deeply undervalued stocks during bear markets to reap the eventual rewards of bull markets. In 1980, the only food stock

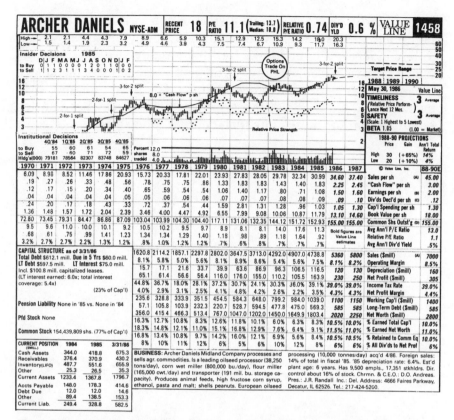

Figure 9-5. A Value Line evaluation of Archer Daniels Midland on May 30, 1986. *Courtesy*: Value Line, 711 Third Avenue, New York, NY 10017.

that looked interesting was Archer Daniels Midland. It had a glamorous "story", placing the stock on the recommended lists of many leading brokerage houses. Technicians loved the stock, especially when it rose above 9 to make a new high of 15. By the next year, Archer was trading below 8. Heinz, on the other hand, was largely ignored, but represented superior investment value, which would eventually be recognized in the forthcoming bull market.

Because investor perceptions are reflected in stock prices, by the time a stock becomes glamorous, it is often reasonably close to being fully valued. With limited upside potential, even in a favored industry group, such a stock is too vulnerable to disappointment and is fraught with risk that is rarely rewarded. Better to buy a deeply undervalued, but high-quality stock, like Heinz, which may be a sleeper now, but is bound to be recognized as a bull market develops and stock groups rotate into fashion. If held over the long term, undervalued quality stocks usually have upside potential that far outweighs their more popular peers.

10

Mutual Fund
Strategy

Mutual funds are a viable alternative to individual stocks for investors who do not have enough capital to diversify their portfolio effectively. It would not be wise to place a dollar limit on who should invest in mutual funds to the exclusion of stocks because it depends on your investment objectives. But as a general rule, investors who are trying to implement the techniques offered in this book should consider mutual funds to properly diversify if they have less than $50,000 in available investment capital.

WHY DIVERSIFY?

The purpose of diversification is to guard against the possibility that the poor performance of any component of a portfolio could overwhelm the performance of the entire portfolio. For instance, if your portfolio had three stocks, two that rose 25% and a third that fell 50%, the portfolio would show no overall gain. Instead, suppose you had 10 stocks, 9 of which gained an average of 10% and 1 that fell 50%; the overall portfolio would show a 4% gain. Even though the nine winners rose less than half as much as the two big gainers of the first portfolio, the overall portfolio did better because the risk was more effectively diversified.

Diversification is achieved by investing in a broad-based configuration of stocks so that a portfolio can show consistent gains despite a variety of changing market conditions. Owning a large list of stocks does not in itself diversify a portfolio. Since stocks within the same industry group tend to move together, a number of different industries should be represented in the portfolio. One step further: since industry groups tend to move together within the same sector, diversification among sectors is important too. For example, transportation stocks comprise one market sector. This sector consists of the air freight, airline, railroad, and trucking industries. If you held a portfolio of 20 railroad stocks, all of your risk would be concentrated in railroad companies, which would move together with the ups and downs of that single industry. Even if the stock market roared ahead in a bull market, with all of your eggs in one basket (or should I say one caboose), you would be taking the unnecessary risk that the portfolio would not participate in the advance.

The same problem, although to a lesser degree, would exist if you bought five stocks in each of the four industry groups (20 stocks in all) of the transportation sector. With just four industry groups represented, it is almost like owning four stocks. With all of them being members of the same sector, there is very little diversification of risk. The transportation sector might participate with the rest of the market, but you are taking a significant and unnecessary risk that the transportation sector may not participate with the rest of the market. Other examples of sectors would be: utility, financial, consumer, energy, high technology, industrial, cyclical (economically sensitive), and metal.

Investing in a mutual fund can reduce the diversification problem. A mutual fund represents a pool of money obtained from investors to be professionally managed. Since this is a stock market book, let us just deal with funds that are invested in the stock market. Most funds have several million dollars under management, allowing them to diversify among large numbers of stocks, industry groups, and sectors.

With a mutual fund that is not specialized in any particular area, an investor has minimized the risk of any single stock, industry group, or sector hurting the overall performance of the investment. Moreover, he can accomplish such impressive diversification, in most funds, with just a $1000 investment minimum. With $5000, he can achieve tremendous diversification by going into five different funds, thereby spreading the risk over five different money management styles.

The decision to diversify with mutual funds rather than through individual stocks is primarily a personal decision, but there are some sensible guidelines that can be of assistance. The amount of diversification recommended is dependent on the amount of capital in your portfolio. For minimum diversification, an investor should have at least three or four market sectors adequately represented in his portfolio at all times.

Let us look at some hypothetical numbers. If you wanted to hold down the commission costs incurred in building your portfolio, you would buy stock in 100-share round lots, rather than incur the extra costs of buying odd lots (less than 100 shares). If you have a minimum of two stocks in each of three market sectors (six stocks), and the average price of a stock you buy is $40, then with purchasing just round lots, the portfolio would cost at least $24,000, plus transaction costs. So, a marginally diversified portfolio of six stocks purchased in 100-share round lots would cost about $25,000.

With less than $25,000 of investment capital, it would be difficult to achieve even a minimum amount of diversification (unless the stocks were low priced) without incurring the heavy transaction costs of odd-lot trades. The $5,000 to $25,000 range of investment capital is perfect for mutual fund investments, although those in the $25,000 to $50,000 range should consider funds as well. Even with $50,000, an investor is just then achieving a fair amount of diversification with twelve 100-share round lots. Beyond $50,000, the investor has the choice entirely open to him whether he wishes to run the portfolio himself or turn over the stock management to a group of mutual funds.

THINGS YOU SHOULD KNOW ABOUT MUTUAL FUNDS

This is not a book about mutual funds, and we will not try to cover all of the nuances of the topic, but there are a few things investors should know about mutual funds that are not as widely known as they should be. It seems as if investors regard mutual funds as the "easy" investment and just buy a fund, without learning what a mutual fund is and some of the differences among them.

A mutual fund is an open-end investment company created to allow smaller investors to pool their investment dollars to form a fund that can benefit from professional portfolio management. Before mutual funds such management was exclusively reserved for the "rich and famous," but with the pooling of resources, small investors can hire the best management money can buy. Of course, one pertinent question to ask about mutual funds is how much money is it costing to buy a hired gun, a subject considered in the "load versus no-load question" discussion below.

The term open-end investment company refers to the practice by mutual funds of selling additional shares to the public after the initial offering is completed. These shares are actually common stock, complete with voting privileges, signifying your ownership of a piece of the investment company. As more investors buy the fund, more stock is issued. It should be noted that closed-end funds are investment companies that issue a fixed number of shares, which are later traded like common stock on the NYSE and other stock exchanges.

Mutual funds trade at their Net Asset Value (NAV), which is calculated by dividing the fund's net assets by the number of shares outstanding at the end of each trading day. Net assets, of course, include both investments and uninvested cash. The NAV is listed in newspapers as the bid price, which is the amount you would receive if you sold your shares. The offer price, the purchase price to enter the fund, depends on whether it is a load or no-load fund.

TO LOAD OR NOT TO LOAD

William Shakespeare probably never pondered this question, but plenty of his readers have, some without really understanding what a load is. Basically, a load is a sales charge, which is stated as a percentage of the net asset value. So, if the Funny Money Fund has a net asset value of $10.00, and there is an 8% load, the offer price would be $10.80; that is, you would have to pay $10.80 to purchase Funny Money. To sell it you would only receive the net asset value of $10.00. If the fund gained two cents of NAV on the day, this mutual fund would show up in the newspaper like this:

	NAV	Offer Price	NAV Change
Funny Money Fund	10.00	10.80	+.02

Honest Injun is a no-load fund, so the offer price is the same as the NAV because there is no sales charge to tack on. Therefore, it is usually listed in the papers with an NL designation under the offer price, signifying that it is a no-load fund.

	NAV	Offer Price	NAV Change
Honest Injun Fund	10.00	NL	+.02

While the names attached to the respective funds might connote that no-loads are more honorable than loads, this is really not the case. As we will discuss later, you have to weigh whether paying a large sales load is really worth it. Both types of funds generally charge similar amounts in management fees to cover the cost of running the fund. The load is a sales charge to either pay for marketing costs or to induce salesmen to hawk their product. While a low-load of 3% or less may have some justification, it is questionable whether any salesman can possibly be worth a more exorbitant charge.

The maximum sales charge allowed by the Investment Company Act of 1940 is 9%, but the National Association of Security Dealers (NASD) has effectively lowered this maximum to 8½% by its Rules of Fair Practice. Because both fund sponsors and sales brokers must be NASD members, the 8½% maximum is the highest sales charge you are likely to see. And since salesmen make their money from commissions, you are likely to see plenty of 8½% loads, along with varying rates of lower load funds.

There are other costs to consider. Some funds, both load and no-load alike, have redemption fees to deter frequent selling, usually less than 1%. These have become especially prevalent with the popularity of mutual fund switching, which is a strategy used by investors who switch back and forth between mutual and money market funds to manage their exposure to the stock market.

Other funds might have a deferred sales charge, which is a back-end load paid when you sell the fund. Some funds using deferred sales charges will offer a sliding scale, reducing the charge to zero after four to six years. It should be noted that both redemption fees and deferred sales charges can be assessed by no-load funds and still maintain their NL status in the newspapers. The NL designation is currently under debate and might become purified in the future, but until that time, it is very important to actually read each fund's prospectus to know whether the charges are being levied.

In 1980, mutual funds were granted the ability to draw cash on a regular basis (not just up front) from the investment pool to meet certain marketing expenses. This is called a 12b-1 fee, which by 1985, already about half of the total mutual funds (both load and no-load) had provisions for, although not all of these had been put into effect. Usually the 12b-1 fee is minimal, just about 0.25% of total assets, but some funds charge 1% or more. Sometimes the 12b-1 plan provision is not printed in a prominent place in the prospectus, or is listed as a "Distribution Plan." The most likely place to begin looking is in the section entitled "Per-Share Financial Information." If the expense ratio to net assets is much higher than 1% of total assets, chances are there is a 12b-1 fee being assessed.

The wide variety of ways that a mutual fund can charge the stockholder makes it imperative to go into these investments with a full awareness of the potential costs. Some mutual funds charge all of these fees—an 8.5% load up front, a 4% or more redemption fee, and a 1% or more 12b-1 fee assessed annually.

This type of abusive fee structure can be found occasionally in the mutual funds of brokerage houses to boost the sales incentives to their salespeople. If someone tries to sell you such a fund, turn the other way; they simply cannot have your best interests in mind, as it would be nearly impossible to do better with this investment than other well-run funds with more reasonable fees. Even a private account at a top investment counselor would rarely cost more than 2% of assets. Should a salesperson be worth appreciably more than that? If you have other investments with that brokerage house already, chances are that your poor investment performance already reflects their hunger for sales commissions at the expense of your well-being. Paying that much for the privilege of investing with them is entirely unnecessary, since there are plenty of quality funds that would be happy to invest your money for a more reasonable sum.

Few investors seem to be aware of another potential fee: the cost of reinvesting their dividends. Mutual funds give you the option of receiving your dividends in cash or reinvesting them into more shares of their fund. Most funds will reinvest your dividends at the net asset value, which is a good way to accumulate more shares. But some funds reinvest their shareholders' dividends at the offer price (NAV plus the load), plus an additional sales charge for each reinvestment. This is a very steep cost to pay for the privilege of reinvesting. If this reinvestment cost is in your fund, you can still keep the fund, but you should elect to take your dividends in cash.

Of course, all mutual funds, load and no-load alike, charge a management fee, usually less than 1%, to cover the costs of managing the fund. While you should be aware of how much the fund is charging for management, they have to earn their money somehow and costs of 1% or less are perfectly acceptable.

To sum up the potentially confusing cost structure, here are the most common ways that mutual funds charge their shareholders:

1. Load—up front, when purchased
2. Deferred Sales Charge—back-end, when sold
3. Redemption Fees—to discourage frequent selling

4. 12b-1 Fee—annual charge

5. Reinvestment fees—to reinvest dividends

MAKING THE LOADED DECISION

Long-term investors might not be too concerned with paying a reasonable load up front, like 3%, since they are likely to hold the fund for several years. In fact, an annual 12b-1 charge might be more distasteful to them, although in the future, it might become difficult to find a fund without an annual fee. Of course, if the 12b-1 charge is just 0.25%, I would not consider it a negative in the investment decision.

More aggressive investors will want to remain in no-load funds, to avoid being charged each time they buy or sell their funds. They will also want to be sure there are no redemption fees that would charge them additionally for frequent selling. If you are planning to buy and sell the same fund within the same year, the transaction costs of a loaded fund are bound to hinder your performance markedly. A no-load fund is just as likely to perform as well as a loaded fund, and your performance might be better because there will ordinarily be less fees subtracted from your piece of the pie.

The decision to buy a load or no-load fund should ultimately not depend on whether there is a load, but more on the type of fund, its management style, and its net performance. The past performance of a fund is a very important criterion for choosing a fund, although it certainly does not guarantee similar performance in the future. Given equal performance, the type and magnitude of the fee structure measured against the frequency of your buy-and-sell decisions can help determine whether you should forgo the loaded funds in favor of a no-load fund.

My personal preference is for no-load funds on the basis that a fund's good performance will create more sales than any other marketing effort. Therefore, if the fund is really terrific, it should be able to generate sufficient sales by simply being a good fund. If a fund needs to charge you extra fees to operate a major sales organization, maybe it is not the best fund available. With more than 1,000 funds to choose from, you can afford to be very selective.

TYPES OF STOCK FUNDS

There seems to be an endless array of mutual funds available, each tailored to a different segment of the investing public. There are funds to fit several different types of income investments, including municipal bonds, "Ginnie Maes," Treasury bonds, and money markets, among others. For the purpose of this book, let us just consider the various stock funds.

Stock funds are run according to the investment style of the fund manager and marketed to the desires of its public. For example, in the 1980s, the overseas markets became popular, which led to significant demand for funds that invested in foreign stock markets—the so-called international funds. Some funds concentrate in certain glamorous regions, like the Pacific Basin, or go even further to specialize in a certain country, like Japan or Korea.

The 1980s also saw the popularizing of funds that specialize in single industry groups. Fidelity Investments is the dominant leader of that movement, and now have a wide array of funds that invest solely in one industry. These specialty funds, whether international or industry group specific, allow ordinary investors to hire professional management in the exact segment of the market they wish to own. Rather than buy 100 shares of one computer stock for $5,000, they can buy a computer fund providing diversification and professional management for as little as $1,000.

Specialty funds give investors the ability to build their own portfolio of stock investments with minimum investment and maximum diversification. For the more experienced investor, a specialty fund can be an ideal vehicle. With a minimum amount of capital, you achieve phenomenal diversification and can choose the areas of the market that you most want to participate in.

For the less experienced investor who recognizes value in the market but has not done the homework necessary to pinpoint which industry groups contain that value, specialty funds are probably not appropriate. By targeting industry groups, you lose a measure of diversification, because stocks within the same industry group tend to move together. For the average investor, decisions regarding how to deploy the assets are probably best left to the professionals.

This leaves us with plenty of funds to choose from in the general stock fund category. Some of these will be very aggressively managed, seeking the highest possible return at the assumption of great risk. Others will be more conservatively managed, either aimed at value investment methods, long-proven companies, or stocks that provide a high yield. Between these general stock funds, there are plenty of choices available to make long-term value investing work admirably with mutual funds.

CHOOSING A FUND

Mutual funds should be chosen according to management style, fund objectives, and performance. The funds' prospectus will briefly discuss the management style of the fund, which should be amenable to your expectations and temperament. The funds' objectives (discussed in greater detail later in this chapter) can be one of the most crucial determinants of your investment's performance. For example, if you buy a gold fund during a period of low inflation, despite it being the best performing gold fund, will still probably fare much worse than an average performing stock fund.

Once you have an optimal mix of funds with suitable objectives and management styles, the decision largely depends on the track record of the fund manager. Although past performance is not a guarantee of future success, a long consistent record of superior performance is the best proxy you have at your disposal for choosing mutual funds among the same fund objective.

The most widely available guide to mutual fund performance is found in *Barron's*, with their "Quarterly Survey of Mutual-Fund Performance," which is based on information gathered by Lipper Analytical Services, Inc. Each quarterly issue lists the 25 best and worst performing funds over 5 different time periods: that quarter, through that year, 1 year, 5 years, and 10 years. It also lists the best performing fund for a wide variety of fund objectives, like growth or income and so on, for a number of different time periods.

The Barron's/Lipper survey also lists almost every fund in existence, giving a variety of information about each fund, including its performance through the year, over the past 12 months, and over 5 years. This should be enough information to lead most investors to a fund that meets his objectives for fund type and performance.

The problem with all of this quantitative hoopla is that, in 1987 at least, many mutual funds are so young that they have not been proven in difficult markets. A newer fund, beginning small, can get lucky and hit on a few big winners to juice up its performance. Some mutual fund companies begin several new funds just to get one that is doing well so they can use it as a drawing card in their promotional material. Of course, some of these new funds take risks and fall flat on their face, so investing in new funds is risky business. Eventually, over time, the startling performance of these high flyers normalizes to what the older funds are doing. Thus, picking a fund on the basis of a short performance record is not advised.

A solid five-year record is the minimum time that is recommended for evaluating a mutual fund. In this way, the fund will have gone through one complete market cycle of a bull and bear market. For a more reliable evaluation, a 10-year record is preferable. While this is certainly no guarantee that the fund will perform well in the future, it will at least show how they have fared through a wide variety of market conditions. Again, consistent performance is to be prized more than a one- or two-year flash in the pan.

MUTUAL FUND SWITCH STRATEGIES

Mutual funds are a wonderful source of diversification, but as we have seen, because each fund is managed according to its own set of objectives and management style, a single mutual fund does not provide as much diversification of risk as a portfolio of them. Since funds are inherently diversified, you do not have to own as many mutual funds as stocks to achieve sufficient diversification. In most cases, a grouping of four to six general stock funds is sufficient to meet most diversification objectives.

The management of a mutual fund portfolio should be handled just like that of a stock portfolio, switching from one fund to the next to meet portfolio objectives, much like the replacement of overvalued stocks with undervalued ones. Before you begin employing a switching strategy, make sure that the funds used do not have any loads, front or back, and do not have any redemption fees for frequent selling. If they do, the strategy is unlikely to prove profitable because of the switching costs involved.

Mutual funds may be more flexible than stocks for moving large amounts of capital, but they can only be sold at the price shown at the close of the day. Therefore, if you put your sell order in at 10 in the morning, you will still get the closing price of the day. Mutual funds are not short-term trading vehicles; the price on close and fee structure limits their ability to be traded like stocks.

Mutual fund switching has become one of the hottest words in the investment world today. In reading *Barron's*, one's head is turned by the variety of mutual fund newsletters offering some remarkable switch strategy that will keep you in the most advantageous position at all times. Nearly all of them are variations on two basic strategies, neither of which makes a lot of sense (or money) in the long term.

One of the new "breakthrough" methods is to always invest in the five best performing mutual funds over a certain period of time, usually six months or so. When 1 of those 5 falls far off the list, say below the top 20, you sell it and buy the new entrant in the top 5. This bit of cleverness usually puts you into the newest funds that are trying to attract money by taking unnecessary risks. It also favors funds that are heavily weighted in a certain industry to maximize the effects of those gains to the portfolio.

Since the market rotates leadership, just when such a fund might hit the top tier of performers, the uptrend of its hot stock group might be petering out. This results in an endless chasing of the tail, as you buy a fund just as its upside potential is minimized and its risk is maximized—the opposite of value investing. While the strategy looks appealing in multicolored glossy pages, like most marketing games it is a psychological trap with little investment justification.

The most common switching strategy is to buy mutual funds when you are bullish on the stock market and switch the capital into money market funds when you are bearish. This strategy can be worth pursuing from a long-term timing perspective so that your percentage of capital invested mirrors the amounts you would have invested in actual stocks. For example, if you felt the market was very close to being overvalued and that with individual stocks you would probably be 80% invested, maybe an 80% invested position in mutual funds makes sense.

But that is not what the endless stream of enticing advertisements suggest you do. Most strategies counsel you to switch frequently between being either 100% invested in the stock market or 100% in cash, requiring fairly definitive statements about an unpredictable animal. This aggressive strategy makes the assumption that someone is able to perfectly time the market on a short-term basis, a claim that many make, but no one (to my knowledge) has been able to prove consistently over long periods of time. An aggressive strategy of switching in and out of the market is a presumptuous act better left to one who is selling his advice than one who is trying to actually profit from his decisions.

A completely noninvested position makes sense only if the market is extremely overvalued from a long-term perspective, but this is a very rare occurrence.

Most investors, over the long haul, find that trying to time the market aggressively on a short-term basis is one of the greatest mistakes they can make.

Switching capital into money market funds is a good way to reduce exposure, but it should be done in the same way as with individual stocks—from a long-term perspective on the basis of value.

A FULLY INVESTED/RISK-ADJUSTED PORTFOLIO STRATEGY

Mutual funds can take advantage of the market timing framework discussed in Chapter 5 and still keep fully invested in the stock market. The easiest way to understand this strategy is to look at a mutual fund portfolio as a proxy for the stock market. Following this strategy, when the market is undervalued, there is less risk and greater upside potential. In those times, you should concentrate your holdings in more aggressive funds. When the market is overvalued, there is greater risk and less upside potential, so it makes sense to batten down the hatches with more conservative funds. In this way, you remain fully invested, but you have adjusted your risk by adjusting your portfolio's composition of fund objectives.

Let us go through an example, using the mutual fund designations found in the quarterly Barron's/Lipper guide. The four types of mutual funds that generally fit our investment objectives are:

1. *Capital Appreciation Fund (CA).* Aggressively seeking profits.
2. *Growth Fund (G).* Seeking long-term growth.
3. *Equity Income Fund (EI).* Normally more than 60% in stocks, with above average yield.
4. *Growth & Income Fund (GI).* Growth objective, with income secondary.

The Equity Income and Growth & Income funds are both oriented toward conservative growth of capital, but there is a difference between the two. The Equity Income funds often have a significant investment in bonds or money market instruments, while the Growth & Income funds are entirely in stocks without any investment in bonds.

The profile on the next page was constructed for a growth-oriented investor who wishes to participate in bull markets, but is trying to reduce exposure in bear markets. The reduction of exposure is accomplished by switching from Capital Appreciation funds to Equity-Income funds.

Despite the ambitious graphic presentations in the following figures, it is impossible to identify consistently the various stages of a bull market. But this is really the greatest advantage of the fully invested/risk-adjusted strategy: the cost of your errors is minimized. Whether you are close to being correct in your assessment of the cycles or not, at least you are fully invested in mutual funds that broadly suit your investment objectives (see Figure 10-1).

By using this strategy, the investor is remaining fully invested in the stock market at all times, except for the portion of the Equity-Income funds that may be invested in bonds. The two Growth and Growth & Income funds remain invested at all times because they are longer-term investments and are ordinarily structured to lessen exposure during bear markets. In addition, the

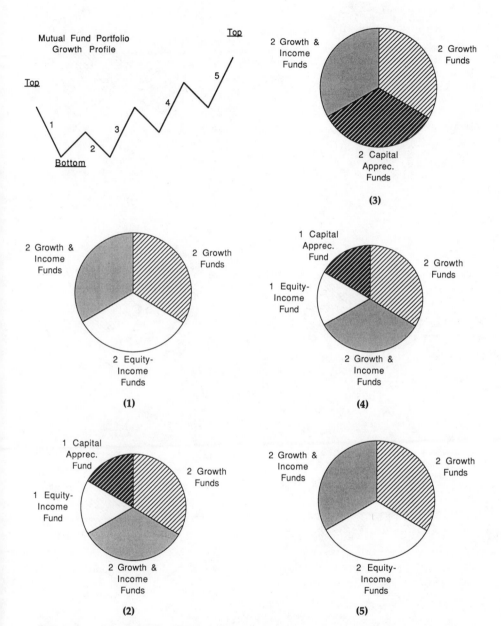

Figure 10-1. Growth profile: The growth investor seeks long-term growth, but reasonable protection when stocks appear fully priced. By using cyclical benchmarks to identify points in the behavioral cycle, an investor can rotate among mutual funds to increase or decrease participation in the market.

267

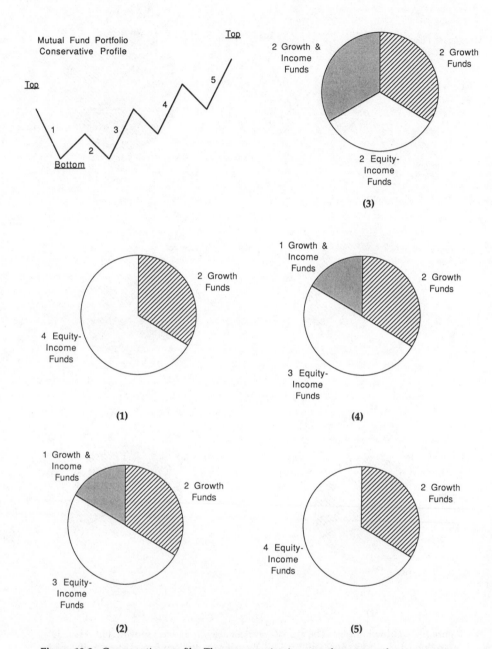

Figure 10-2. Conservative profile: The conservative investor focuses on the preservation of capital with a return on investment, but may do so at the expense of not maximizing the appreciation potential of his assets.

268

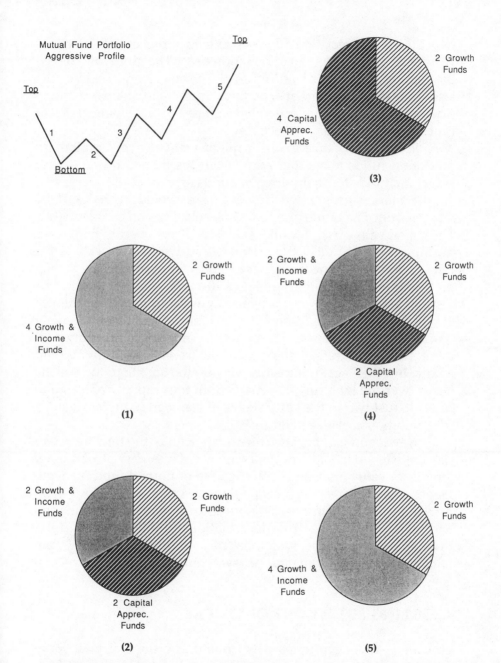

Figure 10-3. Aggressive profile: The aggressive investor seeks to maximize capital appreciation, but does so at somewhat greater risk.

two capital appreciation funds swing to more conservative investments as the risk of overvaluation rises. The more fully priced the market becomes according to the progression of value, the less aggressive the market exposure. You would still have downside risk, but it may be somewhat reduced by switching styles of fund management and objectives.

A more conservative investor might want to avoid capital appreciation funds altogether and switch his money from Growth & Income funds to Equity-Income funds as market risk increased. As the market progressed in value, risk would be reduced by moving from stocks into ordinarily less-volatile income investments. The conservative investor might do as well as the growth investor during a bull market if the advance is driven by lower interest rates, because his income investments will ordinarily be strong participants in the rally (see Figure 10-2).

More aggressive investors generally want to maximize the use of bull markets by shedding Growth & Income funds and moving quickly into capital appreciation funds. Still, this is probably a far more subdued strategy than many aggressive investors would follow. But then again, investors who are too ambitious are usually losers over the long run. The move from four capital appreciation funds to just two in the latter stages is designed to protect against that ambitiousness (see Figure 10-3).

However you want to structure the portfolio, the fully invested/ risk-adjusted portfolio combines many of the best attributes of long-term value investing with the ease of mutual fund management. It recognizes the progression of value in the long-term market cycle, reducing risk at periods of potential overvaluation and taking advantage of undervaluation. All of these long-term value objectives can be accomplished without the risk of missing rallies attendant to conventional switching strategies.

PULLING MONEY OUT OF STOCKS

Of course, there are times when pulling portions of your long-term mutual fund portfolio out of the stock market can be justified. The exemplary case is when the stock market is clearly overvalued compared to competing investments and interest rates are soaring. The most recent example of this was in 1981, when a sharp rise in interest rates sent the Earnings Value Index (Figure 4-2) and the Dividend Value Index (Figure 4-3) plunging to extremely bearish readings while money market funds offered yields near 20%.

But even in 1981, which featured an extraordinary rise in rates, there was no reason to make a knee-jerk decision to convert all of your stock to money market funds. Stocks were still extremely undervalued compared to book values (Figure 5-2). Once the valuations swung back to favor the stock market, it was crucial to reinvest the assets within a matter of weeks or you would have missed out on a meaningful amount of the bull market.

In light of the speed with which the market corrects value imbalances, the decision to remove money from an invested position and place it into cash-equivalents should be given careful consideration. As seen in Chapter 12, over the long term, rash movements of mutual fund investments in and out of stock funds are likely to be counterproductive and hinder overall performance. In conclusion, unless the stock market is terribly overvalued with respect to all of your measures of value and interest rates are overwhelmingly attractive, it is wise from a long-term perspective to retain at least a 50% position in stock mutual funds.

11

Portfolio Strategy

If this book has been successful, every idea mentioned in this chapter should seem a logical extension of what has already been written. We have discussed a wide range of topics that focus on determining value, spanning the spectrum from stock selection to market timing. The goal of this chapter is to integrate these concepts into a realistic and successful portfolio strategy.

Let us first examine a strategy that you can successfully implement with minimal skill and effort. To offer you greater assurance of its utility, I performed a computerized simulation of the strategy over a 10-year period. Specifically, the simulation applied the Return Value Ratio (RVR) to the 30 stocks of the Dow Jones Industrial Average from January 1, 1977 to September 12, 1986. The results were superb, tripling the gain in the Dow, even though only Dow stocks were used. Equally impressive was the near doubling of the S&P 500 during the same time period, while still using just the 30 Dow stocks (see Figure 11.1).

Of course, a computerized simulation is not an accurate test of how well an investor or a particular investment strategy would do in real-life conditions. Frailties of the human decisionmaker and changes in the investment environment usually dilute the

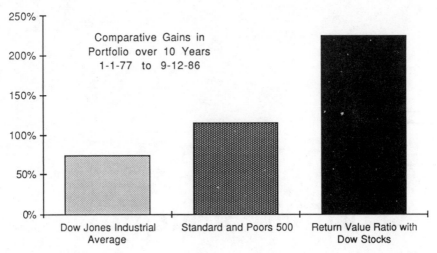

Figure 11-1. Comparative gains in portfolio over 10 years (January 1, 1977–September 12, 1986).

performance of any simulation. However, while the impressive magnitude of the gains might not be duplicated in real life, the simulation did give a fair indication that this value investment strategy makes sense.

For added assurance, other simulations of the RVR have proven equally impressive. These fully computerized tests were done to prove statistical validity, not to show optimal portfolio performance. Nonetheless, a fully invested portfolio of the best-valued RVR stocks performed more than twice as well as a buy-and-hold strategy, and the best-valued RVR stocks outperformed the worst-valued RVR stocks by an incredible 5:1 margin. But since there was no element of human decisionmaking whatsoever, these tests are of little instructive value to this book and will not be discussed any further. Instead, let us take a close look at the 10-year simulation mentioned previously to make use of the several valuable lessons that the exercise had to offer.

The 10-year simulation of the RVR was indeed an exercise, with all of the tedium of a monotoned aerobics instructor. All of the decisionmaking occurred before the simulation began. Once the guidelines were set, the simulation progressed forward in a mechanical fashion without any further human input. Predetermined buy- and sell-points based on the RVR were executed with computerized precision. Even the amount of money invested into each stock was apportioned on a mechanical basis.

Carrying out the dictates of the simulation was frustrating, as I was forced to execute its strict parameters despite a nagging temptation to adjust them to better fit the conditions. The outcome strongly suggested that a consistently implemented logical approach would yield excellent results over the long term. Unfortunately, to be faithful to a logical approach, you have to have one. Hence the first lesson: the need to create a comprehensive plan of investment.

Once the plan was drawn and put into action, three more basic lessons became overwhelmingly clear. All told, the four lessons that emerged were:

1. Write down and implement a formalized portfolio strategy.
2. Buy stocks with consistently superior operating performance.
3. Buy undervalued stocks. Only sell when they become overvalued.
4. Long holding periods are necessary for consistent success.

Let us consider these lessons one by one.

1. *Write Down and Implement a Formalized Portfolio Strategy*. Few investors have a formalized investment strategy and a method of implementation. Most people buy a stock here and there, either on the impulse of a tip or because they have a few spare dollars. Many investors sell stocks only after fears of a decline manage to raise the anxiety level beyond comfortable bounds. Such patchwork methods lead to inconsistent portfolio performance, missing out on buying opportunities as well as opportunities to reap profits.

Before beginning a program of investment, design a portfolio strategy. Write it down. This may sound like busywork, but physically writing down the strategy forces you to place your thoughts into concrete terms. Many investors will be surprised to see gaping holes in their plan, which can be refined after more thought and actual experience.

Designing a portfolio strategy for the simulation was very difficult. Because the simulation was entirely mechanical, the plan needed to cover all possible situations and yet be extremely simple to implement. To give you ideas for the creation of your own plan, listed below are the seven rules I used in this simulation.

1. Every stock selected must be in the Dow Jones Industrial Average.

2. The company must have earned at least a 10% return on capital over the past five years.

3. Buy a 4% position (7% in the early years) with a RVR of 1.75.

4. Buy an additional 3% with a RVR of 2.25.

5. Sell 4% with a RVR of 1.1.

6. Sell the remaining 3% with a RVR of 0.90.

7. Interest earned on the remaining cash balance is apportioned equally for future purchases among the uninvested available stocks.

One Crucial Caveat: The stock market is always changing its parameters for success. Much of these changes are due to changes in interest rates. The parameters were listed only to show that to be consistently profitable, the RVR to buy would have to be much lower than the level to sell. Investors who wish to use the RVR in their portfolio strategy may have to adjust the levels to better fit their investment objectives and the changing conditions of the marketplace.

2. *Buy Stocks with Consistently Superior Operating Performance.* The simulation's rules allowed investment only in the 30 stocks of the Dow Jones Industrial Average. For the time period of 1977–1986, this limited the choices to a mediocre group at best. Many of the stocks were stodgy companies in outdated industries. Companies like Manville Corp., International Harvester (Navistar), and U.S. Steel (USX Corp.) had long lost much of the blue in their chips and were struggling to stay in business.

This was such a weak group of stocks that more than half of the companies did not qualify for the simulation because they could not sustain a rate of 10% earned on capital for five years. At first, the lack of available stocks was a great concern, leading me to question whether 10% was too stringent. This became particularly troublesome when I realized that the portfolio was only 31% invested by the end of 1977, the first year.

In retrospect, this helped the simulation, because early 1977 marked the top for most Dow stocks. The simulation was limited by a one-time investment of funds, so it was advantageous not to be fully invested at times, like in 1977, because it meant that a cash reserve could be deployed in the future to buy stocks when they finally became undervalued.

For most investors, however, this is not the case, since periodically, they have new funds to add to their portfolio. Periodic cash inflows add the needed flexibility to maintain a greater investment in the market. As will be discussed later in this chapter, the cost of not being fully invested can be very high, because market moves occur too quickly for most investors to react. Therefore, always temper your enthusiasm regarding market timing with a dose of realism, for it can be an unpleasant, double-edged sword that can leave you out of potentially profitable market action.

Maintaining the strict return on capital qualifications teaches another good lesson. There are more than 7,000 stocks listed on the various exchanges. The maximum number of stocks needed in most individual investor's portfolios is about 25, apportioning 4% to each stock. Even a large investor might have only 50 stocks, fewer than 1% of the stocks listed in the newspaper. In this case, the other 6,950 stocks (99%) are either not suitable for purchase or will not be purchased because they simply are not needed for diversification purposes.

For most investors, 25 stocks is adequate diversification, so a list of about 100 stocks to choose from lets you select the best 25% of your universe. Even though 100 sounds like a lot, it is still fewer than 2% of the available listed stocks. By considering just the companies that meet your criteria and ignoring the other 98% of the stocks, you are likely to be better informed in your investment decisions and avoid foolish mistakes.

Remain Faithful to Your Strategy

With the abundant number of stocks available, an investor should consider only companies with consistently superior performance. Too many investors buy risky stocks with a "story." Sometimes that means a turnaround situation or a developmental company with no earnings.

Whatever the case, the added risk is unwarranted; the number of losers is going to pull down the performance of your winners. The most successful investor is the one who consistently maximizes upside potential within the confines of reasonable risk. This requires the discipline to invest only in companies that have proven consistently superior long-term performance. To reiterate a comment from the first chapter, *the finest insights of the investment world do not produce winners; they minimize the cost of errors.* By strict application of value techniques to consistently superior stocks, you are more likely to cut down on the number of mistakes you make.

12% Return on Capital

The best indication of financial performance I have found is the return on capital ratio. For the simulation I used a 10% minimum, but I suggest a 12% minimum for real-world investing. Such earnings efficiency shows that a company is maximizing the total capital base of shareholder's equity and long-term debt. Eventually, this superior build-up in equity value should be rewarded with relatively high p/e ratios and stock prices.

Six Years of Consistent Performance

A company should be able to prove financial performance over more than one business cycle. Since the average business cycle is three to five years (usually four), five years should be a minimum and six years is preferable. So, to merit serious consideration, a company should be able consistently to earn a return on capital of 12% or more each (or nearly each) year over a six-year period.

New Companies

The six-year minimum implicitly removes companies that have just begun business. While many of these can be spectacular winners, the risks are too high, considering the chances for disaster and the plethora of fine *proven* companies available. Of course, a company that has been in business for six years and just went public has already proven itself for more than one economic cycle and can be considered for purchase.

Other Financial Requirements

As mentioned, for the simulation, the only financial qualification was a 10% return on capital. But investors should consider other financial requirements that prove steady growth over a six-year-minimum period. Now and then, a company might show a slightly slower year, but taken over a six-year period, all of these attributes should show a 50% or more improvement. On a year-to-year basis, this would come to a 7% minimum compounded increase.

Sales
Earnings
Dividends (if paid)
Cash flow
Book value

Qualities of Winning Stocks

In Chapter 8, we discussed the qualities of superior investments in the belief that top performing companies would eventually be recognized by market participants and accorded higher valuations.

One quality of a winning stock unrelated to corporate performance, is based on the stock market's penchant for driving a stock down to undervalued levels because of perceived weakness or neglect. A stock can be neglected because it is either unpopular or too small to draw adequate institutional coverage:

More Unpopular—More Potential

Four other desirable characteristics of winning stocks were:

Superior ability to increase shareholder value
Market niche leadership
Sales growth with lasting products
Freedom to grow

Conclusion—Hire the Best Résumé

The most successful investor is the one who best manages the best managements. When you buy stocks, you essentially hire management teams for your portfolio. A management team that shows an impressive "résumé" over a six-year minimum (preferably longer) is more likely to perform well for the investor in future business cycles. With 7,000 stocks available in the market, there is no reason to hire an unproven résumé.

3. *Buy Undervalued Stocks. Sell Them Once They Become Over-valued.* Because the simulation was strictly mechanical, it was often frustrating to see opportunities missed because one of the valuation tests was not quite met. I kept saying things to myself like, "If this parameter was just a little easier, the simulation would look a lot better." This is the same "If only . . . " mentality that leads many investors to chase stocks that have already shown big advances and gets them into trouble. I firmly believe that the simulation performed a lot better on a mechanical basis than if I had succumbed to temptation and tampered with the buy-and-sell parameters. This is not to suggest a mechanical approach to the stock market, only to underscore the importance of sticking to your investment discipline.

Buying Undervalued Stocks

With all of the choices available on the various exchanges, there is never a reason to buy a stock that is not undervalued. Equally important to realize is that once a stock becomes undervalued, there is rarely a reason to wait for it to fall lower. If it does fall more, you can always buy more of it. Keep in mind that the market is a game of competitive value; once extreme undervaluation is exposed, the marketplace often moves swiftly to raise the price out of bargain range.

If the stock is undervalued, but your market timing techniques lead you to believe it might fall lower, let your value methods dominate. Take a position in the stock at current levels, and take an additional position once it reaches your expected low price. This way, your portfolio requirements have been satisfied by adding an undervalued stock and the additional purchase can possibly satisfy your desire to get a lower price.

Of course, if your market timing work suggests that the market is at a major long-term bottom, but no stocks are able to hit your buying parameters, perhaps your parameters are too stringent. The goal of a value strategy is to buy undervalued stocks, not to be left out of long-term opportunities. As dictated by the universal concept, undervalued stocks are created by overpessimistic and (therefore) oversold markets. This is another important role of market timing: to suggest a reevaluation of your value investment parameters if they do not coincide with your long-term market timing indicators.

Diversification can be a problem in buying stocks according to value. In the simulation, the varied stocks of the Dow Jones Industrial Average provided natural diversification, because a wide range of industries is represented in the Dow. Ideally, even when considering all available stocks, value investing should lead to a natural diversification. Of course, the ideal does not always occur.

As discussed in Chapter 10, diversification is achieved by investing in a broad-based configuration of stocks so that a portfolio can show consistent gains despite a number of changing market conditions. This requires diversification among individual stocks, their industry groups, and their market sectors. If the portfolio is too concentrated in any of these areas, then it is exposed to too much risk of missing market opportunities. In most cases, a similarly valued stock can be found in another industry group to provide better diversification.

The amount of diversification recommended is dependent on the amount of capital in the portfolio. But for minimum diversification, an investor should have at least three or four market sectors adequately represented in his portfolio at all times. Here are some rough guidelines, depending upon portfolio size:

1. Less than $25,000: use mutual funds for proper diversification.
2. $25,000 to $50,000: 6 to 12 stocks, among 6 or more industry groups.
3. $50,000 to $100,000: 10 to 25 stocks, among 7 or more industry groups.
4. Over $100,000: 20 to 50 stocks, among 10 or more industry groups.

These basic guidelines are meant to show the need to diversify not only among stocks, but also among industry groups and sectors. A portfolio that limits the maximum exposure of each sector to 40%, each industry group to 25%, and each stock to 10% will usually be adequately diversified.

Selling overvalued stocks is the well-deserved reward for all of the patience in choosing a stock and waiting for its price to ripen. Too many investors place too much emphasis on buying and not enough on selling. In many ways, the sell decision is more difficult to make, because you have invested your money and mind in the buy decision, leaving you vulnerable to tricks of the ego.

In the simulation, I set an objective of doubling the value of each stock position. This was based not only on my desire to show large gains, but also on the 2:1 ratio of overvaluation to undervaluation in book values, and earnings and dividends compared with interest rates as shown in Chapter 5. This led me to the buying level on RVR of 1.75 and 2.25, because it averaged 2.0, exactly double the average selling parameters of 1.10 and 0.90 (averaging to 1.0). The actual parameters are not the important lesson to be learned—these can change over time. The lesson to be learned is to set stiff-enough parameters for each side of the transaction so that your discipline strictly to buy undervalued stocks and your patience to sell when they become overvalued is amply rewarded.

A stock is overvalued when its current price rises above the price that fully reflects the expected upside potential. If you sell the stock and it happens to go higher, which it surely will at times, forget about it. The stock has accomplished its purpose in your strategic scheme and opened up the opportunity for new undervalued stocks to carry the ball. There will be a strong temptation to let dreams of unlimited upside potential overrule your powers of reason, but ordinarily, the discipline of your strategic plan will prove correct. To satisfy my sense of greed in the simulation, I used two selling levels, which cut the outstanding risk in the portfolio and still gave my positions a little more running room.

Not all of your stocks will become overvalued by rising to extraordinary levels. Sometimes, even a quality company will fall on hard times, making the stock overvalued relative to its long-term potential. In a quality enterprise, it takes a major event to impair the company's long-term prospects seriously. But if it does happen, cut the string and sell it. The stock will have been bought so cheaply that a small profit can still to be taken. Even if there is a loss, take it, and make room in your portfolio for new undervalued positions with better long-term prospects.

Paring stocks that are overvalued, whether because of high prices or poor long-term prospects, promotes healthy diversification and keeps the portfolio concentrated in undervalued stocks. Whether the overvalued stock can be sold at a gain or loss is not the important point here; only that it is overvalued and should be replaced by another stock which is undervalued. This results in a natural rotation of stock holdings, keeping the value and quality of the portfolio building in a nice upward progression.

4. *Long Holding Periods Are Necessary for Consistent Success.* The most important lesson of the simulation was realizing the advantage of holding stocks for long periods of time, which gave the various companies time to mature from undervalued to overvalued levels. Over the 10-year period, the simulation did not have one loser, certainly a by-product of long-term investing. In fact, the lowest gain was 40%, the average gain per trade was 127%, and the median gain was 116%.

In the Introduction, I mentioned the book *Investment Policy*, by Charles D. Ellis, in which he criticized clients of investment institutions for their short-sighted expectations. Ellis made a brilliant case for setting long time horizons for investment in stocks. Since stocks are much riskier than bonds, he argued, they demand a longer holding period to realize their rewards. The longer the holding period, the greater the percentage of stocks vs. bonds that can be invested in a portfolio, ideally reaching 100% to maximize investment returns over a thirty to fifty year period.

Since it has been statistically proven that stocks outperform Treasury bonds or bills by a wide margin over the long haul, a fully invested portfolio of common stocks is the optimal portfolio asset mix—as long as the holding periods are long enough to realize the potential gains. Most institutions keep an asset mix of about 60% stocks, 40% bonds, which is appropriate, considering their short-term investment viewpoint. But this set-up certainly does not compare to the returns possible if they assumed a long-term fully invested position in stocks. While this might be impractical for institutions, individual investors of independent mind can reap this windfall.

The results of my simulation certainly concur with Ellis's work. Over the entire 10-year period, only 46 transactions took place. Fourteen stocks were purchased, usually at two buying points each, totaling 28 buy decisions. By the close of the simulation, 7 of the 14 stocks were still not overvalued and remained in the portfolio. Nine of the 28 buy points were still held. One more stock, American Brands, representing two buying points, was also not overvalued, but was closed out because it was removed from the Dow.

Again, individual investors cannot outsmart the large, sophisticated investment institutions, but they can exploit the fatal flaw of the client–portfolio manager relationship, which is the overwhelming pressure by clients to expect superior investment performance each quarter. The institutions have all the tools to do well in the market, they just do not have the time to see their investments grow to fruition. Individuals can more than compensate for their inherent disadvantage simply by exercising a long-term investment approach that allows the natural expansion of stock market value to maximize their returns.

This also places the long-term investor ahead of a majority of people who do business with commissioned stockbrokers. There too, the pressure to see performance by clients is compounded by the need for brokers to turn over a commission. A broker who does not sell his clients on the need to sell often or to use heavily commissioned options and futures to hedge their stock positions is not likely to make much money on his stock business. Most brokers have their client's best interests in mind, but they are human, too. A long-term buy-and-hold approach to handling clients is simply not good business for a broker (although it can be), even though it may be good for the client.

Since nearly all of the stock traded on the exchanges either passes through institutions or commissioned stockbrokers, *time* is the one advantage an investor can use to elevate himself above the crowd. This competitive advantage is furthered through buying stocks that have shown the ability to steadily increase the underlying value of their shares by showing strong returns on their total invested capital. Over time, this corporate growth compounds dramatically, and eventually the stock market will recognize the value built up in the business and raise its stock price accordingly.

For example, suppose the fictitious Boomer's Baby Shoes consistently earns a 12% return on capital and pays no dividends. With 20% debt outstanding, Boomer's will show a return on equity of 15% per year. In just five years, Boomer's would double its book value (equity). After 10 years, Boomer's would double it again, now showing book value four times its original amount. After 20 years, book value would be 16 times higher, and so on. Since over time, market values should parallel book values, consistent-growth stocks simply need to be held over the long term to provide outstanding returns to investors.

BENEFITS OF THE TIME HIERARCHY

The benefits of time can be viewed in a hierarchy, with a causative effect from one level to the other. Although value parameters of buy-and-sell decisions are shown as the initial causal element, the ability to set such limits is predicated on the time scope of the investor. For example, a speculator interested in turning over quick profits would set easy buy-and-sell parameters, so the targets would be activated quite frequently. A long-term investor could set strict parameters and still satisfy his profit objectives because his trades, while infrequent, would produce a much higher percentage of winning transactions and considerably larger profits.

Longer-term investment viewpoint:

Allows: Stricter buy-and-sell parameters (within reasonable limits).

Causes: Longer time for each investment.

Causes: Minimized losses and maximized gains.

Causes: Minimized trades, commissions, and taxes paid.

Causes: Consistently maximized portfolio gains.

This hierarchy suggests that maximum investment results are achieved by taking the longest possible investment viewpoint and setting the strictest buy-and-sell parameters reasonable. Of course, to execute this objective perfectly, the investor would have to be able to perfectly predict when stocks are most undervalued and overvalued, which is, of course, not realistic.

A REALISTIC LOOK AT THE TIME HIERARCHY

Because the market is a confluence of so many divergent factors, no one can possibly know exactly how the market values stocks, much less the precise levels of extreme pricing. But over the long term, investors should have a strongly performing portfolio if they maintain the discipline to buy quality stocks at realistically undervalued levels and have the patience to hold them until they are realistically overvalued.

The Return Value Ratio was suggested as a way to measure market value in stocks. Its basic contributions are its investment logic, simplicity, and easy application. But there are other methods that are just as simple, although perhaps not quite as effective. Some investors may want to base their parameters on a relative p/e ratio, buying stocks at a p/e ratio below the market and selling once they move above. Or on the dividend yield, such as buying above 6% and selling at 3%. Whatever indicators of value you feel most comfortable with, the parameters should be consistent with your investment objectives.

For the simulation, I wanted to average a 100% gain on each position, so I made the parameters for buying twice as difficult as for selling, which seemed realistic with regard to the 2:1 multiple that generalizes the level of overvaluation to undervaluation. This objective was only possible because I operated under a long-term time horizon. If I was interested in showing good results over two years, I would have had to move the parameters much closer together and settle for much smaller gains and perhaps a few losses.

Alternatively, if I was working with a 30-year simulation, I might have made the parameters more difficult, hoping to catch extraordinary price valuations to boost the consistency and price gains of the portfolio. But the chances are that I would have stuck close to the 2:1 ratio. If the qualifications were much tighter than those in the 10-year simulation, the objective of lessening risk through strict value parameters might be undermined by missing too much market activity.

This is a common trap to fall into—going to such lengths to minimize risk that you never participate in the market. Remember, as long as civilization is developing and you have a company with good long-term prospects, the passage of time acts like a security net to increase the value of the investment. Given a good company and enough time, the investment should pay off.

AN INESCAPABLE VALUE INVESTMENT ASSUMPTION

Before we leave the lessons of the simulation, it would only be fair to briefly discuss the one assumption that must be made by all value investors:

The world is in a long-term cycle of economic progress, and stock market prices will accurately reflect such progress.

This does not mean that the world economy must continue growing each year without occasional interruptions; merely that civilization will, in general, progress in its economic development. Value investors base their decisions on the belief that despite momentary ups and downs, over the long haul, quality companies will continue to grow and build equity value. Knowing this, they can relish bear markets, combing them for deeply undervalued stocks that will substantially appreciate once the market cycle turns again to the bullish side.

Without this assumption, undervalued quality stocks could fall to zero, irrespective of their assets and earnings power. In a 1929 environment, this might be the case, but such debacles are very rare. Even still, the 1929 crash provided one of the best buying opportunities in market history. The possibility of such steep declines attaches tremendous importance to taking profits in periods of extreme valuation, particularly when confirmed by the market-timing framework.

The long-term perspective that applies to buying stocks is just as important in managing a portfolio. Logically, an investor will always try to maximize the return of his portfolio over the intended portfolio performance period. Because the success of investment institutions is scrutinized every quarter, they try to maximize returns over a three-month period, thereby short circuiting the natural progression of value. Individuals have the advantageous status of independence, not subject to the fickle whims of clients; except for one: Uncle Sam.

TAX CONSIDERATIONS IN SELLING

Pension funds, a primary source of business for investment institutions, do not pay taxes, which gives them the luxury to sell stocks with relatively little cost. Individuals, however, are subject to a hefty tax on their gains; so large, in fact, that it is worth considering whether selling stocks makes any sense at all. This question gains significance after 1986, when the capital gains exclusion is no longer available.

Before 1987, individuals who held stocks for more than six months were allowed to exclude 60% of their capital gain from tax, making the maximum tax rate on capital gains equal to 20%. Many investors, with tax rates far below the maximum 50%, had effective capital gains tax rates in the neighborhood of 15%. After 1986, the capital gains exclusion no longer exists. Instead, gains from the sale of stock are treated as ordinary income. If a married couple earns more than $29,750 (over $28,000 in 1987), their gains are taxed at 28%.

Twenty eight percent might not sound like much, but let us play with the numbers and see how much of a penalty it really is. Suppose, in the first year, you bought stocks for $10,000 and sold them for $15,000. Your gain of $5,000 will be taxed at 28%, reducing the gain to $3,600 after the $1,400 paid in tax. In after-tax money, you have really only made 36% on your investment, not 50%. In the following year, you invested your total $13,600 ($10,000 + $3,600) and made another 50%. Before taxes, that comes to $20,400. After being taxed on the $6,800 gain, the total comes to $18,496.

In two years, after two terrific short-term trades of 50% each, rather than making 125% as you would have had the gains been tax-free, you only made about 85%. In the third year, the market turned lower and you stepped in quickly to cut your losses to just 30% of your $18,496, or $5,549, leaving you with only $12,947. Of course, you get to use the $5,549 loss against your income, but because it is a capital loss, you only get to offset other capital gains or deduct $3,000 of the losses against ordinary income. Since you do not have any capital gains to offset, the loss only gives you a tax benefit of $840 ($3,000 × 28%), placing the remaining $2,549 for use in the following year.

Thus, after three years of investing, two years of which showed spectacular gains of 50%, your total portfolio is only worth $13,787, with the $2,549 loss carried over for use in the next year. This is equal to a gain of about 38%, or just over 11% compounded per year. In simpler terms, it is equal to a single gain of 53%, taxed at 28%. All of this taxing math (sorry, I could not resist) raises the question whether selling stocks is worth considering at all. Because capital gains are now taxed like ordinary income, why not just use stocks like an IRA account, allowing the money to compound tax-free?

The compounding abilities of corporations certainly work in the favor of the long-term value investor. Particularly if the stock was purchased at a favorably low valuation, investors can take a tax-free ride with the fortunes of a steadily growing company. As shown earlier in this chapter, if a company returns 15% on equity over a 20-year period, it would have an equity base 16 times larger than when it was purchased. A $100,000 portfolio of such stocks purchased in 1987 (assuming that the portfolio's performance mirrored the equity values) would be worth $1,600,000 by 2007, a fair amount for most people.

28%: CERTAIN TAX VERSUS POTENTIAL DECLINE

A 28% tax on gains from the sale of stock has the same effect as holding the stock and throwing away 28% of your current gain. With selling, the 28% reduction happens automatically, whereas a stock might not fall by 28%. Moreover, even if the stock falls by 28%, how long is it likely to be so low?

To answer this question, let us look back over the past 40 years, from 1946 forward, a representative sample. Suppose, at the end of 1946, you had bought a portfolio of the Dow Jones Industrial Average and held all of the stocks, only selling when companies in the Dow were replaced. In other words, the performance of your portfolio would perfectly mirror the Dow. At the close of trading in 1946, you would have bought a portfolio representing the Dow worth $177.20. How many times at year-end over the past 40 years do you think your portfolio would show a loss of more than 28%?

Over this 40-year period, the portfolio would have declined 28% or more just two times. The first time occurred after the portfolio retraced its gain after the first year in 1948, when the Dow itself fell a mere 2%, not a significant decline that would justify selling. The second time was in 1974, a real decline, when the portfolio would have fallen 34%, clearly a time that the 28% tax would have been worth it. In conclusion, from one year-end to the next, only one time in 40 years was it worth selling the portfolio and accepting the 28% tax (see Figure 11-2)!

Of course, in all fairness, the Dow Jones Industrial Average did not make any forward progress between 1965 and 1981, a period of 16 years when gains from 1 year would have been extinguished by losses in the next. And there were several severe declines, some of them more than 50%, although only the 1973–1974 decline lasted as long as two years. While it is true that the Dow fell more than 28% just 1 time in 40 years from 1 year-end to the next, depending on when you began investing, you could have sustained several 28% losses over that time period.

It should also be remembered that the Dow is merely an average of 30 stocks, not necessarily a representative sample of the entire market. Fortunately, most stocks do not become overvalued at the same time, except perhaps at monumentous tops like in 1929 or 1972. Usually, the market rotates leadership, allowing investors

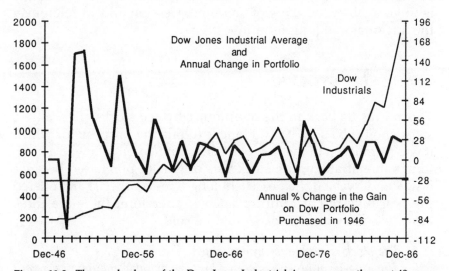

Figure 11-2. The yearly close of the Dow Jones Industrial Average over the past 40 years illustrates that 28% declines (equal to the capital gains tax on sales of stock) seldom occur in the overall stock market.

to replace overvalued stocks with undervalued ones. All of this underscores the importance of intelligent selling, as opposed to a blindfolded buy-and-hold philosophy. Nevertheless, it should also highlight the tremendous burden on the sell decision; because if you do sell, 28% of your gains are automatically taken away.

Therefore, by deciding to sell, you are making the audacious statement that either:

1. The stock will lose more than 28% of its gain, and there is an investment alternative that will perform better than that stock would have; or
2. The stock may not fall, but there is an investment alternative that will perform so well that it will cover the 28% tax and whatever returns the stock would have delivered.

In conclusion, unless you are in the habit of making mistakes deliberately, you should be fairly sure there is excellent justification before selling a stock. The parameters suggested in the following pages are good justification in light of our overall strategy. But outside of those guidelines, anything less than reasonable certainty is to go against the odds of value progression and to relinquish the advantage of long-term investing.

WHY SELL STOCKS?

This brings us back to the question, why sell stocks? Basically, a stock should be sold if it no longer fulfills the purpose for which it was purchased in the first place. Assuming you followed a long-term value strategy, the stock was originally purchased because it was undervalued, had excellent long-term prospects, and offered the best investment return available. Therefore, there are three basic reasons why a stock should be sold:

1. *The stock is no longer undervalued.*
2. *The long-term prospects are no longer favorable enough to warrant holding the stock.*
3. *The stock is nearly fully valued and alternative investments offer better returns at much less risk.*

The first reason is a quantitative decision: Is the stock still undervalued according to your value parameters? If it is fully valued, then its value has been recognized by the marketplace and the stock has accomplished its objectives. In most cases, there will be an undervalued investment to take its place. If there are not any attractive valuations available, then depending on your risk management policy, you can leave the money idle in cash or find a marginally undervalued stock to replace it. Either way, a fully valued stock generally has less upside potential and more risk than the available alternatives.

The second reason is more of a judgment call, one that is fraught with the psychological dilemma, since a company's prospects appear worst when its shares are at depressed levels. Of course, from time to time, even the best companies have difficulty maintaining superior operations, making them candidates for replacement. Ideally, the decision to replace a stock should come when it is still adequately valued, not in a panic-driven fit to sell at low valuations. The quantitative rationalization for selling a stock with weak long-term prospects is to remove stocks that are almost certain to become overvalued in the near future because of poor corporate performance.

The third reason is a matter of risk-management policy, the next topic of discussion. When the stock market is overvalued relative to competing instruments, building a cash position can make sense. It is assumed that all of the portfolio's overvalued stocks will be removed immediately as they become overvalued, but there are often some stocks that linger in a portfolio at levels just below overvaluation (marginally undervalued). In a bear market, these stocks are more likely than deeply undervalued stocks to sustain serious losses. Therefore, when a bear market is suspected, marginally undervalued stocks should be carefully considered as possible sell candidates.

MANAGING RISK

Portfolio strategy is largely a matter of risk management. There are worthwhile risks that can improve portfolio performance and there are unwarranted risks that are more likely to hinder performance. We have already discussed many of these unwarranted risks as they apply to individual investments, such as buying inconsistent companies or overvalued stocks. Essentially, from an overall portfolio standpoint, managing risk becomes a question of deviating from the market standard, which is generally considered to be the Standard & Poor's 500. Basically, there are two types of portfolio risk:

1. *Market risk—risk in the general market. This type of risk, the risk that the stock market will go up or down, cannot be eliminated and, therefore, is not a subject for discussion.*
2. *Opportunity risk—the risk of missing opportunities for profit in the market. Opportunity risk is the basic investor decision: it can be desirable, undesirable, or eliminated entirely.*

THE OPPORTUNITY RISK DECISION

An indexed fund eliminates opportunity risk entirely by duplicating the market averages (popularly the Standard & Poor's 500), making it a plausible alternative to free-choice investing. Any deviation from that standard constitutes the acceptance of opportunity risk. Diversification reduces the risk somewhat by investing in stocks across a wide cross-section of market sectors and industry groups, but a diversified portfolio still has opportunity risk unless it perfectly replicates the market averages.

Throughout this book, I have recommended a disciplined long-term strategy of buying a diversified portfolio of undervalued quality stocks and selling each stock as it becomes overvalued. Since this strategy is obviously a deviation from an indexed fund, it carries opportunity risk, but the strategy is designed to minimize that risk to an acceptable level. By following the strategic disciplines, it is intended that the extra risk will be rewarded by greater upside potential and less downside price risk.

Following a riskier strategy creates risk that could overwhelm the portfolio's upside potential. Any strategy that reduces the long-term time perspective of the investor or allows the purchase of nonundervalued stocks and the sale of nonovervalued ones, automatically increases the opportunity risk and should result in poorer long-term portfolio performance. This would include strategies based exclusively on moving averages, chart formations, or other attempts to short-circuit the maximum utilization of the long-term investment cycle. This type of risk is unwarranted and should be avoided in light of its potentially disastrous effects on long-term portfolio performance.

Basically, a long-term value investor has two intelligent choices regarding risk management policy. The investor can:

1. Always keep the portfolio fully invested.
2. Pursue a passive policy of full investment; always trying to keep a fully invested portfolio, but accepting partial investment if cash alternatives are better valued than available stocks.

Remaining fully invested in a diversified portfolio of undervalued stocks contains more risk than duplicating the market averages, but the risk is more than compensated for by giving the investor the chance to take advantage of profit opportunities in deeply undervalued stocks and avoiding declines in overvalued stocks. Partially invested portfolios are even more risky because of missed opportunities, but could possibly reduce exposure to declining markets to provide more upside potential. Again, the decision to go with a partially invested portfolio should be based on a long-term assessment of available undervalued stocks compared with the cash alternative. Any attempt to take a more aggressive approach to raising cash through short-term market timing or other methods multiples the opportunity risk far beyond warranted levels and undermines your long term value objectives.

THE HUMAN SIDE OF RISK

The competitive nature of many investors pushes them to try to make quick fortunes in the stock market, but as in many things, pursuits of the ego are not always rewarded. Such flings often add risk that is not rewarded. A disciplined long-term value strategy is easy to execute and should provide excellent returns at a reasonable risk. If much greater returns are desired, they can only be accomplished with the assumption of tremendous risks that can seriously endanger the existence of your portfolio. Such windfalls are probably unrealistic, and for those who harbor such ideas I recommend that you take a few minutes to analyze why you are pursuing a dream that only large doses of luck can achieve.

If the purpose is to satisfy some macho (male or female alike) impulse of the ego, your investment record is likely to fall short of meeting the intended gratification. In fact, it is likely to be poor and inconsistent, because you will have a greater tendency to wander from your strategic discipline and succumb to emotional decisions. Remember, according to the behavioral cycle, *investors are generally wrong at emotional extremes.*

It is far better to stay within your abilities and tolerance to risk. In pro football, many quarterbacks with mediocre throwing abilities run very successful offenses by recognizing their limitations and controlling risk. They minimize interceptions by not forcing throws in difficult situations and use a variety of methods to raise the percentage of completed passes. Their teams win consistently because the offense controls the ball and the defense is not burdened by mistakes committed by the offense. Investors should take the same approach to investing. Stay within the limitations of reasonable risk and your portfolio will show consistent gains.

RISK CONSIDERATIONS OF TIME

Throughout this book, I have emphasized that long holding periods are imperative to maximizing the upside potential in stocks. With similar logic, long holding periods in a substantially invested, diversified portfolio of stocks are necessary to maximize the upside potential of a stock portfolio. Again, the basic reason boils down to opportunity risk.

Substantial moves in the stock market are caused by sudden shifts in expectations regarding the balance of value between interest rates and earnings. The competitive nature of the stock market corrects these imbalances very quickly, often too quickly for most investors to react. Therefore, as long as investors are invested in undervalued stocks, and the market recognizes value, investors face a tremendous risk of missing opportunities by not being substantially invested in stocks.

This is particularly true because of the paradoxical behavior of the stock market. In accordance with the behavioral cycle, market tops are created by overoptimism and market bottoms are created by overpessimism. For those trying to aggressively time the market, this psychological dilemma leads most investors to be fully invested at tops and underinvested at market bottoms. When the balance of value shifts, most investors are caught flatfooted, unable to react effectively. This paradox reinforces the emphasis on long-term value investing, which dictates a heavily invested position near undervalued bottoms and suggests caution toward overvalued tops.

FULLY INVESTED PORTFOLIOS

If an investor is always fully invested in undervalued stocks, then the portfolio always has upside potential and there is never a risk of missing a rise in the broad market unless the portfolio is not properly diversified. But to remain fully invested can cause two unwanted problems:

1. If not enough undervalued stocks are available to keep the portfolio fully invested, then an investor will either have to accept less diversification and buy more of the undervalued stocks he already owns; or reduce his value parameters and accept stocks that are not substantially undervalued.

2. If the portfolio is fully invested at a market top, there will not be any available cash to take advantage of deeply undervalued stocks as the market falls and eventually reaches more attractive valuations.

Both of these problems make it undesirable to maintain an absolute policy of full investment in the stock market. While it is hoped that undervalued stocks will not fall as much as the general market, in a bear market nearly all stocks sustain serious declines, particularly those which are overvalued or priced slightly below overvaluation. Such declines create tremendous buying opportunities in new undervalued situations that can yield phenomenal profits over the long-term.

The investor who wishes to remain fully invested at all times should take an approach similar to that mentioned in the last chapter. As valuations rise and overvalued stocks are sold off, there should be a conscious effort to find undervalued stocks that are less likely than others to be affected by a decline. Many institutions employ sophisticated statistical work to define stocks that are less volatile than others, but for the individual investor, this may be an unrealistic endeavor. In addition, because we can afford to be long-term investors by not fighting the quarterly performance game, we can reduce risk by simply becoming more conservative with our investment choices.

Consistency is really the key to a stock retaining its value; consistency in sales and earnings gains, returns on capital, and rising dividend payments. If such a stock is attractively priced relative to interest rates, it will probably retain its value better than other stocks.

The marketplace may reduce its value because of a general decline in stock prices, but because investors will not expect poor corporate performance, its loss in share price might be less than the average stock.

To find a stock that may retain its value better in bear market conditions, you can qualify your value analysis by choosing stocks with a higher earnings yield than the yield on long-term bonds. This is the same test that the legendary Ben Graham used to qualify stocks in both bull- and bear markets, and from my perspective, is certainly fine for use in all markets as well.

Long-term bonds are good for this purpose because they are the most likely alternative to stocks and carry the most similar risk among investment alternatives. Furthermore, bonds are a more stringent test, because when stocks are near extreme valuations, the yield curve is likely to be bullish, in which case long-term bonds yield more than Treasury bills. Use the average yield of twenty-year bonds, since, due to market conditions, the longest maturities sometimes have a lower yield.

Suppose you have just sold an overvalued stock, and although the market is at extreme overvaluation, you would like to keep to your policy of being fully invested. You have done all of your stock selection homework and come up with two (fictitious) stocks: Hot Pants Apparel and Boring Bob's Boot Stores. Hot Pants has shown a spectacular record of growth over the past 6 years and is selling at 30 times earnings. Boring Bob's has a steady 15-year record of good performance and is selling at only 9 times earnings. The average yield on a 20-year bond is 7% and the yield on Treasury bills is 5.5%. The average stock has a p/e of 19, causing the Earnings Value Index to be right on the edge of turning bearish.

The earnings yield on Hot Pants is 3.3% (1 ÷ 30 p/e), about half of the average long-term bond yield. When the stock market yields less than other investment assets, money will flow out of stocks and into better values. Therefore, we want to buy a stock that can favorably compete with other investments. The most common alternative to stocks is the bond market, so with stocks nearing dangerous levels of overvaluation, it is prudent to buy a stock that has a higher earnings yield than the yield on bonds.

In this case, Boring Bob's has an earnings yield of 11.1% (1 ÷ 9 p/e) and such a steady long-term performance that it is almost the equivalent of a bond. Because of its bond-like quality and low earnings yield, it probably has a better chance than Hot Pants Apparel to compete with other investments and withstand a difficult market period. Buying Boring Bob's still keeps us fully invested in the market to participate in the upswing and hopefully provides a better shield against big losses that are very possible with Hot Pants.

The high p/e of Hot Pants makes its price more sensitive to disappointments in either earnings or interest rates. Investor expectations have to be very optimistic to push a p/e ratio up to 30, far above the p/e of the average stock at a time when the Earnings Value Index is suggesting that the average stock is fully valued.

Once the balloon bursts, stocks like Hot Pants often fall precipitously. If the economy weakens, earnings could fall, sending the stock reeling to a more reasonable p/e ratio. If interest rates rise, the p/e ratio for most stocks will fall to bring the stock market back into line with the balance of value. Chances are, Hot Pants would see its p/e ratio fall too, causing the stock price to decline as a multiple of earnings. Either way, because the price of Hot Pants is so inflated relative to underlying value, it poses a greater downside risk in weak markets.

A UNIVERSAL APPROACH TO PORTFOLIO STRATEGY

A policy of full investment, adjustable to a partially invested position, is a more flexible approach that is probably more palatable to most investors. This policy was used in the simulation: if a value parameter was reached, the stock was added to the portfolio. If there was available cash in the portfolio but no new stocks reached a buy point, the cash balance earned interest.

Of course, in the real world, there will be more than just 30 stocks to choose from and there will be more of a tendency to have a greater percentage of capital invested. Additionally, if the market timing framework suggests that the stock market is overvalued or near overvaluation, an investor can take the initiative to sell marginally undervalued stocks from the portfolio.

Stocks that are still attractively valued should remain in the portfolio regardless of what condition the market appears to be in. A portfolio of undervalued stocks is undervalued irrespective of market conditions and should remain in the portfolio to take advantage of the long-term progression of value. Chances are that if your portfolio is fully invested with significantly undervalued stocks near a perceived top, the market is stronger than you think and your market timing analysis is probably incorrect. Clearly, value should be respected more than intuition.

Such a value policy ideally leads to a Darwinistic sort of market timing, another inference from the universal concept. Similar to Darwin's theory of natural selection, optimal investment percentages are achieved by letting undervalued stocks survive in the portfolio and pruning overvalued ones. Darwinistic market timing is a very attractive concept from a universal point of view. Because the market moves in long-term cycles of advance and decline, it would be logical that a value-based natural selection process would produce the best results.

The Darwinistic concept can be adapted to a "relative" RVR method of portfolio management by maintaining a portfolio that is always fully invested in the most advantageously valued stocks. Suppose you have a universe of 80 quality stocks that you feel comfortable placing in your portfolio at any time (given the appropriate valuation). And suppose you would like to be invested in only 20 of them at any one time. Each quarter, review the list to make sure that the 80 stocks are still suitable for investment. If there are any which are not, replace them with stocks that meet your criteria.

Then, on a quarterly basis, rank the 80 stocks according to the RVR. Choose the top 20 among the group and keep updating the list quarterly to keep the portfolio invested in the top 20 RVRs. Of course, allowances can be made for stocks which barely fall out of the top 20 and which are not overvalued. But, on the whole, if you maintain this selection-and-elimination process, your fully invested portfolio should show what previous simulations with the RVR have shown compared with the market averages: significantly reduced losses in bear markets and superior gains in bull markets.

The excellent results are probably due to the minimized opportunity risk (because the portfolio is fully invested) and the reduced exposure to weak markets (because every stock is undervalued). The methodology also eliminates the need to maintain RVR parameters for buying and selling which can become less relevant due to changing market conditions, such as interest rates. By maintaining a fully invested portfolio of the top 20 values you have reduced the potential errors by limiting the amount of potential decisionmaking. The only decisions to make involve the selection of the 80-stock universe and proper diversification, not which ones are actually chosen for investment.

Of course, if you were deeply concerned about the future of your portfolio because you believed the stock market was dangerously overvalued, you always have the option to raise cash by selling the worst-valued stocks in your portfolio. For example, if you wanted to move to a 25% cash position, assuming the stocks were similarly priced, you could sell the 5 worst-valued stocks of the 20, leaving the 15 best-valued stocks in the portfolio. While this would expose you to additional opportunity risk, it is always wise to ease your personal tensions and to protect the long-term future of your portfolio.

There is one problem to consider. Depending on the stocks in your list, this method might lead to the replacement of stocks that have not reached mature valuations, which effectively short-circuits your long-term value strategy. If this is the case, you can consider the following option: begin the portfolio with the best valued quarter of your universe (20 stocks in this example) and let them remain in the portfolio as long as they are in the top half (top 40) of all values. Once a stock drops out of the top half, replace it with a stock that is in the top quarter. In this way, although your portfolio will not contain the best values at all times, the progression of value will have been given more of a chance to work for you and your transaction costs will be much lower.

The decision to use the RVR with buy-and-sell parameters or to choose the relative method is up to you. Your results should be excellent—regardless of which method—as long as you maintain a diversified portfolio of quality stocks that are significantly undervalued compared to the rest of the market and hold them until they become overvalued. Either method has the capacity to be successful, but the results achievable are dependent on your desire and discipline in the course of implementation.

CONSIDERATIONS IN MANAGING OPPORTUNITY RISK

One of our most prized strategic objectives is to minimize the cost of errors. Perhaps the greatest error you can make is to force an investment just to participate in a strong market. If the opportunity is not there, fine; the stock market will be around for a long time and is sure to present you with another buying opportunity. If only marginal or insufficiently undervalued companies are available, the market is very likely to be near the top. Maybe there will be a strong spurt at the end, but such periods of overvaluation ordinarily do not last for too long. Eventually, the overvaluation will be recognized and money will flow out of stocks into other investments.

Remember, stocks are more easily acquired than shed. Once you are in a position, you have made a commitment that this stock is better than any other investment. This is another opportunity cost—the cost of taking money away from other investments that could provide a better return. There are also real entry costs involved: a commission to buy and a commission to sell, plus the tax effects.

The last thing a value investor wants to do is to push his long-term strategy aside and join the crowd in pursuit of a quick buck. Once you join the crowd, you've given up your advantage of long-term value investing to join the loser's game. So, before you make the plunge to buy a stock just to fill the portfolio, ask yourself whether the investment is one that you can live with over the long term and furthers the objectives of your strategic plan.

Some readers, uncomfortable with the universal approach to managing risk, will ask, "In perceived rough markets, what percentage of investment should my portfolio have?" Because value should override intuition, I am reluctant to offer actual percentages, but the following might give you a better grasp of risk management considerations.

As a general guideline, an investor should always try to be fully invested, although a five to 10% cash cushion is perfectly acceptable. Below that, a move to 75% invested should be considered if only marginal purchases are available and the market timing framework suggests the approaching of an overvalued period. A decline to 50% or less invested would be justified only by an overvalued market. If conditions are not that drastic, it could indicate that you are not comfortable with the total size of your allocation to stock investments.

Despite the inability to draw precise portfolio guidelines, I can sum up some of the major points of this book to clarify risk management considerations:

1. *Overall Strategy.* The goal of a strategic value investor is to buy a diversified portfolio of undervalued stocks that have proven superior operating performance over the long haul. Profits are maximized by holding stocks until they are overvalued, at which time they are sold and replaced with new undervalued stocks.

Barring a 1929-like catastrophe, as long as a portfolio contains a diversified group of superior, undervalued stocks, it should be as fully invested as reasonable to reduce opportunity risk.

2. *The Value of Time.* The longer your investment perspective, the better your portfolio performance. This is your advantage over nearly every other market participant. Value investing makes the implicit assumption that given enough time, value will be recognized by the marketplace. Longer holding periods result in greater gains, smaller losses, fewer commissions, and less taxes paid.

After 1986, cutting down on taxes paid is especially important, since for most people, capital gains will be taxed at 28%, a 40% increase over the previous maximum for long-term capital gains and double the amount paid by investors previously in the 35% tax bracket. Since the tax incentive to hold stocks over the long term no longer exists, fewer people are likely to do it, further multiplying our advantage gained by holding undervalued stocks until they are overvalued.

Holding stocks over the long term is the one element that any investor can take advantage of over most other investors, both institutional and otherwise. Through long-term value investing, a greater portion of a stock's upside potential is realized and the opportunity risk of missing potential gains is reduced.

3. *Market Timing Ability.* Some investors have more expertise than others in market timing, but this advantage is minimal over the long term, since aggressive market timing ordinarily results in errors that penalize portfolio performance. Market timing should be limited to concurring with value considerations in order to reduce marginally undervalued holdings from fully invested portfolios and signaling times when only marginal investment opportunities exist.

An investor who recognizes the limitations of market timing and his own abilities to apply it will attempt to implement only long-term judgments into his risk-management policy. Aggressive forays in market timing are the most common way investors raise opportunity risk to injurious levels.

4. Bear Markets. During a bear market, most stocks fall substantially, many to severe undervaluations. To most investors, bear markets are terrifying; but the value investor recognizes them as tremendous opportunities for long-term profit. This places the pruning procedures of overvalued stocks as paramount in importance. Furthermore, market timing can be used to identify the onset of bear markets to allow liquidation of marginally undervalued stocks (overvalued stocks are assumed to be already sold) to make room for bear market bargains. Without bear markets, there would be little reason to be less than fully invested.

Because bear markets exist, it is important to consider a less than fully invested portfolio for two reasons: (1) Severe losses in portfolio value can damage its ability to continue effectively; and (2) the opportunity risk of missing advantageous values produced by bear markets.

5. Bull Markets. Bear market opportunities are harvested in bull markets. Again, the greatest portfolio gains are made by waiting for stocks to mature from undervalued to overvalued levels. Due to market rotation among different industry groups, not all stocks will become overvalued at the same time, creating the opportunity to replace overvalued stocks with undervalued ones.

Bull market profits are best maximized by holding issues until they become overvalued, which lessens the opportunity risk of missing potential gains still harbored by undervalued stocks.

6. Investor Comfort. An investor's strategy should be designed to reflect his ability to handle risk. The best risk policy is one that can keep an investor comfortable with his investments over the longest period of time. If an investor is not comfortable with his risk policy, he will be more likely to sell before stocks are over-valued and significantly raise the opportunity risk of the portfolio.

A portfolio strategy can only be effective if the investor is comfortable with the level of risk assumed. The greater the comfort level, the lower the opportunity risk, because the investor is more likely to hold stocks until they are overvalued.

HOW MUCH MONEY TO INVEST?

This is a crucial decision due to the time hierarchy mentioned earlier in this chapter. The longer each investment can be held, the less the opportunity risk and the greater the probability of consistent long-term gains in the portfolio. If money needs to come out of the portfolio, whether for personal use or to reduce investor anxiety, it will usually necessitate selling an invested position before it is overvalued, which will reduce the portfolio's overall performance.

Therefore, money placed in the portfolio is strictly for investment, without any discretionary strings attached. Once funds are subject to removal, it is no longer investment capital, but speculative money. If the money is pulled out on a frequent basis, it forces you to lose your advantage as a long-term investor and become a speculator. Once you are a speculator, portfolio performance suffers and so does your personal life, as the stock market becomes a bothersome source of unnecessary anxiety.

It is far better to begin small and gain a better sense of your particular comfort level. As you better understand the risk levels you can comfortably tolerate, money can be added to the portfolio with greater confidence. This will help your portfolio performance, because a confident investor will show greater discipline in executing a long-term strategy.

Once you buy the stocks, do not forget about them. While you are in this for the long haul, it is possible for an investment to fizzle out soon after its purchase. This makes it important to keep an ongoing value analysis of each stock, making sure that it still meets your investment criteria. If the investment is no longer a producing member of your portfolio and does not fit in to your strategic plan, discard it in favor of another stock that can fill the bill. Because of your ongoing portfolio analysis, once a stock reaches levels that seem overvalued, you will be physically and mentally prepared to sell the shares.

Finally, keep a list of potential stocks, and update it according to value. Some of these stocks may fall by the wayside, too. Once they do not fit your investment criteria, remove them from consideration. Meanwhile, you should always be looking to upgrade the quality your potential stock list, either by replacing stocks or enlarging the group. Either way, this list should contain the names of the stocks you would most like to own with respect to your strategic plan. Because you are following the companies on a value-rated list, once a stock reaches an attractive price, you will be prepared to add it to your portfolio.

PERSONAL CONSIDERATIONS

In addition to factors solely related to the stock market, there can be personal factors that should be considered and respected. Sometimes an event in one's personal life can impair investment decision making. When such an event occurs, recognize it, and ask yourself whether your investment position is adding to the anxiety. If so, consider raising the cash level of the portfolio by selling off the least undervalued stocks. In this way, even though the event might limit the upside opportunity of the portfolio, it is not going to cause you unnecessary downside risk, both financially and personally.

A good night's sleep is far more important than the stock market. If the market is getting to you, either physically or emotionally, your body or mind is telling you to reconsider the level of risk you are taking. Reviewing investment objectives and policy is necessary to do on a periodic basis. If you become uncomfortable, raise cash until you are comfortable. It might not be your investment methods causing the anxiety, but rather that you have selected too much money to invest.

Executing a successful value investment strategy is a matter of setting realistic goals and policies. Unrealistic goals will cause you to venture outside the limited abilities of market participants to predict moves in the market or in speculative stocks. Successful investment policies generally have two basic qualities: (1) they buy stocks on the basis of value; and (2) take full advantage of long holding periods in order to sell at overvalued levels. The investor who adheres to these two disciplines will minimize risk to a reasonable comfort level and should enjoy consistent success in the stock market.

Appendix A
Interest Rates and Stock Market History, 1950–1986

Date	S&P 500 Yield	Discount Rate	Treas. Bills	Treas. Bonds	Dow Jones Indus.	S&P 500
Jan-50	6.65	1.50	1.07	2.17	199.80	16.88
Feb-50	6.62	1.50	1.12	2.22	203.40	17.21
Mar-50	6.53	1.50	1.12	2.25	206.30	17.35
Apr-50	6.36	1.50	1.15	2.28	212.70	17.84
May-50	6.16	1.50	1.16	2.30	219.40	18.44
Jun-50	6.12	1.50	1.15	2.33	221.00	18.74
Jul-50	6.63	1.50	1.16	2.34	205.30	17.38
Aug-50	6.54	1.75	1.20	2.35	216.60	18.43
Sep-50	6.65	1.75	1.30	2.37	223.20	19.08
Oct-50	6.39	1.75	1.31	2.38	229.30	19.87
Nov-50	6.97	1.75	1.36	2.39	229.30	19.83
Dec-50	7.24	1.75	1.34	2.41	229.30	19.75
Jan-51	6.34	1.75	1.34	2.40	244.50	21.21
Feb-51	6.20	1.75	1.36	2.41	253.30	22.00
Mar-51	6.34	1.75	1.40	2.52	249.50	21.63
Apr-51	6.27	1.75	1.47	2.60	253.40	21.92
May-51	6.23	1.75	1.55	2.68	254.40	21.93
Jun-51	6.30	1.75	1.45	2.69	249.30	21.55
Jul-51	6.25	1.75	1.56	2.68	253.60	21.93
Aug-51	5.96	1.75	1.62	2.60	264.90	22.89
Sep-51	5.75	1.75	1.63	2.58	273.40	23.48
Oct-51	5.77	1.75	1.54	2.65	269.70	23.36
Nov-51	6.18	1.75	1.56	2.69	259.60	22.71
Dec-51	5.99	1.75	1.73	2.72	266.10	23.41

Date	S&P 500 Yield	Discount Rate	Treas. Bills	Treas. Bonds	Dow Jones Indus.	S&P 500
Jan-52	5.82	1.75	1.57	2.74	271.70	24.19
Feb-52	5.99	1.75	1.54	2.72	265.20	23.75
Mar-52	5.94	1.75	1.59	2.71	264.50	23.81
Apr-52	5.96	1.75	1.57	2.64	262.60	23.74
May-52	5.99	1.75	1.67	2.58	261.60	23.73
Jun-52	5.83	1.75	1.70	2.62	268.40	24.38
Jul-52	5.65	1.75	1.81	2.60	276.40	25.08
Aug-52	5.66	1.75	1.83	2.69	276.70	25.18
Sep-52	5.74	1.75	1.71	2.70	272.40	24.78
Oct-52	5.89	1.75	1.74	2.74	267.80	24.26
Nov-52	5.69	1.75	1.85	2.70	276.40	25.03
Dec-52	5.47	1.75	2.09	2.74	286.00	26.04
Jan-53	5.45	2.00	1.96	2.79	288.40	26.18
Feb-53	5.52	2.00	1.97	2.81	283.90	25.86
Mar-53	5.48	2.00	2.01	2.89	286.80	25.99
Apr-53	5.75	2.00	2.19	2.94	275.30	24.71
May-53	5.77	2.00	2.16	3.08	276.80	24.84
Jun-53	5.99	2.00	2.11	3.10	266.90	23.95
Jul-53	5.90	2.00	2.04	2.98	270.30	24.29
Aug-53	5.87	2.00	2.04	2.97	272.20	24.39
Sep-53	6.14	2.00	1.79	2.93	261.90	23.27
Oct-53	5.99	2.00	1.38	2.79	270.70	23.97
Nov-53	5.92	2.00	1.44	2.81	277.10	24.50
Dec-53	5.83	2.00	1.60	2.76	281.20	24.83
Jan-54	5.69	2.00	1.18	2.65	286.60	25.46
Feb-54	5.62	1.75	0.97	2.58	292.10	26.02
Mar-54	5.46	1.75	1.03	2.49	299.20	26.57
Apr-54	5.24	1.50	0.96	2.44	310.90	27.63
May-54	5.02	1.50	0.76	2.51	322.90	28.73
Jun-54	4.99	1.50	0.64	2.52	327.90	28.96
Jul-54	4.77	1.50	0.72	2.44	341.30	30.13
Aug-54	4.63	1.50	0.92	2.45	346.10	30.73
Sep-54	4.57	1.50	1.01	2.49	352.70	31.45
Oct-54	4.43	1.50	0.98	2.51	358.30	32.18
Nov-54	4.52	1.50	0.93	2.54	375.50	33.44
Dec-54	4.45	1.50	1.14	2.56	393.80	34.97
Jan-55	4.38	1.50	1.23	2.65	398.40	35.60
Feb-55	4.32	1.50	1.17	2.71	410.30	36.79
Mar-55	4.33	1.50	1.28	2.70	408.90	36.50
Apr-55	4.19	1.75	1.59	2.77	423.00	37.76
May-55	4.23	1.75	1.45	2.76	421.60	37.60
Jun-55	4.01	1.75	1.41	2.77	440.80	39.78
Jul-55	3.72	1.75	1.60	2.87	462.20	42.69
Aug-55	3.87	2.00	1.90	2.91	457.30	42.43
Sep-55	3.72	2.25	2.07	2.88	476.40	44.34
Oct-55	3.94	2.25	2.23	2.82	452.70	42.11
Nov-55	4.05	2.50	2.25	2.84	476.60	44.95
Dec-55	4.15	2.50	2.54	2.89	484.60	45.37

Date	S&P 500 Yield	Discount Rate	Treas. Bills	Treas. Bonds	Dow Jones Indus.	S&P 500
Jan-56	4.24	2.50	2.41	2.87	474.80	44.15
Feb-56	4.24	2.50	2.32	2.81	475.50	44.43
Mar-56	3.97	2.50	2.25	2.90	502.70	47.49
Apr-56	3.94	2.75	2.60	3.05	511.00	48.05
May-56	4.09	2.75	2.61	2.94	495.20	46.54
Jun-56	4.09	2.75	2.49	2.90	485.30	46.27
Jul-56	3.89	2.75	2.31	2.97	509.80	48.78
Aug-56	3.92	3.00	2.60	3.15	511.70	48.49
Sep-56	4.07	3.00	2.84	3.21	495.00	46.84
Oct-56	4.12	3.00	2.90	3.20	483.80	46.24
Nov-56	4.27	3.00	2.99	3.29	479.30	45.76
Dec-56	4.24	3.00	3.21	3.41	492.00	46.44
Jan-57	4.31	3.00	3.11	3.37	485.90	45.43
Feb-57	4.54	3.00	3.11	3.21	466.80	43.47
Mar-57	4.47	3.00	3.08	3.28	472.80	44.03
Apr-57	4.36	3.00	3.06	3.33	485.40	45.05
May-57	4.18	3.00	3.06	3.44	500.80	46.78
Jun-57	4.04	3.00	3.29	3.66	505.30	47.55
Jul-57	3.95	3.00	3.16	3.67	514.60	48.51
Aug-57	4.17	3.50	3.37	3.68	488.00	45.84
Sep-57	4.31	3.50	3.53	3.67	471.80	43.98
Oct-57	4.54	3.50	3.58	3.75	443.40	41.24
Nov-57	4.67	3.00	3.29	3.48	437.30	40.35
Dec-57	4.64	3.00	3.04	3.07	436.90	40.33
Jan-58	4.48	2.75	2.44	2.97	445.70	41.12
Feb-58	4.47	2.75	1.54	2.98	444.20	41.26
Mar-58	4.37	2.25	1.30	2.94	450.10	42.11
Apr-58	4.33	1.75	1.13	2.79	446.90	42.34
May-58	4.19	1.75	0.91	2.84	460.00	43.70
Jun-58	4.08	1.75	0.83	2.92	472.00	44.75
Jul-58	3.98	1.75	0.91	3.11	488.30	45.98
Aug-58	3.78	1.75	1.69	3.40	507.60	47.70
Sep-58	3.69	2.00	2.44	3.60	521.80	48.96
Oct-58	3.54	2.00	2.63	3.71	539.90	50.95
Nov-58	3.42	2.50	2.67	3.68	557.10	52.50
Dec-58	3.33	2.50	2.77	3.79	566.40	53.49
Jan-59	3.24	2.50	2.82	3.91	592.30	55.62
Feb-59	3.32	2.50	2.70	3.91	590.70	54.77
Mar-59	3.25	3.00	2.80	3.91	609.10	56.15
Apr-59	3.26	3.00	2.95	3.98	617.00	57.10
May-59	3.21	3.50	2.84	4.06	630.80	57.96
Jun-59	3.23	3.50	3.21	4.07	631.50	57.46
Jul-59	3.11	3.50	3.20	4.08	662.80	59.74
Aug-59	3.14	3.50	3.38	4.05	660.60	59.40
Sep-59	3.26	4.00	4.04	4.35	635.50	57.05
Oct-59	3.26	4.00	4.05	4.21	637.30	57.00
Nov-59	3.24	4.00	4.15	4.22	646.40	57.23
Dec-59	3.18	4.00	4.49	4.42	671.40	59.06

Date	S&P 500 Yield	Discount Rate	Treas. Bills	Treas. Bonds	Dow Jones Indus.	S&P 500
Jan-60	3.27	4.00	4.35	4.47	655.40	58.03
Feb-60	3.44	4.00	3.96	4.26	624.90	55.78
Mar-60	3.51	4.00	3.31	4.11	614.70	55.02
Apr-60	3.47	4.00	3.23	4.17	620.00	55.73
May-60	3.51	4.00	3.29	4.15	615.60	55.22
Jun-60	3.40	3.50	2.46	3.93	644.40	57.26
Jul-60	3.49	3.50	2.30	3.78	625.80	55.84
Aug-60	3.43	3.00	2.30	3.71	624.50	56.51
Sep-60	3.55	3.00	2.48	3.72	598.10	54.81
Oct-60	3.60	3.00	2.30	3.85	582.50	53.73
Nov-60	3.51	3.00	2.37	3.88	601.10	55.47
Dec-60	3.41	3.00	2.25	3.87	609.50	56.80
Jan-61	3.28	3.00	2.24	3.87	632.20	59.72
Feb-61	3.13	3.00	2.42	3.78	650.00	62.17
Mar-61	3.03	3.00	2.39	3.76	670.60	64.12
Apr-61	2.95	3.00	2.29	3.79	684.90	65.83
May-61	2.92	3.00	2.29	3.72	693.00	66.50
Jun-61	2.99	3.00	2.33	3.89	691.40	65.62
Jul-61	3.00	3.00	2.24	3.90	690.70	65.44
Aug-61	2.91	3.00	2.39	4.01	718.60	67.79
Sep-61	2.93	3.00	2.28	4.00	711.00	67.26
Oct-61	2.91	3.00	2.30	3.98	703.00	68.00
Nov-61	2.84	3.00	2.48	3.99	724.70	71.08
Dec-61	2.85	3.00	2.60	4.11	728.40	71.74
Jan-62	2.97	3.00	2.72	4.10	705.20	69.07
Feb-62	2.95	3.00	2.73	4.11	712.00	70.22
Mar-62	2.95	3.00	2.72	4.01	714.20	70.29
Apr-62	3.05	3.00	2.73	3.89	690.30	68.05
May-62	3.32	3.00	2.68	3.87	643.70	62.99
Jun-62	3.78	3.00	2.73	3.89	572.60	55.63
Jul-62	3.68	3.00	2.92	4.01	581.80	56.97
Aug-62	3.57	3.00	2.82	3.97	602.50	58.52
Sep-62	3.60	3.00	2.78	3.94	597.00	58.00
Oct-62	3.71	3.00	2.74	3.89	580.70	56.17
Nov-62	3.50	3.00	2.83	3.88	628.80	60.04
Dec-62	3.40	3.00	2.87	3.87	648.40	62.64
Jan-63	3.31	3.00	2.91	3.90	672.10	65.06
Feb-63	3.27	3.00	2.92	3.95	679.80	65.92
Mar-63	3.28	3.00	2.89	3.96	674.60	65.67
Apr-63	3.15	3.00	2.90	4.00	707.10	68.76
May-63	3.13	3.00	2.92	4.00	720.80	70.14
Jun-63	3.16	3.00	2.99	4.01	719.10	70.11
Jul-63	3.20	3.50	3.18	4.02	700.80	69.07
Aug-63	3.13	3.50	3.32	4.00	714.20	70.98
Sep-63	3.06	3.50	3.38	4.06	738.50	72.85
Oct-63	3.05	3.50	3.45	4.09	747.50	73.03
Nov-63	3.14	3.50	3.52	4.13	743.20	72.62
Dec-63	3.13	3.50	3.52	4.16	759.90	74.17

Date	S&P 500 Yield	Discount Rate	Treas. Bills	Treas. Bonds	Dow Jones Indus.	S&P 500
Jan-64	3.05	3.50	3.52	4.16	776.60	76.45
Feb-64	3.05	3.50	3.53	4.14	793.00	77.39
Mar-64	3.03	3.50	3.54	4.19	712.20	78.80
Apr-64	3.00	3.50	3.47	4.22	820.90	79.94
May-64	3.01	3.50	3.48	4.18	823.10	80.72
Jun-64	3.05	3.50	3.48	4.15	817.60	80.24
Jul-64	2.96	3.50	3.46	4.14	844.20	83.22
Aug-64	3.03	3.50	3.50	4.15	835.30	82.00
Sep-64	3.00	3.50	3.53	4.17	963.60	83.41
Oct-64	2.95	3.50	3.57	4.18	875.30	84.85
Nov-64	2.96	4.00	3.64	4.15	880.00	85.44
Dec-64	3.05	4.00	3.84	4.16	866.70	83.96
Jan-65	2.99	4.00	3.81	4.16	890.20	86.12
Feb-65	2.99	4.00	3.93	4.16	894.40	86.75
Mar-65	2.99	4.00	3.93	4.15	896.40	86.83
Apr-65	2.95	4.00	3.93	4.16	907.70	87.97
May-65	2.92	4.00	3.89	4.16	927.50	89.28
Jun-65	3.07	4.00	3.80	4.16	878.10	85.04
Jul-65	3.09	4.00	3.83	4.17	873.50	84.91
Aug-65	3.06	4.00	3.84	4.21	887.60	86.49
Sep-65	2.98	4.00	3.92	4.28	922.20	89.38
Oct-65	2.91	4.00	4.02	4.30	944.60	91.39
Nov-65	2.96	4.00	4.08	4.36	953.30	92.15
Dec-65	3.05	4.50	4.37	4.45	955.20	91.73
Jan-66	3.02	4.50	4.58	4.46	985.90	93.32
Feb-66	3.06	4.50	4.65	4.64	977.10	92.69
Mar-66	3.23	4.50	4.58	4.65	926.40	88.88
Apr-66	3.15	4.50	4.61	4.58	945.70	91.60
May-66	3.30	4.50	4.63	4.61	890.70	86.78
Jun-66	3.36	4.50	4.50	4.67	888.80	86.06
Jul-66	3.37	4.50	4.78	4.77	875.90	85.84
Aug-66	3.60	4.50	4.95	4.84	817.50	80.65
Sep-66	3.75	4.50	5.36	4.82	791.60	77.81
Oct-66	3.76	4.50	5.33	4.73	778.10	77.13
Nov-66	3.66	4.50	5.31	4.75	806.60	80.99
Dec-66	3.59	4.50	4.96	4.68	869.00	81.33
Jan-67	3.51	4.50	4.72	4.43	830.60	84.45
Feb-67	3.36	4.50	4.56	4.49	851.10	87.36
Mar-67	3.29	4.50	4.26	4.50	858.10	89.42
Apr-67	3.24	4.00	3.84	4.56	868.70	90.96
May-67	3.19	4.00	3.60	4.81	885.70	92.59
Jun-67	3.19	4.00	3.53	4.92	872.50	91.43
Jul-67	3.15	4.00	4.20	4.92	888.50	93.01
Aug-67	3.11	4.00	4.26	5.01	912.50	94.49
Sep-67	3.07	4.00	4.42	5.04	923.40	95.81
Oct-67	3.07	4.00	4.55	5.24	907.50	95.66
Nov-67	3.18	4.50	4.72	5.48	865.40	92.66
Dec-67	3.09	4.50	4.96	5.44	887.20	95.30

Date	S&P 500 Yield	Discount Rate	Treas. Bills	Treas. Bonds	Dow Jones Indus.	S&P 500
Jan-68	3.13	4.50	4.99	5.26	884.80	95.04
Feb-68	3.28	4.50	4.97	5.24	847.20	90.75
Mar-68	3.34	5.00	5.16	5.48	864.80	89.09
Apr-68	3.12	5.50	5.37	5.34	893.40	95.67
May-68	3.07	5.50	5.65	5.45	905.20	97.87
Jun-68	3.00	5.50	5.52	5.32	906.80	100.53
Jul-68	3.00	5.50	5.31	5.15	905.30	100.30
Aug-68	3.09	5.50	5.08	5.11	883.70	98.11
Sep-68	3.01	5.50	5.20	5.15	922.80	101.34
Oct-68	2.94	5.50	5.35	5.31	954.00	103.76
Nov-68	2.92	5.50	5.45	5.42	964.90	105.40
Dec-68	2.93	5.50	5.94	5.74	968.60	106.48
Jan-69	3.06	5.50	6.13	5.85	935.40	102.04
Feb-69	3.10	5.50	6.12	5.95	931.50	101.46
Mar-69	3.17	5.50	6.01	6.17	916.50	99.30
Apr-69	3.11	6.00	6.11	5.95	927.40	101.26
May-69	3.02	6.00	6.03	5.99	954.90	104.62
Jun-69	3.18	6.00	6.43	6.22	894.80	99.14
Jul-69	3.34	6.00	6.98	6.21	844.00	94.71
Aug-69	3.37	6.00	6.97	6.12	825.50	94.18
Sep-69	3.33	6.00	7.08	6.38	826.70	94.51
Oct-69	3.33	6.00	6.99	6.38	832.50	95.52
Nov-69	3.31	6.00	7.24	6.61	841.10	96.21
Dec-69	3.52	6.00	7.81	6.86	757.20	91.11
Jan-70	3.56	6.00	7.87	6.91	782.90	90.31
Feb-70	3.68	6.00	7.13	6.59	756.30	87.16
Mar-70	3.60	6.00	6.63	6.61	777.60	88.65
Apr-70	3.70	6.00	6.50	6.71	771.70	85.95
May-70	4.20	6.00	6.83	7.11	691.90	76.06
Jun-70	4.17	6.00	6.67	7.17	699.30	75.59
Jul-70	4.20	6.00	6.45	6.77	712.80	75.72
Aug-70	4.07	6.00	6.41	6.93	731.90	77.92
Sep-70	3.82	6.00	6.12	6.79	756.40	82.58
Oct-70	3.74	6.00	5.90	6.77	763.70	84.37
Nov-70	3.72	5.75	5.28	6.51	769.30	84.28
Dec-70	3.46	5.50	4.87	6.18	821.50	90.05
Jan-71	3.32	5.00	4.44	6.06	849.00	93.49
Feb-71	3.18	4.75	3.69	5.96	879.30	97.11
Mar-71	3.10	4.75	3.38	5.74	901.30	99.60
Apr-71	2.99	4.75	3.85	5.79	932.50	103.04
May-71	3.04	4.75	4.13	6.19	925.50	101.64
Jun-71	3.10	4.75	4.74	6.23	900.50	99.72
Jul-71	3.13	5.00	5.39	6.19	887.80	99.00
Aug-71	3.18	5.00	4.93	6.09	875.40	97.24
Sep-71	3.09	5.00	4.69	5.83	901.20	99.40
Oct-71	3.16	5.00	4.46	5.72	872.10	97.29
Nov-71	3.31	4.75	4.22	5.64	822.10	92.78
Dec-71	3.10	4.50	4.01	5.78	869.90	99.17

Date	S&P 500 Yield	Discount Rate	Treas. Bills	Treas. Bonds	Dow Jones Indus.	S&P 500
Jan-72	2.96	4.50	3.38	5.73	904.70	103.30
Feb-72	2.92	4.50	3.20	5.77	914.40	105.24
Mar-72	2.86	4.50	3.73	5.76	939.20	107.69
Apr-72	2.83	4.50	3.71	5.85	958.20	108.81
May-72	2.88	4.50	3.69	5.74	948.20	107.65
Jun-72	2.87	4.50	3.91	5.69	943.90	108.01
Jul-72	2.90	4.50	3.98	5.67	925.90	107.21
Aug-72	2.80	4.50	4.02	5.55	958.30	111.01
Sep-72	2.83	4.50	4.66	5.62	950.70	109.39
Oct-72	2.82	4.50	4.74	5.65	944.10	109.56
Nov-72	2.73	4.50	4.78	5.43	1001.20	115.05
Dec-72	2.70	4.50	5.07	5.57	1020.30	117.50
Jan-73	2.69	5.00	5.41	5.89	1026.80	118.42
Feb-73	2.80	5.50	5.60	6.09	974.00	114.16
Mar-73	2.83	5.50	6.09	6.16	957.40	112.42
Apr-73	2.90	5.50	6.26	6.07	944.10	110.27
May-73	3.01	6.00	6.36	6.11	922.40	107.22
Jun-73	3.05	6.50	7.19	6.17	893.90	104.75
Jul-73	3.04	7.00	8.01	6.35	903.30	105.83
Aug-73	3.16	7.50	8.67	6.69	883.70	103.80
Sep-73	3.13	7.50	8.29	6.11	910.00	105.61
Oct-73	3.05	7.50	7.22	5.89	967.60	109.87
Nov-73	3.36	7.50	7.83	5.92	879.00	102.03
Dec-73	3.70	7.50	7.45	5.99	824.10	94.78
Jan-74	3.64	7.50	7.77	6.25	857.20	96.11
Feb-74	3.81	7.50	7.12	6.22	831.30	93.45
Mar-74	3.65	7.50	7.96	6.52	874.00	97.44
Apr-74	3.86	8.00	8.33	6.74	847.80	92.46
May-74	4.00	8.00	8.23	6.69	830.30	89.67
Jun-74	4.02	8.00	7.90	6.57	831.40	89.79
Jul-74	4.42	8.00	7.55	6.67	783.00	82.82
Aug-74	4.90	8.00	8.96	6.78	729.30	76.03
Sep-74	5.45	8.00	8.06	6.79	651.30	68.12
Oct-74	5.38	8.00	7.46	6.81	638.60	69.44
Nov-74	5.13	8.00	7.47	6.54	642.10	71.74
Dec-74	5.43	7.75	7.15	6.44	596.50	67.07
Jan-75	5.07	7.25	6.26	7.98	659.10	72.56
Feb-75	4.61	6.75	5.50	7.81	724.90	80.10
Mar-75	4.42	6.25	5.49	8.05	765.10	83.78
Apr-75	4.34	6.25	5.61	8.34	790.90	84.72
May-75	4.08	6.00	5.23	8.21	836.40	90.10
Jun-75	4.02	6.00	5.34	8.08	845.70	92.40
Jul-75	4.02	6.00	6.13	8.20	856.30	92.49
Aug-75	4.36	6.00	6.44	8.53	815.50	85.71
Sep-75	4.39	6.00	6.42	8.53	818.30	84.67
Oct-75	4.22	6.00	5.96	8.36	831.30	88.57
Nov-75	4.07	6.00	5.48	8.26	845.50	90.07
Dec-75	4.14	6.00	5.44	8.20	840.80	88.70

Date	S&P 500 Yield	Discount Rate	Treas. Bills	Treas. Bonds	Dow Jones Indus.	S&P 500
Jan-76	3.80	5.50	4.87	8.01	929.30	96.86
Feb-76	3.67	5.50	4.88	8.01	971.20	100.64
Mar-76	3.65	5.50	5.00	7.93	988.60	101.08
Apr-76	3.66	5.50	4.86	7.77	992.60	101.93
May-76	3.76	5.50	5.20	8.09	988.80	101.16
Jun-76	3.75	5.50	5.41	8.04	985.60	101.77
Jul-76	3.64	5.50	5.23	8.01	993.20	104.20
Aug-76	3.74	5.50	5.14	7.94	981.60	103.29
Sep-76	3.71	5.50	5.08	7.81	994.40	105.45
Oct-76	3.85	5.50	4.92	7.72	952.00	101.89
Nov-76	4.04	5.25	4.75	7.71	944.60	101.19
Dec-76	3.93	5.25	4.35	7.35	976.90	104.66
Jan-77	3.99	5.25	4.62	7.49	970.60	103.81
Feb-77	4.21	5.25	4.67	7.71	941.80	100.96
Mar-77	4.37	5.25	4.60	7.74	946.10	100.57
Apr-77	4.47	5.25	4.54	7.68	929.10	99.05
May-77	4.57	5.25	4.96	7.73	926.30	98.76
Jun-77	4.60	5.25	5.02	7.60	916.90	99.29
Jul-77	4.59	5.25	5.19	7.61	908.70	100.18
Aug-77	4.72	5.75	5.49	7.64	872.30	97.75
Sep-77	4.82	5.75	5.81	7.60	852.80	96.23
Oct-77	4.97	6.00	6.16	7.74	823.50	93.74
Nov-77	5.02	6.00	6.10	7.80	828.30	94.28
Dec-77	5.11	6.00	6.07	7.93	818.20	93.82
Jan-78	5.32	6.50	6.44	8.15	781.10	90.25
Feb-78	5.49	6.50	6.45	8.23	763.60	88.98
Mar-78	4.62	6.50	6.29	8.20	756.20	88.82
Apr-78	5.42	6.50	6.29	8.33	794.70	92.71
May-78	5.20	7.00	6.41	8.44	838.60	97.41
Jun-78	5.19	7.00	6.73	8.49	840.30	97.66
Jul-78	5.25	7.25	7.01	8.65	831.70	97.19
Aug-78	4.93	7.75	7.08	8.42	887.90	103.92
Sep-78	4.97	8.00	7.85	8.44	878.60	103.86
Oct-78	5.11	8.50	7.99	8.62	857.70	100.58
Nov-78	5.45	9.50	8.64	8.70	804.30	94.71
Dec-78	5.42	9.50	9.08	8.86	807.90	96.11
Jan-79	5.33	9.50	9.35	8.93	837.40	99.71
Feb-79	5.48	9.50	9.32	9.00	825.20	98.23
Mar-79	5.41	9.50	9.48	9.01	847.80	100.11
Apr-79	5.35	9.50	9.46	9.05	865.00	102.07
May-79	5.58	9.50	9.61	9.13	837.40	99.73
Jun-79	5.53	9.50	9.06	8.85	838.70	101.73
Jul-79	5.50	10.00	9.24	8.86	837.00	102.71
Aug-79	5.30	10.50	9.52	8.90	873.60	107.36
Sep-79	5.31	11.00	10.26	9.13	878.50	108.60
Oct-79	5.56	12.00	11.70	9.90	840.40	104.47
Nov-79	5.71	12.00	11.79	10.34	815.80	103.66
Dec-79	5.53	12.00	12.04	10.11	836.10	107.78

Date	S&P 500 Yield	Discount Rate	Treas. Bills	Treas. Bonds	Dow Jones Indus.	S&P 500
Jan-80	5.41	12.00	12.00	10.53	860.70	110.87
Feb-80	5.24	13.00	12.86	12.25	878.20	115.34
Mar-80	5.87	13.00	15.20	12.28	803.60	104.69
Apr-80	6.05	13.00	13.20	11.18	786.30	102.97
May-80	5.77	12.00	8.58	10.13	828.20	107.69
Jun-80	5.39	11.00	7.07	9.80	869.90	114.55
Jul-80	5.20	10.00	8.06	10.21	909.80	119.83
Aug-80	5.06	10.00	9.13	11.00	947.30	123.50
Sep-80	4.90	11.00	10.27	11.28	946.70	126.51
Oct-80	4.80	11.00	11.62	11.70	949.20	130.22
Nov-80	4.63	12.00	13.73	12.12	971.10	135.65
Dec-80	4.74	13.00	15.49	12.21	946.00	133.48
Jan-81	4.80	13.00	15.02	11.88	962.10	132.97
Feb-81	5.00	13.00	14.79	12.64	945.50	128.40
Mar-81	4.88	13.00	13.36	12.48	987.20	133.19
Apr-81	4.86	13.00	13.69	12.98	1004.90	134.43
May-81	4.98	14.00	16.30	13.44	979.50	131.73
Jun-81	5.03	14.00	14.73	12.71	996.30	132.28
Jul-81	5.18	14.00	14.95	13.37	947.90	129.13
Aug-81	5.16	14.00	15.51	13.84	926.30	129.63
Sep-81	5.69	14.00	14.70	14.48	853.40	118.27
Oct-81	5.65	14.00	13.54	14.38	853.20	119.80
Nov-81	5.54	13.00	10.86	12.96	860.40	122.92
Dec-81	5.57	12.00	10.85	13.28	878.30	123.79
Jan-82	5.95	12.00	12.28	14.19	853.40	117.28
Feb-82	6.06	12.00	13.48	14.20	833.20	114.50
Mar-82	6.28	12.00	12.68	13.51	812.30	110.84
Apr-82	5.99	12.00	12.70	13.34	845.00	116.31
May-82	5.97	12.00	12.09	13.23	846.70	116.35
Jun-82	6.28	12.00	12.47	13.90	804.40	109.70
Jul-82	6.31	11.50	11.35	13.53	818.40	109.38
Aug-82	6.32	10.00	8.68	12.74	832.10	109.65
Sep-82	5.63	10.00	7.92	12.05	917.30	122.43
Oct-82	5.12	9.50	7.71	11.15	988.70	132.66
Nov-82	4.92	9.00	8.07	10.56	1027.80	138.10
Dec-82	4.93	8.50	7.94	10.53	1033.10	139.37
Jan-83	4.79	8.50	7.86	10.60	1064.30	144.27
Feb-83	4.74	8.50	8.11	10.86	1087.40	146.80
Mar-83	4.59	8.50	8.35	10.61	1129.60	151.88
Apr-83	4.44	8.50	8.21	10.46	1168.40	157.71
May-83	4.27	8.50	8.19	10.51	1212.90	164.10
Jun-83	4.26	8.50	8.79	10.91	1221.50	166.39
Jul-83	4.21	8.50	9.08	11.37	1213.90	166.96
Aug-83	4.35	8.50	9.34	11.80	1189.20	162.42
Sep-83	4.24	8.50	9.00	11.64	1237.00	167.16
Oct-83	4.25	8.50	8.64	11.56	1252.20	167.65
Nov-83	4.31	8.50	8.76	11.74	1250.00	165.23
Dec-83	4.32	8.50	9.00	11.87	1257.60	164.36

Date	S&P 500 Yield	Discount Rate	Treas. Bills	Treas. Bonds	Dow Jones Indus.	S&P 500
Jan-84	4.27	8.50	8.90	11.74	1258.90	166.39
Feb-84	4.59	8.50	9.09	11.94	1164.50	157.25
Mar-84	4.63	8.50	9.52	12.38	1162.00	157.44
Apr-84	4.64	9.00	9.69	12.64	1152.70	157.60
May-84	4.72	9.00	9.83	13.40	1143.40	156.55
Jun-84	4.86	9.00	9.87	13.42	1121.10	153.12
Jul-84	4.93	9.00	10.12	13.16	1113.30	151.08
Aug-84	4.62	9.00	10.47	12.51	1212.80	164.42
Sep-84	4.54	9.00	10.37	12.27	1213.50	166.10
Oct-84	4.62	9.00	9.74	11.97	1199.30	164.82
Nov-84	4.61	8.50	8.61	11.55	1211.30	166.27
Dec-84	4.68	8.00	8.06	11.51	1189.00	164.48
Jan-85	4.51	8.00	7.76	11.44	1238.20	171.61
Feb-85	4.30	8.00	8.27	11.47	1283.20	180.88
Mar-85	4.37	8.00	8.52	11.80	1268.80	179.42
Apr-85	4.37	8.00	7.95	11.45	1266.40	180.62
May-85	4.31	7.50	7.48	11.03	1279.40	184.90
Jun-85	4.21	7.50	6.95	10.43	1314.00	188.89
Jul-85	4.14	7.50	7.08	10.49	1343.20	192.54
Aug-85	4.23	7.50	7.14	10.55	1326.20	188.31
Sep-85	4.32	7.50	7.10	10.60	1318.00	184.06
Oct-85	4.28	7.50	7.16	10.49	1351.60	186.18
Nov-85	4.06	7.50	7.24	10.05	1432.90	197.45
Dec-85	3.88	7.50	7.10	9.53	1517.00	207.26
Jan-86	3.90	7.50	7.07	9.39	1534.90	208.19
Feb-86	3.72	7.50	7.06	8.92	1652.70	219.37
Mar-86	3.50	7.00	6.56	7.95	1757.40	232.33
Apr-86	3.43	7.00	6.06	7.38	1807.10	237.98
May-86	3.42	6.50	6.15	7.52	1801.80	238.46
Jun-86	3.36	6.50	6.21	7.56	1867.70	245.30
Jul-86	3.43	6.00	5.83	7.26	1809.90	240.18
Aug-86	3.36	5.50	5.53	7.32	1843.50	245.00
Sep-86	3.43	5.50	5.21	7.60	1813.50	238.27
Oct-86	3.49	5.50	5.18	7.69	1817.00	237.36
Nov-86	3.40	5.50	5.35	7.51	1883.70	245.09
Dec-86	3.38	5.50	5.53	7.37	1924.10	248.61

Appendix B
Recent History
of Stock Market
Values, 1967–1986

Date	Yield	S&P 500 P/E Ratio	Treas. Bills	DVI	EVI	S&P 500
Jan-67	3.51	15.26	4.72	1.49	1.39	84.45
Feb-67	3.36	15.89	4.56	1.47	1.38	87.36
Mar-67	3.29	16.30	4.26	1.54	1.44	89.42
Apr-67	3.24	16.68	3.84	1.69	1.56	90.96
May-67	3.19	17.56	3.60	1.77	1.58	92.59
Jun-67	3.19	18.16	3.53	1.81	1.56	91.43
Jul-67	3.15	18.39	4.20	1.50	1.29	93.01
Aug-67	3.11	18.20	4.26	1.46	1.29	94.49
Sep-67	3.07	17.98	4.42	1.39	1.26	95.81
Oct-67	3.07	17.94	4.55	1.35	1.23	95.66
Nov-67	3.18	17.40	4.72	1.35	1.22	92.66
Dec-67	3.09	17.67	4.96	1.25	1.14	95.30
Jan-68	3.13	17.43	4.99	1.25	1.15	95.04
Feb-68	3.28	16.67	4.97	1.32	1.21	90.75
Mar-68	3.34	16.21	5.16	1.29	1.20	89.09
Apr-68	3.12	17.29	5.37	1.16	1.08	95.67
May-68	3.07	17.74	5.65	1.09	1.00	97.87
Jun-68	3.00	18.26	5.52	1.09	0.99	100.53
Jul-68	3.00	18.25	5.31	1.13	1.03	100.30
Aug-68	3.09	17.31	5.08	1.22	1.14	98.11
Sep-68	3.01	17.44	5.20	1.16	1.10	101.34
Oct-68	2.94	17.92	5.35	1.10	1.04	103.76
Nov-68	2.92	17.97	5.45	1.07	1.02	105.40
Dec-68	2.93	18.14	5.94	0.99	0.93	106.48

Date	S&P 500 Yield	P/E Ratio	Treas. Bills	DVI	EVI	S&P 500
Jan-69	3.06	17.45	6.13	1.00	0.93	102.04
Feb-69	3.10	17.41	6.12	1.01	0.94	101.46
Mar-69	3.17	16.87	6.01	1.05	0.99	99.30
Apr-69	3.11	16.95	6.11	1.02	0.97	101.26
May-69	3.02	17.63	6.03	1.00	0.94	104.62
Jun-69	3.18	17.11	6.43	0.99	0.91	99.14
Jul-69	3.34	16.51	6.98	0.96	0.87	94.71
Aug-69	3.37	16.41	6.97	0.97	0.87	94.18
Sep-69	3.33	16.36	7.08	0.94	0.86	94.51
Oct-69	3.33	16.15	6.99	0.95	0.89	95.52
Nov-69	3.31	16.18	7.24	0.91	0.85	96.21
Dec-69	3.52	15.08	7.81	0.90	0.85	91.11
Jan-70	3.56	14.93	7.87	0.90	0.85	90.31
Feb-70	3.68	14.49	7.13	1.03	0.97	87.16
Mar-70	3.60	15.43	6.63	1.09	0.98	88.65
Apr-70	3.70	15.53	6.50	1.14	0.99	85.95
May-70	4.20	13.58	6.83	1.23	1.08	76.06
Jun-70	4.17	14.18	6.67	1.25	1.06	75.59
Jul-70	4.20	14.53	6.45	1.30	1.07	75.72
Aug-70	4.07	15.00	6.41	1.27	1.04	77.92
Sep-70	3.82	15.44	6.12	1.25	1.06	82.58
Oct-70	3.74	15.48	5.90	1.27	1.09	84.37
Nov-70	3.72	15.44	5.28	1.41	1.23	84.28
Dec-70	3.46	16.71	4.87	1.42	1.23	90.05
Jan-71	3.32	17.43	4.44	1.50	1.29	93.49
Feb-71	3.18	18.14	3.69	1.72	1.49	97.11
Mar-71	3.10	18.73	3.38	1.83	1.58	99.60
Apr-71	2.99	20.15	3.85	1.55	1.29	103.04
May-71	3.04	19.85	4.13	1.47	1.22	101.64
Jun-71	3.10	19.29	4.74	1.31	1.09	99.72
Jul-71	3.13	18.95	5.39	1.16	0.98	99.00
Aug-71	3.18	18.56	4.93	1.29	1.09	97.24
Sep-71	3.09	18.71	4.69	1.32	1.14	99.40
Oct-71	3.16	18.24	4.46	1.42	1.23	97.29
Nov-71	3.31	17.46	4.22	1.57	1.36	92.78
Dec-71	3.10	18.31	4.01	1.55	1.36	99.17
Jan-72	2.96	19.03	3.38	1.75	1.55	103.30
Feb-72	2.92	19.40	3.20	1.83	1.61	105.24
Mar-72	2.86	19.41	3.73	1.53	1.38	107.69
Apr-72	2.83	19.08	3.71	1.53	1.41	108.81
May-72	2.88	18.66	3.69	1.56	1.45	107.65
Jun-72	2.87	18.58	3.91	1.47	1.38	108.01
Jul-72	2.90	18.45	3.98	1.46	1.36	107.21
Aug-72	2.80	19.09	4.02	1.39	1.30	111.01
Sep-72	2.83	18.46	4.66	1.21	1.16	109.39
Oct-72	2.82	18.36	4.74	1.19	1.15	109.56
Nov-72	2.73	19.23	4.78	1.14	1.09	115.05
Dec-72	2.70	19.11	5.07	1.07	1.03	117.50

Date	S&P 500 Yield	P/E Ratio	Treas. Bills	DVI	EVI	S&P 500
Jan-73	2.69	19.23	5.41	0.99	0.96	118.42
Feb-73	2.80	18.53	5.60	1.00	0.96	114.16
Mar-73	2.83	17.50	6.09	0.93	0.94	112.42
Apr-73	2.90	17.11	6.26	0.93	0.93	110.27
May-73	3.01	16.44	6.36	0.95	0.96	107.22
Jun-73	3.05	15.42	7.19	0.85	0.90	104.75
Jul-73	3.04	15.53	8.01	0.76	0.80	105.83
Aug-73	3.16	15.11	8.67	0.73	0.76	103.80
Sep-73	3.13	14.58	8.29	0.76	0.83	105.61
Oct-73	3.05	15.10	7.22	0.84	0.92	109.87
Nov-73	3.36	13.46	7.83	0.86	0.95	102.03
Dec-73	3.70	12.25	7.45	0.99	1.10	94.78
Jan-74	3.64	12.51	7.77	0.94	1.03	96.11
Feb-74	3.81	12.16	7.12	1.07	1.16	93.45
Mar-74	3.65	12.08	7.96	0.92	1.04	97.44
Apr-74	3.86	11.40	8.33	0.93	1.05	92.46
May-74	4.00	10.99	8.23	0.97	1.11	89.67
Jun-74	4.02	10.67	7.90	1.02	1.19	89.79
Jul-74	4.42	9.86	7.55	1.17	1.34	82.82
Aug-74	4.90	8.70	8.96	1.09	1.28	76.03
Sep-74	5.45	7.69	8.06	1.35	1.61	68.12
Oct-74	5.38	7.92	7.46	1.44	1.69	69.44
Nov-74	5.13	8.07	7.47	1.37	1.66	71.74
Dec-74	5.43	7.33	7.15	1.52	1.91	67.07
Jan-75	5.07	7.99	6.26	1.62	2.00	72.56
Feb-75	4.61	8.72	5.50	1.68	2.09	80.10
Mar-75	4.42	9.82	5.49	1.61	1.85	83.78
Apr-75	4.34	9.36	5.61	1.55	1.90	84.72
May-75	4.08	10.14	5.23	1.56	1.89	90.10
Jun-75	4.02	10.84	5.34	1.51	1.73	92.40
Jul-75	4.02	10.94	6.13	1.31	1.49	92.49
Aug-75	4.36	10.08	6.44	1.35	1.54	85.71
Sep-75	4.39	10.74	6.42	1.37	1.45	84.67
Oct-75	4.22	11.19	5.96	1.42	1.50	88.57
Nov-75	4.07	11.47	5.48	1.49	1.59	90.07
Dec-75	4.14	11.70	5.44	1.52	1.57	88.70
Jan-76	3.80	12.68	4.87	1.56	1.62	96.86
Feb-76	3.67	13.21	4.88	1.50	1.55	100.64
Mar-76	3.65	13.12	5.00	1.46	1.52	101.08
Apr-76	3.66	13.13	4.86	1.51	1.57	101.93
May-76	3.76	13.02	5.20	1.45	1.48	101.16
Jun-76	3.75	12.24	5.41	1.39	1.51	101.77
Jul-76	3.64	12.29	5.23	1.39	1.56	104.20
Aug-76	3.74	12.23	5.14	1.46	1.59	103.29
Sep-76	3.71	11.50	5.08	1.46	1.71	105.45
Oct-76	3.85	11.15	4.92	1.57	1.82	101.89
Nov-76	4.04	11.02	4.75	1.70	1.91	101.19
Dec-76	3.93	11.02	4.35	1.81	2.09	104.66

Date	S&P 500 Yield	P/E Ratio	Treas. Bills	DVI	EVI	S&P 500
Jan-77	3.99	10.93	4.62	1.73	1.98	103.81
Feb-77	4.21	10.62	4.67	1.80	2.02	100.96
Mar-77	4.37	10.21	4.60	1.90	2.13	100.57
Apr-77	4.47	10.01	4.54	1.97	2.20	99.05
May-77	4.57	9.99	4.96	1.84	2.02	98.76
Jun-77	4.60	9.86	5.02	1.83	2.02	99.29
Jul-77	4.59	9.92	5.19	1.77	1.94	100.18
Aug-77	4.72	9.72	5.49	1.72	1.87	97.75
Sep-77	4.82	9.24	5.81	1.66	1.86	96.23
Oct-77	4.97	8.98	6.16	1.61	1.81	93.74
Nov-77	5.02	9.04	6.10	1.65	1.81	94.28
Dec-77	5.11	8.75	6.07	1.68	1.88	93.82
Jan-78	5.32	8.48	6.44	1.65	1.83	90.25
Feb-78	5.49	8.34	6.45	1.70	1.86	88.98
Mar-78	4.62	8.18	6.29	1.47	1.94	88.82
Apr-78	5.42	8.50	6.29	1.72	1.87	92.71
May-78	5.20	8.93	6.41	1.62	1.75	97.41
Jun-78	5.19	8.90	6.73	1.54	1.67	97.66
Jul-78	5.25	8.83	7.01	1.50	1.62	97.19
Aug-78	4.93	9.51	7.08	1.39	1.49	103.92
Sep-78	4.97	9.28	7.85	1.27	1.37	103.86
Oct-78	5.11	9.02	7.99	1.28	1.39	100.58
Nov-78	5.45	8.41	8.64	1.26	1.38	94.71
Dec-78	5.42	8.26	9.08	1.19	1.33	96.11
Jan-76	3.80	12.68	4.87	1.56	1.62	96.86
Feb-76	3.67	13.21	4.88	1.50	1.55	100.64
Mar-76	3.65	13.12	5.00	1.46	1.52	101.08
Apr-76	3.66	13.13	4.86	1.51	1.57	101.93
May-76	3.76	13.02	5.20	1.45	1.48	101.16
Jun-76	3.75	12.24	5.41	1.39	1.51	101.77
Jul-76	3.64	12.29	5.23	1.39	1.56	104.20
Aug-76	3.74	12.23	5.14	1.46	1.59	103.29
Sep-76	3.71	11.50	5.08	1.46	1.71	105.45
Oct-76	3.85	11.15	4.92	1.57	1.82	101.89
Nov-76	4.04	11.02	4.75	1.70	1.91	101.19
Dec-76	3.93	11.02	4.35	1.81	2.09	104.66
Jan-77	3.99	10.93	4.62	1.73	1.98	103.81
Feb-77	4.21	10.62	4.67	1.80	2.02	100.96
Mar-77	4.37	10.21	4.60	1.90	2.13	100.57
Apr-77	4.47	10.01	4.54	1.97	2.20	99.05
May-77	4.57	9.99	4.96	1.84	2.02	98.76
Jun-77	4.60	9.86	5.02	1.83	2.02	99.29
Jul-77	4.59	9.92	5.19	1.77	1.94	100.18
Aug-77	4.72	9.72	5.49	1.72	1.87	97.75
Sep-77	4.82	9.24	5.81	1.66	1.86	96.23
Oct-77	4.97	8.98	6.16	1.61	1.81	93.74
Nov-77	5.02	9.04	6.10	1.65	1.81	94.28
Dec-77	5.11	8.75	6.07	1.68	1.88	93.82

322

Date	S&P 500 Yield	P/E Ratio	Treas. Bills	DVI	EVI	S&P 500
Jan-78	5.32	8.48	6.44	1.65	1.83	90.25
Feb-78	5.49	8.34	6.45	1.70	1.86	88.98
Mar-78	4.62	8.18	6.29	1.47	1.94	88.82
Apr-78	5.42	8.50	6.29	1.72	1.87	92.71
May-78	5.20	8.93	6.41	1.62	1.75	97.41
Jun-78	5.19	8.90	6.73	1.54	1.67	97.66
Jul-78	5.25	8.83	7.01	1.50	1.62	97.19
Aug-78	4.93	9.51	7.08	1.39	1.49	103.92
Sep-78	4.97	9.28	7.85	1.27	1.37	103.86
Oct-78	5.11	9.02	7.99	1.28	1.39	100.58
Nov-78	5.45	8.41	8.64	1.26	1.38	94.71
Dec-78	5.42	8.26	9.08	1.19	1.33	96.11
Jan-79	5.33	8.54	9.35	1.14	1.25	99.71
Feb-79	5.48	8.44	9.32	1.18	1.27	98.23
Mar-79	5.41	8.26	9.48	1.14	1.28	100.11
Apr-79	5.35	8.29	9.46	1.13	1.28	102.07
May-79	5.58	8.08	9.61	1.16	1.29	99.73
Jun-79	5.53	7.67	9.06	1.22	1.44	101.73
Jul-79	5.50	7.71	9.24	1.19	1.40	102.71
Aug-79	5.30	8.06	9.52	1.11	1.30	107.36
Sep-79	5.31	7.76	10.26	1.04	1.26	108.60
Oct-79	5.56	7.44	11.70	0.95	1.15	104.47
Nov-79	5.71	7.40	11.79	0.97	1.15	103.66
Dec-79	5.53	7.42	12.04	0.92	1.12	107.78
Jan-80	5.41	7.66	12.00	0.90	1.09	110.87
Feb-80	5.24	7.91	12.86	0.81	0.98	115.34
Mar-80	5.87	7.15	15.20	0.77	0.92	104.69
Apr-80	6.05	6.96	13.20	0.92	1.09	102.97
May-80	5.77	7.30	8.58	1.34	1.60	107.69
Jun-80	5.39	7.53	7.07	1.52	1.88	114.55
Jul-80	5.20	7.81	8.06	1.29	1.59	119.83
Aug-80	5.06	8.05	9.13	1.11	1.36	123.50
Sep-80	4.90	8.53	10.27	0.95	1.14	126.51
Oct-80	4.80	8.73	11.62	0.83	0.99	130.22
Nov-80	4.63	9.12	13.73	0.67	0.80	135.65
Dec-80	4.74	9.06	15.49	0.61	0.71	133.48
Jan-81	4.80	9.03	15.02	0.64	0.74	132.97
Feb-81	5.00	8.78	14.79	0.68	0.77	128.40
Mar-81	4.88	9.03	13.36	0.73	0.83	133.19
Apr-81	4.86	9.09	13.69	0.71	0.80	134.43
May-81	4.98	8.89	16.30	0.61	0.69	131.73
Jun-81	5.03	9.05	14.73	0.68	0.75	132.28
Jul-81	5.18	8.84	14.95	0.69	0.76	129.13
Aug-81	5.16	8.94	15.51	0.67	0.72	129.63
Sep-81	5.69	7.92	14.70	0.77	0.86	118.27
Oct-81	5.65	7.96	13.54	0.83	0.93	119.80
Nov-81	5.54	8.19	10.86	1.02	1.12	122.92
Dec-81	5.57	8.07	10.85	1.03	1.14	123.79

Date	Yield	S&P 500 P/E Ratio	Treas. Bills	DVI	EVI	S&P 500
Jan-82	5.95	7.80	12.28	0.97	1.04	117.28
Feb-82	6.06	7.70	13.48	0.90	0.96	114.50
Mar-82	6.28	7.56	12.68	0.99	1.04	110.84
Apr-82	5.99	7.60	12.70	0.94	1.04	116.31
May-82	5.97	7.70	12.09	0.99	1.07	116.35
Jun-82	6.28	7.74	12.47	1.01	1.04	109.70
Jul-82	6.31	7.50	11.35	1.11	1.17	109.38
Aug-82	6.32	8.50	8.68	1.46	1.36	109.65
Sep-82	5.63	8.87	7.92	1.42	1.42	122.43
Oct-82	5.12	9.80	7.71	1.33	1.32	132.66
Nov-82	4.92	10.50	8.07	1.22	1.18	138.10
Dec-82	4.93	11.12	7.94	1.24	1.13	139.37
Jan-83	4.79	11.50	7.86	1.22	1.11	144.27
Feb-83	4.74	12.00	8.11	1.17	1.03	146.80
Mar-83	4.59	12.32	8.35	1.10	0.97	151.88
Apr-83	4.44	12.80	8.21	1.08	0.95	157.71
May-83	4.27	13.00	8.19	1.04	0.94	164.10
Jun-83	4.26	13.35	8.79	0.97	0.85	166.39
Jul-83	4.21	13.44	9.08	0.93	0.82	166.96
Aug-83	4.35	13.18	9.34	0.93	0.81	162.42
Sep-83	4.24	13.32	9.00	0.94	0.83	167.16
Oct-83	4.25	13.11	8.64	0.98	0.88	167.65
Nov-83	4.31	13.22	8.76	0.98	0.86	165.23
Dec-83	4.32	12.47	9.00	0.96	0.89	164.36
Jan-84	4.27	12.43	8.90	0.96	0.90	166.39
Feb-84	4.59	11.81	9.09	1.01	0.93	157.25
Mar-84	4.63	11.37	9.52	0.97	0.92	157.44
Apr-84	4.64	11.28	9.69	0.96	0.91	157.60
May-84	4.72	10.72	9.83	0.96	0.95	156.55
Jun-84	4.86	9.96	9.87	0.98	1.02	153.12
Jul-84	4.93	9.77	10.12	0.97	1.01	151.08
Aug-84	4.62	10.97	10.47	0.88	0.87	164.42
Sep-84	4.54	10.26	10.37	0.88	0.94	166.10
Oct-84	4.62	10.25	9.74	0.95	1.00	164.82
Nov-84	4.61	10.19	8.61	1.07	1.14	166.27
Dec-84	4.68	10.05	8.06	1.16	1.23	164.48
Jan-85	4.51	10.84	7.76	1.16	1.19	171.61
Feb-85	4.30	10.93	8.27	1.04	1.11	180.88
Mar-85	4.37	10.71	8.52	1.03	1.10	179.42
Apr-85	4.37	10.89	7.95	1.10	1.16	180.62
May-85	4.31	11.22	7.48	1.15	1.19	184.90
Jun-85	4.21	11.60	6.95	1.21	1.24	188.89
Jul-85	4.14	11.83	7.08	1.17	1.19	192.54
Aug-85	4.23	11.50	7.14	1.18	1.22	188.31
Sep-85	4.32	11.43	7.10	1.22	1.23	184.06
Oct-85	4.28	12.02	7.16	1.20	1.16	186.18
Nov-85	4.06	13.00	7.24	1.12	1.06	197.45
Dec-85	3.88	13.78	7.10	1.09	1.02	207.26

Date	S&P 500 Yield	P/E Ratio	Treas. Bills	DVI	EVI	S&P 500
Jan-86	3.84	13.57	7.07	1.09	1.04	208.19
Feb-86	3.62	14.74	7.06	1.03	0.96	219.37
Mar-86	3.40	15.72	6.56	1.04	0.97	232.33
Apr-86	3.67	15.77	6.06	1.21	1.05	237.98
May-86	3.32	16.97	6.15	1.08	0.96	238.46
Jun-86	3.33	17.02	6.21	1.07	0.95	245.30
Jul-86	3.41	16.99	5.83	1.17	1.01	240.18
Aug-86	3.37	17.01	5.53	1.22	1.06	245.00
Sep-86	3.46	15.67	5.21	1.33	1.22	238.27
Oct-86	3.48	16.55	5.18	1.34	1.17	237.36
Nov-86	3.37	17.16	5.35	1.26	1.09	245.09
Dec-86	3.32	16.42	5.53	1.20	1.10	248.61

Bibliography

Burke, Michael L., ed. *Investors Intelligence* (newsletter). New Rochelle, NY: Chartcraft, Inc.

Davis, Dick. *The Dick Davis Digest* (newsletter). Miami Beach, FL: Dick Davis Digest.

Ellis, Charles D. *Investment Strategy*. Homewood, IL: Dow Jones-Irwin, 1985.

Fisher, Kenneth L. *Super Stocks*. Homewood, IL: Dow Jones-Irwin, 1984.

Fosback, Norman G. *Market Logic* (newsletter). Fort Lauderdale, FL: Institute for Econometric Research.

George, Wilfred R. *Tight Money Timing*. New York: Praeger, 1982.

Graham, Benjamin. *The Intelligent Investor*. New York: Harper & Row, 1973.

Graham, Benjamin, and David Dodd. *Security Analysis* (4th ed.). New York: McGraw-Hill, 1962.

Hurst, J. M. *The Profit Magic of Stock Transaction Timing*. Englewood Cliffs, NJ: Prentice-Hall, 1970.

Prechter, Robert R., Jr., and Alfred J. Frost. *The Elliott Wave Principle*. Chappaqua, NY: New Classics Library, 1981.

Pring, Martin J. *Technical Analysis Explained*. New York: McGraw-Hill, 1980.

_____ , *How to Forecast Interest Rates*. New York: McGraw-Hill, 1981.

Train, John. *The Money Masters*. New York: Harper & Row, 1980.

Weinstein, Stan. *The Professional Tape Reader* (newsletter). Hollywood, FL: Radcap.

Index